Understanding the Policymaking Process
in Developing Countries

Understanding the Policymaking Process in Developing Countries
provides a uniquely comprehensive and practical framework for development practitioners, policymakers, activists, and students to diagnose
and improve policy processes in developing countries across a wide
range of issues. Based on the classic policy sciences approach, the book
offers over 100 diagnostic indicators keyed to identify problems of
policy processes, policy content, bureaucratic behavior, stakeholder
behavior, and national-subnational interactions. This multi-disciplinary
framework is applied to a host of policy problems that particularly
plague countries experiencing the "under-development syndrome,"
including aborted programs and projects, policy impasses, distorted
implementation, unnecessary harm and conflict, and shortsighted initiatives. These points are illustrated through cases from Africa, Asia, and
Latin America. Based on the developing countries' distinctive challenges, the book also offers recommendations on improving policy
content and institutions to address the typical limitations.

WILLIAM ASCHER is Professor of Government and Economics at
Claremont McKenna College. He has authored or edited nineteen
books on political economy of development, natural resource and
environmental policy, political psychology, forecasting methodology,
physical infrastructure policy, and conflict-sensitive development.
Ascher has twice won the Harold D. Lasswell Prize for best article in
Policy Sciences and his book *Bringing in the Future* won the International Political Science Association's Levine Prize for the best public
policy book of 2009. He has worked with the World Bank, USAID, and
the EPA. He directed the Duke Center for International Development
and served as Dean of the Faculty at Claremont McKenna College.

Understanding the Policymaking Process in Developing Countries

WILLIAM ASCHER

Claremont McKenna College

CAMBRIDGE
UNIVERSITY PRESS

CAMBRIDGE
UNIVERSITY PRESS

University Printing House, Cambridge CB2 8BS, United Kingdom

One Liberty Plaza, 20th Floor, New York, NY 10006, USA

477 Williamstown Road, Port Melbourne, VIC 3207, Australia

4843/24, 2nd Floor, Ansari Road, Daryaganj, Delhi – 110002, India

79 Anson Road, #06–04/06, Singapore 079906

Cambridge University Press is part of the University of Cambridge.

It furthers the University's mission by disseminating knowledge in the pursuit of
education, learning, and research at the highest international levels of excellence.

www.cambridge.org
Information on this title: www.cambridge.org/9781108417617
DOI: 10.1017/9781108277990

© William Ascher 2017

First published 2017

Printed in the United Kingdom by Clays, St Ives plc

A catalogue record for this publication is available from the British Library.

Library of Congress Cataloging-in-Publication Data
NAMES: Ascher, William, author.
TITLE: Understanding the policymaking process in developing countries / William Ascher.
DESCRIPTION: 1 Edition. | New York : Cambridge University Press, 2017.
IDENTIFIERS: LCCN 2017030759 | ISBN 9781108417617 (Hardback) |
ISBN 9781108405515 (Paperback)
SUBJECTS: LCSH: Developing countries–Economic policy. | Developing countries–Politics
and government. | BISAC: POLITICAL SCIENCE / Economic Conditions.
CLASSIFICATION: LCC HC59.7 .A83553 2017 | DDC 320.609172/4–dc23
LC record available at https://lccn.loc.gov/2017030759

ISBN 978-1-108-41761-7 Hardback
ISBN 978-1-108-40551-5 Paperback

To the development practitioners, of organizations big and small, striving to meet the daunting challenges of development

Contents

Tables

Acknowledgments

My exposure to the potentials and pitfalls of formulating, advocating, and implementing development initiatives has come from listening to the travails of hundreds of government officials, analysts, and activists across a broad range of institutions. Anyone who has attended the presentations by the International Fellows of the Duke Center for International Development, or has worked with the dedicated staff of the World Bank, the Asian Development Bank, the Inter-American Development Bank, and the U.S. Agency for International Development, cannot help but understand that whatever insights this book may have are based as much on their practical experiences as on the academic scholarship that necessarily dominates the volume's citations.

Rather than name hundreds of these people, I will single out Sudhir Shetty, Jennie Litvack, and Konstantin Atanesyan, who brought me into crucial learning experiences through World Bank work, and Craig Hammer, also of the World Bank, whose efforts to apply the policy sciences framework to development work has been a major inspiration for this volume. I owe a huge intellectual debt to Natalia Mirovitskaya, through myriad discussions, and always polite arguments, in the pursuit of our co-authored and co-edited works. A recent collaboration with Garry Brewer, Shabbir Cheema, and John M. (Jay) Heffron also leaves its fingerprints all over this volume. Finally, the exposition in this book would have been even more stilted were it not for the dedicated editing, among other enormous contributions, by Barbara Hirschfelder-Ascher.

I

Challenges to Effective Development Policymaking

The purpose of this book is to orient citizens, activists, students, planners, and policymakers to contribute more effectively to the public policy processes of developing countries, through greater understanding of the dynamics and pitfalls of these processes. One premise of the book is that in each specific context, readily available knowledge is limited by three vital factors: stakeholders' and policymakers' assumptions and true preferences, the range of paths through which policy initiatives can be channeled, and the technical and political obstacles that can undermine sound policy initiatives. Without guidance on how to understand the origins of dysfunctions of the process, identify the appropriate range of stakeholders who ought to be involved, or identify the opportunities to navigate the policy process more effectively, sound policy initiatives may falter or become seriously distorted.

It is also true that planning, policy selection, implementation, and evaluation are intricately intertwined – these aspects must be considered as a whole. Therefore, this book is not only a guide and a critical assessment of the governmental policy processes across the whole range of policies, but it also tries to illuminate the interactions among all of the decision functions involved in this policy process. This is necessary both for maneuvering within existing processes and for developing more effective processes.

THE DEVELOPMENT CONTRIBUTOR'S CHALLENGE

A crucial insight for understanding the challenges in trying to contribute to sound development is that *everyone* is an outsider with regard to major aspects of the policy process. Obviously foreign development practitioners are outsiders. Individual citizens and groups outside of government are not privy to many of the deliberations within government. Yet even within government ranks, a planner or policymaker of one agency is an "outsider" with respect to the inner machinations of other agencies. Top leaders of the national government are outsiders with respect to subnational governments, and they have no realistic way to know everything about the thoughts and actions of staff within the agencies over whom these leaders ostensibly have authority. Therefore, in addition to the practical problem that misperception often abounds, the analytic challenge is for all participants to be able to make reasonable inferences about the motivations and perceptions of others involved in the development-policy process. Much of this book is devoted to suggesting suitable diagnostic indicators to make these assessments.

SEVEN KEY PROBLEMS IN PURSUING SOUND DEVELOPMENT-POLICY INITIATIVES

To make this guide as useful as possible, it is organized around seven fundamental problems commonly encountered in the pursuit of sound development-policy initiatives. They are:

Support of Ill-Fated Initiatives. Without understanding and anticipating how seemingly sound initiatives will be weakened or distorted, or without the capacity to prevent this from happening, anyone involved in the formulation or support of particular policies runs the risk of endorsing an ill-starred effort. This could supplant more promising initiatives, as well as discredit the endorser. Many donor governments, international assistance agencies, and NGOs have fallen into the trap of supporting initiatives based on weak intelligence. For example, the U.S. Agency for International Development supported a major Kenyan project to introduce genetically-modified cassava, only to learn that insufficient preliminary research missed the new strain's vulnerability to cassava mosaic disease, leading to 30 percent crop losses (East African Magazine 2006).

Another form of intelligence – to which policymakers critical to the approval and enactment of a sound initiative might not be sufficiently committed – may be lacking. Development practitioners and aid agencies may be sucked into supporting initiatives that falter when the government's commitment declines, as in the failure of the Bangladesh government to deploy half of the $400 million Health and Population Sector Program fund, provided by a host of bilateral and multilateral agencies.[1] This fund, holding more than half of all foreign assistance aid directed to health in Bangladesh, was suspended by a new government in 2002 (Batkin et al. 2006, 32). The UK Department of International Development's self-assessment also noted that "None of the HPSP reforms had been fully implemented by that point [2002], and there is no evidence of increases in productivity or in the quality of essential health services. The proportion of health in the GoB budget fell and there is also no evidence of increased efficiency or equity in distribution of funding" (Batkin et al. 2006, 32).

Considerable waste of resources and embarrassment have also come from endorsing initiatives that are substantially implemented but with problematic modifications. In many developing countries, bilateral donors, multilateral assistance agencies, and international conservation NGOs have supported the establishment of protected areas, only to find that local people have been displaced without adequate provision for their livelihoods (Brandon 2014). A World Wildlife Fund (2004, 13) assessment of over 200 conservation areas in developing countries concluded that ineffective conservation often resulted from failing to enforce project provisions, including inadequate resources for monitoring and community participation. In particular, management practices of protected areas often depart substantially from the legal property rights arrangements, as documented for Ecuador and Peru by Naughton-Treves et al. (2006, 40).

Rejection of Sound Knowledge or Recommendations. One of the great frustrations of many participants is that the development-policy process effectively ignores their input even if their contributions are based on solid information and expertise. In many cases the input goes unheeded, even when it is accompanied by resource transfers contingent on complying with the advice. The most prominent instances are the decisions of many governments not to comply with the conditions formally required by international financial institutions, such as the International Monetary Fund and the World Bank (Dreher 2006; 2009; Mosley, Noorbakhsh, and Paloni 2003). Yet on a more micro level, virtually all advisors have seen their advice neglected, even if it has been received with respect and appreciation. This author (among others) was consulted by a leader of a prominent Asian political party on the issue of

---

[1] The British, Canadian, German, Japanese, Swedish, and U.S. bilateral foreign assistance agencies, plus the European Union, the UN Family Planning Agency, the UN Children's Fund, the World Bank, and the World Health Organization.

whether the party platform should include a call for a minimum wage regulation. The "outsiders" pointed out that the minimum wage would reduce the better-paying employment prospects for the unemployed and workers in the informal sector, precisely the voters whom the party needed to attract. The advice was ignored; what the party leaders believed (perhaps correctly) was that low-income voters would view a minimum wage favorably even if it went against their true interests.

Impasses Blocking the Enactment of Sound Initiatives. Antagonism among groups, or between stakeholder groups and the government, frequently undermines efforts to forge constructive accords. Mills et al. (2012, 15) note that assessments of South Africa's health insurance policymaking have demonstrated "how the opposition of key stakeholders to the particular equity goals and key design features within insurance proposals, and the failure to manage this opposition, resulted in a policy stalemate."

Understanding the factors that exacerbate the relations among groups may hold the potential to bring groups together. Even when an initiative would in fact be favorable to a particular group, influential members of that group may not agree with this assessment, perhaps because of lack of information or trust. For example, low-income groups rarely embrace government initiatives to reduce subsidies on gasoline and diesel, yet based on analysis of twenty countries in Africa, Asia, Latin America, and the Middle East, Del Granado, Coady, and Gillingham (2012, 2234) conclude that "[f]uel subsidies are a costly approach to protecting the poor due to substantial benefit leakage to higher income groups; in absolute terms, the top income quintile captures six times more in subsidies than the bottom." Thus, these subsidies benefit higher income people far more, and deny the government the savings that could be devoted to programs for the poor. Or perhaps the stakeholders fear that supporting or acquiescing to the initiative would lead to damaging future measures. If fuel subsidies are reduced, would this pave the way for the reduction of other subsidies that benefit the poor more than others? In other cases, repressive actions by the government or the armed forces worsen the impasse by sowing distrust. The governance status of Indonesia's regions of the island of New Guinea has been in impasse since the fall of President Suharto in 1998, in no small part because of the heavy-handed military suppression of the independence movement (Chauvel 2011).

Sometimes impasses can be circumvented by bringing the initiative through other channels. For example, to help the poor to overcome the costliness and rigidities of many judicial systems, the Commission on Legal Empowerment of the Poor (2008, 26) recommends that "reformers might also address the demand for judicial services [for the poor] by encouraging or requiring resolution of more disputes (at least in the first instance) in the administrative bureaucracy rather than the courts." Another strategy of pursuing different channels is the shift from national-level arenas to subnational arenas. For example, the European Union has recommended that Nigerian community-self-help advocates should target local governments to establish social funds involving participatory community development (Ifeka 2001, 462). However, continued reliance on less promising channels may be frozen because of lack of knowledge and experience regarding alternatives, legal rigidities, difficulties in mobilizing support for the shift, or sheer inertia.

Ineffective or Incoherent Enactment of Initiatives. Behind many of the ill-fated endorsements, but going considerably beyond that problem, is the fact that formal policy provisions are often distorted or ineffective in their application. The most obvious scenario is the incomplete enactment of formal provisions pursuing sound objectives; in fact, except for policies that simply involve setting a rate (e.g., the government bond interest rates), it is a rare policy that is precisely and fully implemented. However, it is important to recognize that the problem may not lie with the implementers, but rather with the weaknesses of the formal policies, particularly insufficient funding or cumbersome procedures.

A much less obvious problem is that many formal policies lack provisions to adapt to the changing conditions or varying contexts in which they are applied. In Thailand, Khotsing (2013, 6) notes that in addition to avoiding or delaying the granting of community title deeds, title deed officers confront legal rigidities that limit their function. In Brazil, the constitutional requirement that a proportion of the national budget and state and local taxes be devoted to education helps to lock in the commitment to education, but Alston et al. (2004, 7) note that this makes it more difficult to adapt to unexpected contingencies. More generally, they argue that "the initial high level of constitutionalization of public policy produced great rigidity in public policy in general" (Alston et al. 2004, 9). Raczynski and Muñoz-Stuardo (2007, 655) critique Chile's education policies on the grounds that "a standardized and rigid design has been preferred, that imposes changes on schools and does not take into account their specific problems and potential." Kinsey and Binswanger (1993) documented the rigidities of resettlement programs (focusing principally on Burkina Faso,

Guatemala, Indonesia, Kenya, Malaysia, and Zimbabwe), resulting in both economic and environmental problems.

Inadequate Accommodation for Groups Excessively Deprived by Policy Initiatives. Policy initiatives often have severe impacts on particular groups, whether intended or not. Although deliberate or inadvertent causes of what one would consider to be excessive deprivations are likely to have very different roots, the outcome is problematic all the same. Often, policymakers simply do not anticipate some of the consequences. Kothari and Pathak (2009, 2), after citing estimates of the number of people living in protected areas as between 2.5 and 3 million, note that the enactment of India's Wild Life Protection Law, following the Supreme Court's ruling that protected areas needed to be designated within a year, had the consequence that "[m]any state governments quickly complied with the order without any comprehensive assessments of rights, hence depriving thousands of people of their due rights; or conversely they allowed all rights in [protected areas] (as in Rajasthan) without assessing their impacts on the ecosystem."

In addition, the *termination* of policies, programs, or projects may be mis-timed in either direction. Premature terminations do not allow the provisions to demonstrate their positive impacts, or do not afford enough time needed for alternatives to be developed and enacted. For example, following Indonesia's decentralization, the withdrawal of the national government's provision of health services to internally displaced persons in 2003 left these people dependent on the inadequate resources of the subnational government units (Brussets et al. 2004; Massie 2008, 2).

In contrast is the failure to terminate policies that should have been ended sooner. For example, Argentina's peso-dollar convertibility, which began in 1991, endured far beyond its usefulness in the face of trade and financial imbalances (Jiri 2002). It caused enormous damage to Argentines, particularly the most vulnerable. The failure to terminate policies in a timely fashion often indulges particular groups at the expense of others, just as premature termination not only undermines potentially fruitful policies, but also deprives those stakeholders who invested their resources in good faith the chance (or time) to take advantage of the policies. For them, adequate lead time for termination occurs, and, often, compensation, may be compelling.

Avoidable Conflict Stemming from Policy Initiatives and Their Enactment. Although the bulk of policies, programs, and projects meet with some resistance, some policy designs, communications, and implementation approaches lead to avoidable destructive conflict. For example, Winichakul (2008, 26) argues that in Thailand the centrist, urban-oriented governments have been blind to the urban and central-region biases of government policies: "promises of tax benefits, industrial parks, more electric trains in Bangkok and measures to solve Bangkok's traffic jams, export promotions, and investment stimuli are seen in the urban-biased view as national interests and legitimate policies." His point is that this discourse denied the legitimacy of the complaints of the largely rural-based leftist-populist movement. Both the weakness of pro-poor policies by the centrist governments and their dismissive rhetoric increased the polarization and contributed to the political violence that erupted in 2010 and has continued sporadically since then.

Shortsightedness. Policymakers often fail to adopt farsighted initiatives recommended by development practitioners, either taking no action in the face of pressing problems or adopting shortsighted initiatives. Although this can result in ill-fated initiatives, or the futility of development practitioners when their advice is ignored, special problems arising from shortsightedness need to be addressed. The scope of the challenge includes not just whether policymakers and implementers pursue farsighted initiatives, but also whether stakeholders in general can be induced to pursue their own farsighted actions, as well as support the government's efforts.

Examples of shortsighted policies, programs, and projects can be found in virtually all sectors, from energy, physical infrastructure, and environment to education and health. Highways in sub-Saharan Africa are often opened with great fanfare, but the maintenance funds – often a less attractive investment – are typically neglected (Benmaamar 2006), with the result that the highways crumble prematurely. Resettlement programs may serve the short-term goal of alleviating congestion in high-density areas, but the conflicts with existing residents in the resettlement areas can have highly destructive long-term consequences. The early neglect of investment in urban upgrading has perpetuated urban degradation that would now require far more disruption and investment to reverse. Kombe and Kreibich (2012: 13) note for Tanzania that "[t]he failure of the slum clearance approaches, site and service and squatter upgrading strategies of the 1960s, 70s and 80s has demonstrated the exorbitant costs of retrofitting unsustainable settlement structures and left the state and its administration at crossroads."

Because of the short-term pain of abandoning popular but distorting tax exemptions, many governments have been unwilling to undertake sound tax reforms that would lead to better investment decisions by discouraging investments that are sufficiently profitable only because of the exemptions.

The rates of natural resource extraction for more immediate government revenues are frequently excessive even when world prices are low. For renewable resources, such as timber and fish, excessive extraction also risks the long-term problems of deforestation, desertification, collapse of fish stocks, and so on. When governments receive windfall revenues, policymakers often spend them profligately even when available projects and programs lack adequate rates of return. In the sphere of national security, policymakers frequently resort to heavy-handed tactics to suppress threats, increasing the likelihood of greater future antagonism.

STRUCTURING THE ANALYSIS

For each of these problematic outcomes, one can identify and analyze several malfunctions in planning, policy selection, implementation, and/or evaluation—and the interactions among these functions. In turn, these malfunctions are related to dynamics seen in some developing countries. The crucial next step is to provide diagnostic tools to aid in identifying relevant malfunctions and dynamics.

While it is clear that planning, selection, implementation, and evaluation are useful distinctions, a more nuanced set of categories has proven even more useful for identifying the resources, political aspects, technical challenges, and potential malfunctions of the policy process. This set, a core component of the policy sciences framework,[2] offers seven functions – which are not "stages," despite how they have been misconstrued by superficial critiques,[3] because they go on continually and interactively. However, if one wishes to follow a particular initiative, the process can be applied to follow that initiative as all of these functions shape it (or may kill it).[4] In other words, the multiple efforts are a continual swarm of activity, but once an initiative – whether a vague campaign promise or a detailed policy proposal – is on the table, it can be followed sequentially through time.

---

[2] In particular, Lasswell and Kaplan 1950; Lasswell 1971; Brewer and deLeon 1983; Lasswell and McDougal 1992.

[3] E.g., Nakamura 1987; Sabatier 1999. They both confuse functions for sequences or stages. Susan Clark (2011) gets it right: "Because these are functions or activities of decision making and not stages, they are often carried out simultaneously, rather than sequentially, and they are often mixed together in complex ways."

[4] That is why Brewer and deLeon (1983) segment the process into initiation, estimation, selection, implementation, evaluation, and termination.

TABLE 1.1 *Functions of the Decision Process*

Intelligence	Gathering and analysis of information, formulation of alternatives and other "technical" planning
Promotion	Efforts to secure preferred policies or outcomes
Prescription	Establishment of rules and norms (including laws, regulations, and allocative, as well as non-formal rules)
Invocation	Determination which prescription(s) ought to apply to a particular case
Application	Concrete carrying out of the prescription deemed to be applicable in each case
Termination	Elimination or significant change in policies, programs, projects, etc.
Appraisal (ex post evaluation)	Evaluation of outcomes according to criteria regarded as appropriate

Sources: Lasswell and Kaplan 1950; Lasswell 1963; Lasswell 1971

These functions are both activities and outcomes; therefore, we can evaluate each activity by using appropriate criteria (e.g., the honesty of persuasive efforts, which are part of the "promotion" function), and we can think of each function in terms of its outcome (e.g., people are duped into favoring a policy because of promotion efforts that are dishonest propaganda). Armed with this understanding of decision functions, we can then examine how they are likely to play out distinctively in developing countries, using an example that reflects the much broader set of initiatives to establish conditional cash transfers in many developing countries.

Addressing these seven problems entails a heavy analytic burden. They can be briefly summarized as follows:

1. To avoid supporting ill-fated initiatives, one must be able to anticipate the distorting influences that may affect the initiative as it proceeds through the policy process. This includes anticipating the possibility that some stakeholders may resist initiatives that in fact are in their interest, and assessing strategies for both conveying the consequences of the initiative and reducing the likelihood that acquiescing to this initiative would bring greater risk to the stakeholders.

2. The development practitioner has to appreciate that others may have very different views of the practitioner's role: Is it regarded as appropriate only to provide technical advice that does not go beyond

tactics of enactment? Does suggesting "second-best approaches" in light of existing constraints reduce the pressure to remove these constraints and pursue technically optimal policies? Some development practitioners may limit their input to the technically optimal advice, consciously ignoring the fact that policymakers may not follow it. Nevertheless, any participation in decision-making that is not oppositional may be taken as an endorsement of the initiatives.

3. To try to avoid the rejection of sound knowledge or recommendations, it is crucial to diagnose the analytical limitations of others and oneself. One's advice may still be ignored for a host of reasons, but understanding the difference between one's understanding and that of others is often crucial though frequently unexamined. This requires "an analysis of analysis" – what is the knowledge base of others; what assumptions do they hold that might be quite different from one's own?

4. To avoid neglecting more promising channels for pursuing a constructive initiative, it is crucial to identify the full scope of potential arenas through which an initiative may be channeled. The arenas range from executive agencies to legislatures to the courts, at levels from the international to the humblest local commune. This, in turn, requires an assessment of the resources that can be more effective in one arena rather than another, as well as the full range of relevant actors requiring consideration. Relevant actors include not only planners, policymakers, and other active participants, but also stakeholders whose positive or negative reactions are anticipated.

5. To overcome impasses that block the enactment of sound initiatives, one must diagnose problems of the policy process per se, and understand the psychology associated with various aspects of the policy process in order to anticipate otherwise surprising reactions to policy initiatives. These analytical challenges hold as well for understanding how to minimize destructive conflict arising from policy disputes and the consequences of the implementation of policies.

6. To overcome the problems of inconsistent or incoherent policy implementation, one must understand the multiple ways in which planning, policy choice, and the implementing institutions are intertwined (Pritchett, Woolcock, and Andrews 2010). This requires an integrated view of the policy process, resisting the temptation to

blame one slice of the process for policy shortfalls or distortions, but avoiding the "one size fits all" over-generalizations about these patterns across different countries. Ignoring the interaction is one reason for the huge number of disappointing diagnoses of policy failures focusing too narrowly on one slice of the policy process. So many failures are blamed on poor planning, without recognizing that the policy objectives, the pressures to act before adequate intelligence can be gathered and the analysis completed, and the uncertain prospects of enactment in light of other actions that leaders will take in the future are also in play. Other failures are attributed to the selection of excessive regulation, even though the rationale may be the concern that moderate regulations would be more difficult to prosecute. Yet other failures are blamed on weak or irresponsible implementation, even though policymakers may have deliberately left the implementation functions with insufficient resources.

7. To help in providing sufficient flexibility in formal provisions and implementation, it is crucial to understand why policymakers often feel compelled to adopt rigid policies. It is also important to understand why implementers often add rigid rules in undertaking their tasks.

8. To reduce the risk that policies will excessively harm particular stakeholders, one must be able to diagnose whether the deprivation is deliberate or not; and, if not, what knowledge needs to be brought to policymakers to convince them to moderate the policy. To help with appropriate timing and compensatory measures when policies are terminated, one must understand why the risks of mis-timed termination occur, and be able to anticipate the impacts of termination.

9. To minimize shortsighted policies, one must recognize when intelligence weaknesses limit the capacity to visualize impressive future benefits, and to have confidence that the path to successful long-term gains will be obtained. Policymakers championing farsighted policies need to project the credibility of their commitment and capacity to achieve the long-term goals. The prescription process has to permit farsighted considerations to receive due attention even when haste and crisis shorten time horizons for many participants. Inter-agency rivalries need to be held in check, lest agencies take shortsighted actions in their struggle for resources and standing. Ongoing appraisal must be effective enough to recognize

when existing initiatives are shortsighted, and the capacity to terminate such policies must be strong enough despite the opposition of vested interests.

10. In many cases one can address these problems by identifying strategies to adapt policies, institutions and processes, on the principles that some policies are more appropriate for the conditions of developing countries, and that more coherent, more responsive institutions and procedures are likely to yield better policies.

2

The Policy Process in Developing Countries Really Is Different

It is reasonable to ask why one cannot read some of the currently available texts on the policymaking process to learn how policies are made in developing countries and how to navigate the process more effectively. Yet even if these books do an excellent job of guiding the reader through the policy process,[1] they are focused overwhelmingly on the processes and problems encountered in developed countries. Just as wise economists realize that the dynamics encountered in developing countries are different from those in developed countries, posing different problems and requiring the exploration of different patterns, the policy-making process in developing countries also requires different foci and perspectives. The typical differences between the modal developing and developed country contexts affect all three of the categories of analytics, choosing policies, and implementation.

First, though, it may be necessary to preempt nitpicking about what is meant by "developing countries." Obviously a huge range of nations fall under this designation: from the so-called FCS countries that are in "Fragile and Conflict Affected Situations" to highly stable countries; from the countries with the lowest per capita incomes, such as Malawi or Nepal, to the "upper middle-income countries," such as Mexico or Thailand. However, recognizing that this label has been used in very

---

[1] Among the best of these are the books authored by Brewer and deLeon 1983, Clark 2011, and Howlett 2011 and the volumes edited by Brunner et al. 2005 and Fischer and Miller 2006. The useful Organisation for Economic Co-operation and Development publication *A Governance Practitioner's Notebook: Alternative Ideas and Approaches* (Whaites et al. 2015) is a compendium of pithy insights on development challenges and the practitioner's roles within the policy process.

different ways, what is important for our purposes is to clarify that we are interested in the set of countries that pose the greatest challenges in interacting on the broad range of policy issues. In this regard, it is useful to think about a "syndrome" of underdevelopment, which begins – but is not limited to – low per capita income. It is clear that important anomalies exist if only per capita income was the sum total of the definition. For example, Equatorial Guinea is classified by the World Bank as a high-income country, overwhelmingly because of the oil and gas exports. The World Bank is correct in its classification as "high income" – the per capita national income of Equatorial Guinea, at nearly US\$17,000 in 2014[2] is greater than that of Costa Rica or Panama. Yet roughly two-thirds of the population of Equatorial Guinea live below the poverty line,[3] and the economic instability of the country is evidenced by the fact that the 2014 per capita income was only fourth-fifths of what it had been two years before. Clearly, poverty and economic volatility should not be ignored as part of the syndrome. And, typically, the syndrome is also marked by low capital accumulation, underdeveloped capital markets, and low levels of productivity.

Another point requiring clarification is that positing that developing countries are different does not invalidate the broad policy sciences framework employed in this book. Regarding the policy sciences framework, the categories of decision functions are useful regardless of the differences in the conditions, trends, institutions, and options that policy-makers in any country face. It has been shown to be effective in assessing challenges and processes regarding specific issues, such as population (Montgomery, Lasswell, and Migdal 1979), political development (Brewer and Brunner 1975), and human rights (Nagan 1990).

Political economy is usefully defined as the study of institutions, resource allocation, and benefit distribution, taking into account polit-ical as well as economic factors, which motivate relevant actors and thereby shape resource allocation and benefit distribution.[4] The most

---

[2] This is in constant internal dollars at purchasing power parity – the best way to compare across countries. World Bank Database, http://databank.worldbank.org/data/reports .aspx?source=2&country=GNQ&series=&period=.

[3] The *African Economic Outlook 2012* ventures the following: "Equatorial Guinea has the characteristics of a low income country while having one of the highest per capita GDPs in Africa. About 75% of the population live below the poverty threshold and get no benefit from the oil economy."

[4] Many other definitions exist, reflecting the fact that economics as an entire field of economics historically had been labeled "political economy. Some of the vagueness is

prominent (but by no means exclusive) analytic methodology consists of efforts to trace out the implications of these actors' efforts to optimize their multiple objectives, assuming some form of rationality but acknowledging uncertainty. The hope motivating political economy approaches is that stylized models, with or without empirical data, will generate insights on causes and remedies of the problems of growth and distribution.

Drazen (2008) argues that political economy approaches are just as serviceable for studying developing countries as developed countries because the core political economy assumptions hold for both: government officials often pursue objectives beyond maximizing social welfare; they have to negotiate with other actors to stay in power and accomplish their objectives; and they operate under uncertainty.[5]

It is worth noting that the policy sciences approach is not antagonistic toward the tenets of political economy. The policy sciences incorporate the premise of multiple objectives by elaborating multiple value categories. The social process model of the policy sciences also includes any participants involved in or affected by social interactions.

The distinctiveness of developing countries, then, is not in the analytical framework or highest-level premises, but rather in the different economic, political, governance, and sociocultural trends and conditions that shape the challenges that the policy process faces.

---

illustrated in Edward J. Mishan's prominent text, *Introduction to Political Economy*, which states that "it is possible, for the most part, to use as close synonyms the terms 'political economy,' 'normative economics,' 'welfare economics' and 'allocation economics,' without risk of confusion" (Mishan 1984/2013, 19). "Political economy" can also be applied as the label for the economic analysis of political behavior (Weingast, Shepsley, and Johnsen 1988), essentially equivalent to the analytic framework labeled "public choice" (Mashaw 1989). The variety of what is labeled "political economy," is amply demonstrated by the range of articles found in the *Journal of Political Economy*, *European Journal of Political Economy*, and *International Journal of Political Economy*.

[5] Drazen's "political economy" elements include four sets of actors: 1) policymakers (from the top through the bureaucracy); 2) stakeholders (who influence but do not make formal policy decisions), many of whom organize in interest groups with which government leaders often have to negotiate); 3) those who choose leaders (which may extend beyond domestic actors); and 4) a subset of these actors that the leader "assembles" to keep him or her in power. Leaders have multiple motives, not just maximizing social welfare; the actors who chose leaders, operating with imperfect information, have to decide, based on past performance, and expectations, whether to continue to support the leaders. Finally, various mechanisms shape the processes that determine whether leaders will stay in power; various mechanisms determine policy choices; the differences within each set of mechanisms will determine the nature of policies that emerge.

ECONOMIC DEFICITS

Numerous differences between developing and developed countries stem directly from the lower economic capacity of lower-income countries. While developing countries can grow economically at a far higher rate than developed countries when conditions are ripe, their declines during bad times are typically also more extreme. Much of policymaking in developing countries entails coping with crisis.

Typically, developing countries are prone to more acute class or ethnic conflicts, which are exacerbated by scarcer resources. Therefore, policy choices are more likely to be fraught with contention and the possibility of destructive conflicts emerging from these choices. Such conflicts also make it more likely that some groups will resist particular policies, both in their formulation and in their implementation. In many cases, this also contributes to the instability of policy, as do irregular turnovers of government leaders. Reducing conflict potential may require less ambitious policies.

Lower educational levels often make it more difficult for citizens to have constructive understandings of policy content, or to have the knowledge and resources to participate effectively and peacefully. Therefore, policy discourse and the day-to-day interactions between government officials and representatives of stakeholders are more narrowly confined to the better educated. When lower income, less educated groups do get mobilized, their interactions with policymakers are likely to be more confrontational and less nuanced in terms of signaling policy and outcome preferences.

Lower economic levels generally mean lower *budgetary* resources per capita, often exacerbated by weaker tax effort. Bird, Martínez Vázquez, and Torgler (2008, 55) note that "[m]any developing countries need to spend more on public infrastructure, education, health services and so on, and hence they need to increase their tax effort – tax revenue as a percentage of gross domestic product (GDP) – if they want to grow and to be less poor." One might suppose that developing countries richly endowed with exportable natural resources would be less vulnerable to budget stress, yet governments of countries dependent on raw material exports often find it difficult to impose higher taxes when taxpayers expect the export revenues to fund government operations, and the volatility of export prices also exacerbates the budget problems. This volatility can make the planning and execution of projects and programs far more difficult.

Another important consequence of limited budget resources is that government personnel are often underpaid in relation to what they would consider to be sufficient for an appropriate lifestyle. The temptations to engage in corruption, and to rationalize it as necessary and therefore appropriate, are correspondingly high as well. This often undermines the efficient and fair application of regulations and service provision, as personnel in front-line roles such as inspecting, policing, and teaching try to exact greater compensation in their roles. Table 2.1 demonstrates the much greater prevalence of corruption in lower-income countries. There are exceptions: Rwanda, a lower-middle-income country, is at the 44th rank out of 168; 53 high-income or upper-middle-income countries have worse rankings. High-income Argentina is ranked 107th; high-income Venezuela is ranked 160th. Nevertheless, the pattern is clear that countries are more prone to corruption when government personnel perceive themselves to be severely underpaid.

Lower economic resources also typically mean less investment in the analytical functions of the policy process. Fewer resources are available to train planners and other policy experts, or to gather and maintain relevant information. The United Nations Secretary-General's Independent Expert Advisory Group on a Data Revolution for Sustainable Development (IEAG 2014, 12) points out that for the fifty-five key indicators of progress toward meeting the Millennium Development Goals, "there is no five-year period when the availability of data is more than 70% of what is required." These knowledge gaps, combined with the greater volatility of most developing countries compared to developed countries, increases the importance of building adaptation into policymaking. Root, Jones, and Wild (2015) argue that greater policy adaptability is required, yet adaptation also implies uncertainty about what policies will be in place over time and exemplifies the consequence of rigidity addressed above.

The lack of prior economic success contributes not only to greater economic vulnerability. Developing countries have less cushion in terms of maintaining the physical well-being of their populations. The economic meltdowns in the relatively developed country of Greece was certainly a horrendous experience for Greeks, but it pales in comparison to the devastation that low-income countries face in times of economic disaster. Greeks did not starve; Ethiopians, South Sudanese, and Papua New Guineans have. The precarious situation in many developing countries often leads to lower tolerance for failure regarding government plans and specific policies. A secondary consequence of this is that the governments of developing countries have greater incentive to suppress negative information, which impoverishes the analytical capability of their own analysts.

TABLE 2.1 *Corruption Levels and Per Capita Income*

Corruption perceptions index	70–91	60–69	50–59	40–49	30–39	20–29	10–19	0–9
High-income countries (52)	26 (50%)	7 (13%)	11 (21%)	4 (8%)	2 (4%)	1 (2%)	1 (2%)	
Upper-middle-income countries (42)		1 (2%)	3 (12%)	9 (21%)	18 (43%)	5 (12%)	4 (10%)	
Lower-middle-income countries (44)		1 (2%)	3 (7%)	4 (9%)	17 (39%)	15 (35%)	4 (9%)	
Low-income countries (30)					10 (33%)	13 (43%)	5 (17%)	2 (7%)

Sources: for the corruption perceptions (higher scores indicate less corruption), Transparency International 2016. Corruption perceptions index 2015, 6–7. For income categories, World Bank. 2016 (http://data.worldbank.org/about/country-and-lending-groups).

The same thinness of resources also hampers the enactment functions. Even aside from corruption, the certainty that regulations will be enforced is undermined when enforcement personnel are spread thinly. For example, for India's highly bio-diverse Uttarakhand forest, covering 38,000 km², there is only one forest guard per 10.5 km²; "safeguarding such a vast area has become a challenge for the department ... In most cases, neither this level of funding nor staffing are available" (Sahani 2015). Limited numbers of police officers or health inspectors similarly limit the effectiveness of regulation. By the same token, the scarcity of government personnel available to implement programs often dictates greater reliance on unofficial implementers. For example, cash transfer programs are frequently implemented by village head men or community activists, over whom policymakers are not likely to be able to exert the same degree of control.

Finally, perhaps the most complex consequence of greater economic fragility and poverty is that they typically dictate more interaction with development assistance agencies, whether multilateral (e.g., the International Monetary Fund, World Bank, regional development banks, the UN Development Programme, and the UN Economic Commissions for each region) or bilateral (e.g., the U.S. Agency for International Development, the UK Department for International Development). They provide a wide range of resources: funding, training, intelligence, policy advice, coordination with other governments, and so on. As mentioned in Chapter 1, what role they, and other external development organizations, should play is often a matter of contention.

Some of these organizations, in particular the World Bank and the regional development banks, have provided crucial funding, in the form of grants and loans, without which many programs and projects in developing countries would have been totally infeasible. The International Monetary Fund and the World Bank, along with the governments of developed countries, have also provided loans and loan guarantees that have kept many developing countries from being cut off from private banks, which could result in economic collapse. Yet, they provide not only guidance, but also frequently require adherence to policy reforms that in some occasions government leaders would be loath to undertake. In many circumstances, these "conditionalities" have been highly controversial for both practical political and ideological reasons. For one thing, these organizations typically have their greatest influence when countries are in greatest need of their support, which typically is an economic crisis that calls for unpopular austerity measures. For another thing, the conditionalities may be perceived as threats to a nation's sovereignty and as the dominance of the "North" over the "South." Globalization critics have denounced the so-called "Washington Consensus," an unfortunately misnamed set of economic policy precepts that, despite including the "redirection of public expenditure priorities toward sectors with both high economic returns and the potential to improve income distribution," has been demonized as serving the interest of the wealthy.

The more general issue is that policymakers face internal demands, and different time horizons, than the external development organizations. Maintaining eligibility for these resources often constrains the policy choices that government leaders would otherwise prefer – whether or not good for the country. However, as elaborated in Chapter 3, the situation is not clear-cut, as international development agencies do not share the same development approaches.

ECONOMIC STRUCTURE

The structure of the economy, as distinct from the economic level, is equally relevant. Overall, the underdevelopment syndrome features dependence on a limited range of important industries; raw materials dependence is common. Low per capita income and a dominant agriculture sector often go hand in hand. Of course, dependence on agriculture means vulnerability to weather and, for countries that depend on agricultural exports, to collapses in agricultural export prices.

Dependence on hydrocarbons is often even more problematic, because their international prices are typically more volatile. This is one reason why the major hydrocarbon-exporting countries, even if judged as "high income" by the World Bank's classification (sensibly based solely on per capita income at purchasing power parity), share some of the elements of the underdevelopment syndrome. High prices can bring enormous revenues relative to other industries, leading very often both to greater opportunities for corruption and greater conflict (Ross 2013). Low prices wreak havoc on government budgets, often elevated above sustainable levels during boom times.

Developing countries tend to have larger informal sectors (unregulated or minimally regulated economic activity, such as street vending, domestic service, unregistered small businesses, for which reporting is correspondingly limited). In many respects these individuals and enterprises effectively fall outside of government regulation as well as government programs, either because the scale of their operations is too small for some regulations to be useful, or because they evade regulation and taxation. Yet in low-income countries, the proportion of enterprises and workers in the informal sectors is often far greater. The first and most obvious consequence is, by definition, reduced capacity to enact regulations. Taxable income is under-reported. Less obvious, but often very important, is the limited information available to analysts and policymakers. In addition, a larger informal sector restricts the government's capacity to extend such programs as pension plans and loan programs.

The combination of low labor mobility across regions, the fact that some regions are likely to have much larger rural populations, and the uneven concentration of industries typically account for greater income and infrastructural disparities across regions within developing countries. One implication is that national policies, if uniform, may have less effective impacts in some regions compared to others. Another implication of obvious political consequence is that insofar as different regions have different ethnicities, the perception of neglect some regions may feel can fuel ethnic animosities and destructive conflict. Inter-group animosities may also serve as a rationalization for favoring intragroup stakeholders in both the formulation of policies and their implementation.

Because the frustrations of lack of economic success often lead to frequent changes in policies, it is frequently difficult to isolate the consequences of a particular policy from the impacts of prior policies. These past frustrations also erode the credibility of governments, both in terms of faith that policy initiatives will be successful, and in confidence that political leaders are sincere in the initiatives that they pursue.

The fact that some segments of the population (e.g., farmers, rural populations in general, small shop owners, and casual labor in cities) often lack the resources to organize on a sustainable basis, the density and breadth of interest groups are typically lower in developing countries. Therefore, effective interaction with policymakers is more likely to be skewed. In addition, if a commitment to limit the damage to stakeholders who suffer from the policies exists, it involves a more limited set of stakeholders.

Insofar as developing country economies are more agriculturally based, larger proportions of the population are rural, making it more difficult to reach them with policies or to monitor their behavior and the fates of projects and programs. Developing countries also tend to have greater disparities in income across regions, which also exacerbate policy debates. The responsiveness of the economy to policies is often hampered by low labor mobility, unwillingness to take risks by people on the edge of subsistence, and the unwillingness to depart from traditional folkways.

A combination of historical, economic, and political reasons has left developing countries with relatively larger state sectors than developed countries. In decolonized countries, the leaders of independence movements commonly maintained a strong hand in controlling the economy as well as the government; the countries that had been within the Soviet sphere have typically gone only part way in dismantling their state-owned enterprises. The lack of private domestic capital (or at least the inability to muster private domestic capital for domestic investment), and low levels of international capital (whether disinterested or discouraged) also prompted governments to opt for state-controlled and state-directed economies. Politically, dismantling state enterprises, at the risk of increasing unemployment, and the sometimes-well-founded fear privatization would further enrich the wealthy, have held back the more or less continuing efforts to reduce state sectors (Gwartney, Hall, and Lawson 2014; Nellis 2012).

This has two fundamental implications for policymaking. First, the personnel within the state sector are often crucial stakeholders not only because their actions can shape the success or failure of government initiatives, but also because they may constitute a formidable voting bloc. Second, in contrast to most developed countries, the ongoing project of state-sector reform is a mainstay of policy challenges facing many developing countries. While fairly marginal changes in the role of the state are common in developed countries, in most developing countries the proposals for reform are far more substantial, increasing the stakes and the level of contestation.

POLITICAL AND GOVERNANCE ASPECTS

The problems of governance for developing countries are clearly rooted in the lower-income levels outlined above. Table 2.2, which divides countries into the conventional World Bank categories of low-income, lower-middle income, upper-middle income, and high income, demonstrates a consistent pattern of greater difficulties for poorer countries in each of the governance categories of the World Bank's rankings. The countries suffering from the most acute governance problems, scoring at the bottom of the 0 to 100 ranking scale (e.g., Somalia scoring zero for "rule of law" for both 2013 and 2014) are within the low-income category across all six of the governance and political stability dimensions of the World Bank

TABLE 2.2 *Average Governance Rankings for World Bank Gross National Income (GNI) Per Capita Categories*

(*0 to 100 scale*)

Income level	Number	Control of corruption	Government effectiveness	Political stability	Regulatory quality	Rule of law	Voice and accountability
Low income[a]	31	22	18	25	23	22	25
Lower-middle income[b]	51	34	33	34	33	33	37
Upper-middle income[c]	53	46	47	48	45	46	47
High income[d]	73	77	75	75	77	74	71

a. 2014 GNI per capita less than US$1,045 (World Bank Atlas Method)
b. 2014 GNI per capita more than US$1,045 and less than US$4,125 (World Bank Atlas Method)
c. 2014 GNI per capita more than US$4,125 and less than US$12,736 (World Bank Atlas Method)
d. 2014 GNI per capita more than US$12,736 (World Bank Atlas Method)
Source: World Bank Database; World Bank Worldwide Governance Indicators 2015
http://data.worldbank.org/data-catalog/worldwide-governance-indicators

assessment. The differences in average scores for the lower-middle-income countries, the upper-middle-income countries, and the high-income countries are also completely consistent across all six categories (e.g., Singapore scoring 100 on "regulatory quality"; Finland scoring 100 on "rule of law").

However, the relationship between lower economic capability on the one hand, and the problems of governance and political stability on the other, goes both ways: governance problems hobble economic progress.

In many developing countries, the political formula, entailing beliefs about the appropriate form of government and appropriate ways that policies ought to be formulated, is highly contested. Developing countries are likely to have relatively greater disagreement on fundamental economic, social, and political doctrines. This brings into question not only the legitimacy and survival of a particular government and the policies that it is trying to undertake, but also greatly complicates the motivations behind supporting or opposing particular policy initiatives. One common response to ineffective policies (typically exacerbated by scarcer resources) is to reshuffle the policymaking institutions. In short, it is not just the government leaders who often face challenges to their authority, it is also the policymaking practices.

Thus, the application of policies, and the conduct of projects and programs, also have to cope with the greater conflict and violence potential in developing countries. Administrators may be deterred from applying regulations, or allocating benefits according to the formal policies, when the specter of violence is present. Therefore, it is not surprising that the risk profiles of developing countries tend to be quite different than those of wealthier, more politically stable nations. Policymakers facing imminent threats of economic downturns of uncertain magnitude, regime change, insurrection, or other extreme events are less likely to focus on the longer term.

The sustainability of developing countries' policies, programs and projects is also compromised by the relativity high turnover among leaders, subordinate administrators, planners, and external development practitioners. This erodes institutional memory, useful informal connections, and social capital. The political will to accomplish long-term objectives may thus be undermined by personnel instability on any and all levels.

Political instability, on top of economic disappointments, also increases the likelihood of military governments and greater power of the armed forces in general. To be sure, the "military-industrial complex," denoting strong ties between the civilian and military establishments, and high defense spending, are common in some developed countries, most notably the United States. In many policy areas, from technology export to geopolitical alliances and foreign assistance, national security concerns may well trump other concerns. However, in many developing countries, even where democratically-elected governments exist, the interests of the military often must be accommodated to a greater extent than in developed countries. One very important aspect of this is the prevalence of a wide range of industries owned and operated by the military (Brömmelhörster and Paes 2003). Industrial policies in such countries as China, Egypt, Indonesia, and Pakistan must take into account the vast industrial holdings of the armed forces.

SOCIOCULTURAL CONDITIONS

Insofar as the traditional norms of loyalty to family, clan, or ethnicity compete with more "modern" norms of impartiality, predicting the behavior of government officials and state service providers may be far less certain. The idea that these decisions ought to be made on the basis of strict neutrality may be accepted in the formal directives that government officials are required to serve, but the counter-norm of responsibility to one's ingroup means that bureaucrats have to struggle with these opposing self-demands (Riggs 1964).

Although corruption has some of its roots in poverty and the rejection of government authority, in many developing countries it has also become embedded within the culture as "normal," though still highly regrettable. One implication is that in many developing countries governmental actions are viewed with great skepticism, due to the expectation that corrupt motives may be behind them. Accusations of corruption, whether justified or not, frequently become political weapons.

Illustrating the Approach: The Thai Conditional Cash Transfer Initiative

Background. Despite strong pressures to redress income inequality in Thailand, no Thai government has developed a significant conditional cash transfer (CCT) program, although many other countries, including some in Southeast Asia (including the Philippines and, quite notably, Indonesia), have established prominent ones. These programs provide cash to low-income households with children, generally transferring the monthly funds to the mother. Eligibility typically requires regular healthcare for the children and school attendance if they are of school age. Thailand had a modest transfer program in the mid-1990s, but that was criticized for its weaknesses in addressing the poorest populations (Subbarao and Rudra 1996). In fact, Thailand remains very weak in social safety net programs in general: less than two-thirds of one percent of Thailand's GDP is devoted to social safety net programs, compared to 1.6 percent for developing countries across all world regions, and almost none of Thailand's poverty gap has been reduced through social safety net programs (World Bank Group 2015, 22, 28).

However, in 2015 UNICEF and the Thai Health Promotion Foundation, working with the Ministry of Social Development and Human Security and the Ministry of Public Health, secured a modest governmental pilot program for cash transfers to poor families with young children, the Child Support Grant Programme (Chanmorchan et al. 2015). UNICEF (2013) had noted two years earlier that "[t]here currently is no programme to help families cover the significant costs of providing children 0–6 with nutritious food, adequate clothing and early learning materials such as books."

The research, other sources of knowledge, and program design that have gone into the consideration of CCT programs in Thailand exemplify the *intelligence* function, entailing the gathering and analysis of information, the formulation of alternatives, and other "technical" planning efforts. The brief in favor of CCTs is the combination of providing cash to the most vulnerable, improving the health and education of children, and ultimately contributing to economic productivity through strong human capital. The initiative was developed by domestic NGO activists, the well-respected non-profit, non-governmental Thailand Development Research Institute, and the UNICEF analysts.

However, support for CCTs is hardly unanimous (Ortiz 2007; Tabbush 2010; De Brauw and Hoddinott 2011). CCTs have been criticized as paternalistic in pressuring the poor to comply rather than to make free choices. Some regard them as distractions from more fundamental economic restructuring, or as encouraging dependency. A straightforward economic concern is the high administrative costs that may render them less productive than other investments. Some have raised the concern that unless health and education services are bolstered, the quality of the services would be limited, for both old and new beneficiaries. CCTs have been criticized as excluding families too poor or too remote to fulfill the conditions. A feminist critique is that CCTs put undue burdens on the women who bear the burden of complying with the conditions, and set parents against one another. Some have argued that they encourage women to have more children in order to receive greater transfers.

Part of the intelligence challenge, therefore, has been to assess the impacts of CCTs in those contexts where they have been enacted, and the reactions to them in political as well as economic respects. The World Bank, the regional development banks, and academic researchers have conducted substantial research on this (Grosh et al. 2008; Barrientos 2012; Barrientos 2013; Alderman and Yemtsov 2013; Park, Lee, and Lee 2015; Molina-Millan et al. 2016). One of the concerns regarding the sustainability of CCT programs is the unsurprising finding that in Latin America non-recipients of CCT benefits are less likely to reelect incumbents who enact the programs, even if recipients are more likely to support the reelection of incumbents (Correa and Cheibub 2015). Ocampo (2009, 133) notes the Paraguayan business sector's opposition to CCTs when, in 2009, the government expanded safety net transfers to the poor in reaction to the Great Recession. Ocampo also notes the difficulty of managing CCT programs when the bulk of the population is very poor:

The controversy among interest groups is heightened by opposition to conditional cash transfers to the most vulnerable sectors voiced by business entrepreneurs and opportunist politicians. These transfers are more generous and available to more people than under the previous administration, which increased competition for them and complicated access. Conditional transfers are justified in 'exceptional times' and until better alternatives can be introduced. However, they are not a panacea nor are they easy to allocate fairly, since it is hard to discriminate between the poor and the destitute based on income alone, and everybody is affected by inadequate education and public health services characterised by low coverage and/or poor quality.

Of course, uncertainty inevitably remains as to whether the specific conditions in Thailand would conform to the various patterns found in other countries. Nevertheless, considerable research on the Thai context has set the stage for reasonably well-informed invention of CCT initiatives (Pannarunothai, Patmasiriwat, and Srithamarongsawat 2004; Boonyarattanasoontorn 2006; Dixon 2009), including survey findings that the Thai public is relatively favorable to welfare programs (Chandoevit 2010).

The Child Support Grant Programme demonstrates some of the intricacies of the *promotion* function, which covers the set of activities to try to secure preferred policies or outcomes. In terms of the program-design aspect of the promotional effort, the initiative adopted the tactic of beginning with a pilot program. This reduced the risk faced by the military government of approving a long-term program that not only may arouse opposition, but also undermine its stance as a caretaker government. In terms of the persuasive aspect of the promotion effort, UNICEF tried to preempt criticism by invoking "international experience" in its argument that some of the qualms about CCTs are unfounded. Most notably, a UNICEF "frequently asked questions" document, to preempt concern that poor families will have more children in order to get more grants, states that "International experience has been that child support grants do not encourage poor families to have more children than they otherwise would have. It is also notable that Thailand's birth rate is falling, and it is government policy to try to support families who want to have more children" (UNICEF 2013). In fact, the evidence is quite mixed (Grosh et al. 2008, 39; Fiszbein, Schady, and Ferreira. 2009, 121), although the assessments do indicate that the effects are modest, whether positive or negative. The UNICEF staff also asserted that contrary to the concern that CCT investments are relatively unproductive, "[a]n expanded Child Support Grant programme in Thailand will be a highly cost-effective way of addressing inequality and persistent child poverty" (Davin 2016). This may be true, but evidence is not provided.

Another promotional effort is reflected in the reportage of the survey findings cited above that the Thai public favors welfare programs (Chandoevit 2010). Here again, the evidence is very weak. The World Values Survey (2016), in its most recent (2013) interview wave for Thailand, revealed that nearly 50 percent of Thai respondents indicated a preference of a score of six or higher on the ten-point scale, where one signifies the strongest support for making incomes more equal; with ten indicating the strongest rejection of this position. In fact, 12 percent of respondents indicated the strongest agreement with the statement "We need larger income differences as incentives for individual effort."

It is significant that Thai groups that might oppose conditional cash transfers do not have to make unpopular public pronouncements of their opposition; they can try to influence much more quietly through participation, formal or informal, in the national budget process. One of the lessons here is that some promotional influences on policies may not be visible through monitoring of available communications.

The Thai cabinet's approval of the Child Support Grant Programme is an instance of policy adoption; in the jargon of the policy sciences, this is termed the *prescription* function. This slightly misleading term was chosen in order to avoid the idea that norms, rules, and requirements of action need to be formally established. The formal rules – laws, regulations, appropriations legislation, and so on – receive so much attention that it is easy to neglect the huge role of informal rules. These informal rules frequently are more difficult to identify, precisely because they are less formal, and because they are of two types. One type of informal rule simply exists in broad acceptance of how to proceed and behave; e.g., the legislators of the political party with the most legislative seats chair the legislative committees, even if there is no constitutional provision to this effect. Sometimes these rules are more enduring than formal ones. The second type of informal rule (which also can be labeled the "effective" rule) is how a formal rule is actually enacted; e.g., some communities formally eligible for program funding are excluded, while ineligible communities do receive the funding. Or the budget actually spent on a particular project or program is higher or lower than the budget formally approved and appropriated. Establishing this second variety of informal rule rests clearly on which policies are deemed as appropriate for each case, and how these decisions are carried out. Often, too much attention is paid to the formal laws and regulations, neglecting the often crucial importance of the "effective" laws and regulations. The fact that the Child Support Grant Programme is a one-year pilot program reflects the flexibility of the initiative in that, as a pilot, the program provides the opportunity to be adapted if and when the program is made more permanent.

The process required to select beneficiaries of the Child Support Grant Programme reveals considerable care taken to clarify whether the program's provisions will be invoked in the case of a particular family (Chanmorchan et al. 2015).[6] This *invocation* function – the process of determining whether a particular rule should apply to a particular case – is often overlooked, even though it is making effective policy, magnified to the degree that it serves as a precedent for subsequent decisions. Thus, the Child Support Grant Programme process affords potential discretion

---

[6] Chanmorchan (et al. 2015, 5) present a flowchart: the local administration introduces the project to potential target groups, either by volunteers or administrative staff, issuing a document of eligibility that triggers to process of registration, but leaving open the possibility of objections. The examination of birth certificates, which, if deemed as confirming eligibility, is recorded. With this information – and the birth certificate – the central government's administration records and organizes grant-receiver information, including the recording of birth information, and transfers funds to the provincial government to distribute to the beneficiary.

regarding which communities are approached and when; whether an objection is recognized as valid; and whether birth certificates are valid and qualify in terms of the child's age, as judged by both the provincial and central governments.

Whether the Child Support Grant Programme reaches the appropriate beneficiaries depends on the strength of the *application function*. This is the concrete carrying out of the prescription determined to be applicable in each case, but often provides wide latitude in how this is accomplished, and therefore also shapes the outcomes. The reliance on volunteers as well as government officials in contacting potential recipients is perhaps a sign of administrative weakness. If the governmental administrative capacity is weak, it might be attributable to the approved policy (that is, the pre-scription) that does not provide enough funding for government officials to take the full load of reaching potential beneficiaries. The earlier cash transfer program of the mid-1990s bypassed the poorest areas that could not match the central government's contribution. Subbarao and Rudra (1996, 37) judged that

> It is not clear that the village fund transfers can serve the intended purpose in the villages inhabited by predominantly poor. Those villages will have very little private resources to augment the government contribution. Ironically, the poorest villages are often short-changed ... The current uniform allocation rule (of 12,000 baht for every village no matter whatever the incidence and severity of poverty) is not very helpful for predominantly poor villages.

Thus, in some cases what seem to be application weaknesses may be more accurately attributed to policymakers' disinterest in fuller implementation. Another possibility regarding the pilot program, though, is that the strategy of relying on some volunteers reflects an intention to encourage community activism. In short, the application function may have programmatic and governance implications.

The pilot nature of the Child Support Grant Programme reflects a strategy of the *termination* function, which is the elimination or significant change in policies, programs, projects, and so on. The pilot program's limitation to one year of grants (although the assessment is scheduled for two years) has its termination built in, in contrast to many policies and programs that have no pre-determined termination date. The limited dur-ation of the Child Support Grant Programme largely avoids the resentment stemming from the disappointment of cutting programs in which stake-holders have invested hopes and resources. However, the pilot program does not cut off the possibility of a longer-term program in the future.

The heavy involvement of the Thai Development Research Institute (TDRI) in monitoring the impact of the pilot program reflects the commitment of the Child Support Grant Programme to the ongoing *appraisal* function, which is the evaluation of outcomes according to criteria regarded as appropriate. Appraisal, which is variously termed "ex-post (or post-hoc)" evaluation or assessment, is, of course, essential for determining whether a policy, program, or project ought to be continued, modified, or terminated. One might ask, "Why not simply consider appraisal as a variant of the intelligence function?" Distinguishing between the two functions is useful because it draws attention to distinctive analytical and political issues involved in assessing initiatives that have already been enacted. The uncertainty about the causes of positive or negative performance leaves open different evaluations by supporters and opponents of the existing policy. Supporters may give the policies the benefit of the doubt and opponents the opposite. Yet the uncertainty may also open space for promotional efforts, as can be seen in the arguments for or against CCTs.

Another distinctive aspect of appraisal is the challenge of making sense of the targets reached in relation to the targets announced when the initiative was launched. Is an initiative successful because it has reached or even exceeded the targets, for instance in terms of the number of beneficiaries reached or the gains in education or health? But are the priorities reflected by the targets shared by others? What if the targets were deliberately chosen to be so modest that their achievement should not be regarded as impressive? If targets are not reached, could this be because they were deliberately overly ambitious, in order to extort implementers to put in the maximum effort. Or because external conditions simply did not permit realistic targets to be reached? Or as priorities change, the targets have lost their relevance in fostering sound development, even though they may have considerable political significance? Stubborn adherence to particular targets can distract from pursuing better initiatives.

The analytic challenge may even be deeper: sound policymaking requires an assessment of how well a policy performs compared to possible alternatives. Appraisal is thus much more than evaluating what to make of the accomplishments; it depends on different conceptions of what might have been achieved; It other words, what could have been accomplished with other alternatives. This is not simply a result of promotional efforts to validate or discredit particular development approaches, but also reflects different outlooks that both weigh different outcomes differently and have very different expectations as to what could have been done with alternatives. For example, for CCTs that have been in place for many years, in such countries as Mexico, Brazil, and Indonesia, the appraisal of their success hinges on different theories as to what alternative expenditures of the same funds could have accomplished if they had been devoted to different programs.

Yet, despite the distinctive issues that arise with the appraisal function, both the intelligence function and the appraisal function are the interactive essence of policy analytics. Much of the intelligence inputs that went into the formulation and advocacy of the Child Support Grant Programme were based on appraisals of prior programs in other contexts. And as the consequences of the Child Support Grant Programme emerge and are measured, the debate will continue over whether alternative policies could be more successful, with advocates of alternative policies citing positive results when these other policies were enacted, either in Thailand or elsewhere.

IMPACTS ON THE POLICY PROCESS DUE TO DISTINCTIVE CHARACTERISTICS OF DEVELOPING COUNTRIES

With the fine-grained distinctions among the functions of the decision process, we can now be more specific as to how the syndrome of underdevelopment shapes the governmental policy process.

The intelligence function is often compromised in developing countries because of the economic deficits that beggar the government's analytic efforts. The economic diversity of developing countries and the limited information about the informal sector, as mentioned previously, limit the intelligence available to planners and policymakers.

In addition, the information that reaches planners may be skewed because only certain groups are able to convey their preferences. Time may also be scarce, denying policymakers the opportunity to gather sufficient information before actions are to be taken. For example, resettlement programs are sometimes initiated before soil, climatic, and hydrological studies are completed.

In addition, limited budgets exacerbate agency rivalries that may motivate government agencies to withhold information from other agencies. To the degree that developing countries are more politically and ideologically polarized, the interpretation of trends and the likely consequences of policy alternatives will also be more polarized. With less known about "facts on the ground," self-interested assertions are more difficult to dispel. In other words, the intelligence function is far from being strictly technical.

The promotion function tends to have a wider and more confrontational nature in developing countries that lack consensus on the political formula, lack effective channels of participation, or experience greater levels of desperation and resentment by the have-nots. A seemingly second-order issue may be fraught with political significance because the impasse on this issue may topple the government. Without routine mechanisms to try to influence policy, stakeholders are prone to more highly confrontational acts. While strikes and extra-legal provocations are not common in developed countries (for example, French farmers blockading roads), they are far less violent than the food riots that in some countries are seen as the only way to force the government to act. Insofar as the military sees the nation's economic strength as a core component of national security, actions viewed as threatening economic strength, such as strikes or boycotts, may be suppressed.

In terms of the content of the policies under consideration, the options likely to be considered typically are more extreme in relation to the existing policies, reflecting the demands by some stakeholders to escape from existing economic and social limitations. However, in light of the weaker intelligence and greater uncertainty in general, policymakers may be highly ambivalent about risking major departures. One possible outcome may be strong rhetoric with little major change. The heightened importance of the armed forces in many developing countries, as mentioned earlier, is likely to keep their enterprises more immune to privatization than state enterprises directly controlled by the government.[7]

In terms of the processes of formally selecting policies, some groups tend to be more dominant than others in developing countries. The typically greater imbalance in resources and organization between higher- and lower-income stakeholders translates into an imbalance of influence over policy outcomes, except when the poor escalate the confrontations as a promotional strategy. Grass-roots participation through formal channels by the broad range of stakeholders is more difficult; indeed, perhaps the most common explanation of policy failures in developing countries is the neglect of participation. A typical diagnosis is offered by Sah (2013, 3) for the failure of Nepal's education reforms, in tracing weak implementation to an inadequate prescription process: "The causes

---

[7] However, China recently appears to be an exception, as the government has been making a concerted effort to dismantle some of the Peoples' Liberation Army's enterprises.

of weak implementation of policies in the field could be because of formulating the policies without giving adequate consideration to the participation of those who are affected by them. To make [the] policy cycle more effective, the feedback and suggestions from the school stakeholders was [*sic*] required to increase ownership on the developed policy." Similarly, for stalled Nigerian family support programs of the 1990s, the post mortems maintain that although "for policies to be successful they should involve target groups, ... the programmes failed to take this important aspect of policy implementation into consideration. Most of the time, the target beneficiaries were not involved at the planning stage." (Makinde 2005, 65–66). This lack of participation can also be interpreted as an intelligence failure, in the lack of knowledge of needs (Ugwuanyi and Chukwuemeka 2013, 34).

In reaction to concerns over inadequate or imbalanced participation, developing country governments frequently have opened up the formal process to explicit participation by various groups outside of government. In Colombia, the 2006 efforts to formulate a national policy for early childhood development included "over 57 consultations ... in most districts in planning zones of Bogotá with an emphasis on poor districts" (O'Gara, Long, and Vargas-Barón. 2008, 55). These openings range from minimal solicitations of stakeholders' views to formal negotiations. Development practitioners – working for government, international aid agencies, NGOs, universities, or other institutions – simply may solicit people's concerns, either in a one-shot fashion or over an extended period, but with no implication that the participation has standing beyond expressing needs and wants. Some of the techniques have been controversial. One long-standing approach, "participatory rural assessment," a widespread technique used by development practitioners on the ground, has provided information previously unknown to planners and policymakers, but it also has been criticized for the risks of poorly sampling community opinion and the difficulties of determining the validity of respondents' claims (Priest 2014). Respondents believing that their input is not taken seriously are likely to resent the time they have devoted to these efforts, and also may fear that their responses may be used against them. Poteete (2002, 4) notes, with respect to Botswana and Ghana, that "[o]fficials who are rewarded for the use of participatory techniques for their own sake and do not see these techniques as means to achieve other goals may be content with superficial forms of participation, such as the solicitation of information." Often a substantial discrepancy exists between policymakers' assessments that they are providing genuine participation, and the more jaded perceptions of stakeholders.

An important but often overlooked distinction is whether solicitation of stakeholder input focuses on outcome preferences or policy preferences. Simply soliciting preferred outcomes puts stakeholders into a more passive position. How much stakeholders regarded this interaction as meaningful participation in shaping policy, or as simply providing intelligence to the policymakers, varies greatly – but is important for development practitioners to gauge.

Some developing country governments formalize "stakeholder negotiations" by organizing a prescription format designed to reach a consensus agreement with key stakeholders. Through such a mechanism to seek common ground and demonstrate concern for stakeholders' views, governments hope to elicit support for its policies, often attributed to the deliberations. Stakeholder negotiation formats vary considerably in terms of the range of groups that the government involves, and the degree to which outcomes of the negotiations are considered to be binding.

One particularly prominent variant of stakeholder negotiation, "concertation," was originally pioneered in Western Europe but has been employed in developing countries, particularly Latin America (Berger and Compston 2002). Typically involving a smaller number of peak organizations, often the major business and labor organizations, concertation focuses on finding common ground to reach "social pacts," often to check inflation,[8] but sometimes to reach broader development policy accords. For example, in 1994 the South African government established the National Economic, Development and Labour Council (NEDLAC), with representatives from Business Unity South Africa, the three major apex labor organizations, numerous government agencies, and six "community" organizations (specifically the Women's National Coalition, South African National Civics Organization, South African Youth Council, Disabled People South Africa, the National Association of Cooperatives of South Africa, and the Financial Sector Coalition), "to consult, 'co-ordinate' and negotiate on issues relating to economic, labour, and development issues pertaining to the [Reconstruction and Development Programme]." (Naidoo and Maré 2015, 417–418). Because the involved organizations typically are dominated by major modern-sector groups, concertation often excludes representation of the informal-sector groups and other less "peak" organizations. South Africa has hundreds of NGOs not affiliated with the six organizations represented on the NEDLAC, and

---

[8] Blake 1996; Cordova 1987.

only one of the 30 organizations within Business Unity South Africa – the National African Farmers' Union – represents small farmers, and its problems have resulted in the formation of a competing African Farmers' Association of South Africa (Mahala 2013).

Because of the multiple and often more obvious imbalances in participation in formal policy selection outlined above, government offices in developing countries are more likely to be closely tied ("captured") by a particular group, firm, industry, or labor organization. Of course, because governments consist of multiple agencies with different mandates and linkages to stakeholders outside of government, it is unlikely that "government" as a whole is fully captured by any one particular set of stakeholders. Yet it certainly is possible that policy choices, particularly regulations, are highly dependent on the inputs of particular stakeholders (World Bank and Inter-American Development Bank 2005). However, industry-group personnel frequently have essential information and expertise to formulate regulations. They also may have the knowledge of how stringent the regulations can be without triggering defiant non-compliance or a politically unacceptable backlash. Therefore, the question of whether the dependence is healthy or unhealthy requires a nuanced analysis.

Insofar as government offices in developing countries are under staffed, both the invocation and application functions are weakened. People deserving of government benefits are often under-served because of the backlog of processing; regulations are under-enforced for lack of inspectors. More complicated invocation issues arise from the tendency of developing countries to have regulations that are either highly restrictive or entail extreme punishments. In such cases, both the courts and the bureaucracies who interface directly with stakeholders (police, inspectors, social-assistance workers, etc.) may be reluctant to deem cases as fitting even when formally they do fall under the formal provisions. And because of lower monitoring capacity to assess whether these state personnel do invoke the rules faithfully with respect to the formal criteria, these state officials have more discretion to reflect their affective orientations toward residents, ranging from contempt to great empathy. Sometimes this reflects ethnic, religious, linguistic, or class affinities or differences; sometimes it reflects the degree to which these "street-level bureaucrats" are threatened or at least beleaguered.

The judicial system, in determining which laws, regulations, or other rules should be applied, is clearly central to the invocation function, and is marked by serious deficiencies in many developing countries. In addition to the inaccessibility to the poor that the Commission on Legal Empowerment of the Poor (2008) assesses, the contested independence of the judiciary leaves open more opportunity for arbitrary applications. On a more fundamental constitutive level, the struggle over the degree of judicial autonomy is heightened by two distinctive problems that may arise in the relationships between the judiciary and the top political leadership. First, lawsuits targeted against the government's invocation of laws and regulations will put the courts and the political leadership at odds when the courts decide in favor of those opposing these invocations. In some instances, the judiciary, in questioning the constitutionality of the prescriptions themselves, may be challenging the legitimacy of the top political leadership. Second, even more challenging for countries with contested political formulas is a court challenge of how the government decides policies and enacts them. When a Supreme Court, or its functional equivalent, declares that the government is in violation of the formula of governance, the stakes are obviously very high. This has led to efforts to emasculate judicial independence. Helmke and Rosenbluth (2009, 358) note that

Throughout the twentieth century, Mexican and Argentine judges may have enjoyed secure life tenure on paper, but most were routinely dismissed with every change in government. Following the third-wave transitions to democracy, newly minted constitutional courts in Russia and Peru were immediately rendered impotent by presidents whose powers they sought to limit. Since the 1990s, governments from Egypt and Zimbabwe to Bolivia, Ecuador, and Pakistan have dealt with recalcitrant judges through a combination of forced resignations, impeachments, and arrests. No doubt courts in poorer and newer democracies are especially vulnerable to institutional instability ... Argentina, Bolivia, and Ecuador have continued to experience profound institutional instability on the court even as democracy has become otherwise consolidated.

Although implementation efforts may be challenged by problems related to all of the aforementioned functions, they are most directly undermined by the lower administrative capacity directed to the application function in lower-income countries that are short of budgetary resources and adequately educated and trained government personnel. In addition, insofar as implementation requires cooperation by stakeholders outside of government, the cooperation and compliance important for enactment may be undermined by resistance due to dissatisfaction with perceived unfairness of the prescription and invocation processes. It is also possible that people who see a discrepancy between prescriptions and the practical applicability of these prescriptions may view the prescriptions themselves as cynical posturing. With lower monitoring capacity of developing country governments, defiance has a better chance of avoiding detection and negative sanctions.

The challenges that developing country governments face in deciding whether to *terminate* a policy, program, or project begin with the greater desperation of existing beneficiaries. Low-income beneficiaries in low-income countries are more marginal in their economic and social status; higher-income beneficiaries typically feel more vulnerable than their counterparts in developed countries when termination initiatives are under consideration. This vulnerability compounds the distinctive ethical and political issues of the termination function. Insofar as the current policies and programs draw in stakeholders who, in good faith, have devoted their hopes and resources to avail themselves of the existing opportunities and benefits, the ethical question of whether the government must soften the blow of changing the incentives is more acute for more vulnerable stakeholders.

The resistance to termination initiatives is often exaggerated in developing countries by the greater uncertainty of termination impact, further compounded by the typical divergence in expectations between government officials and the stakeholders, as well as among different stakeholder groups. For the development practitioner to be sensitive to these differences, the straightforward diagnostic would seem to be the discrepancies across actors. However, the challenge is to take into account the hyperbole that some stakeholders might employ to mobilize support and put greater pressure on the government.

The *appraisal* of existing policies, programs, and projects – whether undertaken by government planners and policymakers or by stakeholders outside of government – is typically challenged to a greater degree in developing countries for the same reasons (weak information about how the opaque informal sector is faring, limited information-gathering and assessment capabilities, agency rivalries that prompt information withholding, and so on) as for intelligence in general. Frequent policy changes make it more difficult to separate the impacts of current policies from previous ones. These limitations permit highly politicized, exaggerated claims of great success or abject failure that cannot be discredited with trusted information.

The appraisal of the performance of the government itself also is more contested when there is widespread skepticism as to whether the rule of law and impartial invocations and applications of policies are observed. The most prevalent criticism is that high government officials favor their own ethnic, religious, or linguistic groups. Even when this is not true, it is extremely difficult to disabuse people of this presumption, in light of the limited information that people have of how other groups as a whole are faring. The poorer the economic information accessible to stakeholders, the more likely that assumptions about the distributional consequences of policies are largely projections of presumed favoritism.

Development practitioners need to be prepared for the prevalence of highly critical appraisals. The focus of attention is typically on problems, not on what is going smoothly; often even more so for the informal evaluations of stakeholders who are unfamiliar with the constraints under which policies and programs operate. The general frustrations that beset developing countries exacerbate this negativity. In addition, positive evaluations coming from government sources are often seen as self-serving and therefore dismissed. Albert O. Hirschman (1963, 245; 1975), in his classic review of policy histories in Brazil, Chile, and Colombia, coined the term *"fracasomania"* (or "failure complex"), attributing exaggerated negative evaluations to a range of potential explanations, from a defeatist mindset to the political advantages of portraying current initiatives as unlikely to succeed or minimizing the accomplishments of the preceding regime.

3

The Expert's Risk: Endorsing Ill-Fated Initiatives

One of the most discouraging outcomes of involvement in the policy process is the regret – and often ignominy – of supporting an initiative that proves to be futile or seriously flawed once it has gone through the gauntlet of the decision process. It is one thing if one has the clout to keep a sound initiative on track. Yet, with the multiple processes involved in every policy process, no one can be totally certain that initial intentions will be fulfilled. All participants deciding whether to endorse an initiative, whether explicitly or implicitly, have strong incentives to ask whether the initiative will be successful. These participants need to identify the patterns that could undermine or distort the initiative. Determining whether an initiative will succeed, both in terms of its survival largely intact through the policy process, and its success if implemented as such, is an intimidatingly complex challenge. It involves gauging the likelihood of survival of the government, its second thoughts about maintaining a policy in the face of opposition, and the effectiveness of whatever eventually does get implemented. One must look for indirect indicators to determine whether one's endorsement is likely to be appropriate. These would have to be indicators of the government's commitment and capabilities – some of which are assessed in this chapter.

Consider the reputational damage the World Bank Group suffered from its support of the Chad–Cameroon Oil Pipeline, ambitiously intended both to bring desperately needed income to Chad, and to induce the Chadian government to channel the oil revenues constructively. Leibold (2011, 167) summarizes:

[T]he World Bank approved funding for the Chad-Cameroon Oil Pipeline on the premise that resource extraction would reduce poverty in Chad. Critics argued that the Chadian government, with its questionable record on corruption, would surely squander Chad's oil revenue, thereby following the usual trajectory of the resource curse. In response, the World Bank required Chad to institute certain measures to ensure that oil revenue would be used for development purpose. This novel scheme–considered the World Bank's great "experiment" in combating corruption in oil–led development included a revenue management law and a local and international monitoring component. Some believed that in these measures the World Bank had found a viable solution to the resource curse.

From the project's very inception, however, its implementation was fraught with problems ... Nongovernmental organizations (NGOs) alleged that the Bank failed to listen to their concerns about corruption and human rights abuses. They begged the Bank to consider delaying the project until more thorough anticorruption measures could be instituted. The Bank nevertheless moved forward with the project. Despite the Bank's novel revenue management scheme, Chad's President, Idriss Déby, shocked the global community by using Chad's initial oil royalties to purchase weapons. The situation deteriorated as Déby openly manipulated the Bank's revenue laws and oversight bodies. Ultimately, the Bank determined that it could not remain as a project lending partner, and it withdrew officially from the project in 2008. At first glance the World Bank's great experiment appears to have utterly failed ... [T]the Bank failed in the case of the Chad-Cameroon Oil Pipeline because the Bank (1) did not adequately consider the local context; (2) failed to listen to all of the stakeholders within Chad; (3) did not ensure that all parties realized benefits from third-party coordination, thereby creating a culture hostile to intervention; and (4) failed to institute firm measures to ensure Chad's continuing compliance, which was crucial given the Bank's diminishing leverage in the project.

The prescription that the World Bank was counting on being enacted was the combination of spending on the pipeline and budgetary discipline. The World Bank staff was aware, of course, of the risk of corruption, but presumably this intelligence was deemed as less important than the projection that the revenues from the pipeline would be attractive enough not to risk the financing.

The irony of the failure to induce governance improvements is that the financial success of the initiative, due to efficient construction, higher-than-expected deliveries, and high oil prices made the Chadian government far less beholden to World Bank. The World Bank Groups' Independent Evaluation Group (xiii) reported:

The oil revenue accruing much sooner and in higher amounts than anticipated was a major factor underlying the program's failure to achieve its development objectives in Chad. The management arrangements devised for a comparatively limited amount of oil revenue cracked under the weight of the much larger revenue that materialized. The larger revenue also generated temptations and competing claims that were in part associated with the re-emergence of political instability and violent rebellion. The slow efforts at capacity building were undercut by the more rapid inflow of oil money. And the oil revenue much greater than the total of foreign aid sharply altered the initial leverage calculus of the program. Despite notable isolated achievements, mainly in road construction and access to water, the World Bank Group's broad objective of helping Chad reduce poverty and improve governance was not met. Measured against this objective, the overall program outcome was unsatisfactory.

This case demonstrates that the analysis of whether to endorse an initiative is essentially a feasibility assessment, but one has to go far beyond the feasibility of the provisions announced in the initiative to achieve its goals without unacceptable negative consequences. It has to assess whether these provisions will survive in decent shape as they are formalized and whether these official policies will be enacted. Are other objectives – such as increasing the government's weaponry or personal enrichment – likely to swamp the stated goals? Are the time horizons of government leaders consistent with the pursuit of multi-year projects such as the construction of a pipeline? Yet, it also points to the complex relationships between external development practitioners and government leaders. In addition, the case was reasonably evaluated as successful in some important respects. The World Bank's Independent Evaluation Group (2009, xiii), never shy about criticizing project weaknesses, assessed several core aspects of the project as successful: "The main oil development and pipeline construction project was a physical, technical, and financial success." Thus, another key theme of the case – and challenges encountered by cases throughout this book – is the challenge of evaluation when performance is radically different for different dimensions.

To explore the kinds of risks that this case epitomizes, this chapter raises the analytical questions that one should ask, not to assess the technical feasibility of policies as formulated by planners, but rather to assess what happens thereafter: how committed are the government leaders; how will going through the gauntlet of the decision process change the initiative; what obstacles to its enactment need to be examined?

The framework outlined in previous chapters will direct this chapter in the following ways. First, the assessment of the malfunctions associated with ill-fated initiatives will begin with the possibility that the prescription function is masking an unwillingness of the policymakers to pursue the initiative. Note that the analysis need not begin with the intelligence function, although it is typically listed as the "first" function in the standard lists of functions. These functions are not in a fixed sequence, and beginning with the prescription function is warranted by the fact that if indeed top leaders fundamentally lack commitment, other issues are far less important. To assess the seriousness of commitment, development practitioners must examine the accuracy of their own intelligence function because of the conditioning factors that can send misleading signals, such as "restriction by partial incorporation," risk aversion as the costs of the initiative unfold, goal displacement, and divergent interests and time horizons – all defined and illustrated below. This is complemented by reviewing diagnostic indicators of commitment.

Beyond this scenario of lack of top leadership commitment, other potential policy malfunctions need to be addressed. The potential for intelligence malfunctions is addressed by identifying dynamics that prompt overconfidence on the part of policymakers: generalization from past success, several patterns leading to under-estimates of opposition, unanticipated resistance within the national and subnational bureaucracies, government analysts' self-censorship of doubts, and under-valuation of low-probability risks.

The dynamics that lead to malfunctions involved in the invocation and application functions include budgetary incrementalism that may reduce inter-agency conflict but constrains gearing up for new initiatives, bureaucratic rivalries that cause inter-agency conflict, and conflicting objectives between national officials and subnational officials mandated to implement the initiatives.

Several quite different scenarios are relevant to these questions. One scenario entails an initiative serving the interests of the policymakers at the expense of the common interest. The policymakers may adorn the rhetoric accompanying this initiative with language invoking national interests and the public good; the potential endorser must look more closely at both the impacts of the initiative if faithfully carried out, and the likelihood that the government will alter the policies over time.

One variant of this scenario is an initiative proposed by a government agency to pursue its particular mandate but without an assessment of the initiative's overall impact on other outcomes under the authority of other agencies. The decision as to whether one should endorse this agency's initiative needs to be based on an assessment of its overall impact, including whether devoting the resources to this initiative would erode the funds, regulations, or operations of other initiatives that would be more constructive overall.

For example, to preserve some of the initiatives highlighted in India's 2014–2015 central ("Union") budget for educational technology, expanded rural infrastructure, and so on, the government decreased the central healthcare budget by 20 percent (Kalra 2014; ICRA Research Services 2015). Another example would be launching resettlement programs into environmentally sensitive areas that would undermine conservation and ecotourism, as in Brazil, India, and Indonesia.

A second scenario involves initiatives that lack a serious commitment on the part of the policymakers. This has an important temporal dimension: the commitment may be regarded by policymakers initially as serious, but lacks careful consideration of future difficulties that could puncture the enthusiasm for the initiative. The endorser risks whatever credibility is lost by being associated with the initiative, plus the sacrifice of resources that the endorser has devoted to the initiative.

A third scenario involves policymakers' commitment to the common interest within their jurisdiction, but the initiative unravels as it goes through the decision process. The policy choice simply may be misguided because of some weakness in the analysis and design; it may be because of opposition by sufficiently powerful stakeholders, or because of the technical infeasibility of enactment. Any of these problems could result in modifications in the initiative that lead to poor outcomes.

Especially with respect to expensive new initiatives, the typical politics of budgeting raises the risk that resources allocated to the initiative in the long run will be inadequate. Budgetary incrementalism – modest increases or decreases for each agency from one budget cycle to the next[1] – reflects a strategy to reduce the conflict among agencies. Mogues (2013, 3) notes that "it is to be expected that incremental budgeting is more pronounced in domestic spending. Incrementalism has been viewed in Africa as a compromise solution to avoiding budget conflicts between agencies, and has also been the default outcome of input-based budgeting systems." Top government officials are often torn between putting the resources into major new programs or projects, and keeping the peace within the whole set of government agencies. When government revenues decline, the commitment to complete major projects often gives way to maintaining agency budgets across the board. Dim, Okorocha, and Okpduwa (2016) state that

a damming [sic] report from the Abandoned Projects Audit Commission which was set up by the Ex-President Goodluck Jonathan in 2011 revealed that 11,886 federal government projects were abandoned in the past 40 years across Nigeria ... A lot of public projects in the Nigerian construction industry failed as a result inadequate funding, and the difference between the national annual budget and the budget actual[ly] released.

---

[1] The classic expositions of this pattern are Wildavsky 1964 and Wildavsky 1997. The application to developing countries can be found in Caiden and Wildavsky 1980.

GAUGING GOVERNMENT LEADERS' COMMITMENT

An obvious challenge for anyone deciding whether to endorse an initiative is whether policymakers are sufficiently committed to pursue the policy even if greater political or financial costs arise, or if yet other objectives would have to be sacrificed. Some policy announcements are simply rhetoric, or do not stand up in the face of more opposition than the government leaders anticipated.

This problem of possible lack of commitment can be assessed in terms of the political economy insights regarding the conditions under which top-level policymakers have "ownership" of the initiatives they formulate or agree to follow.[2] The simple political economy premise that policymakers have multiple objectives that certainly go beyond the maximization of social welfare means that truly embracing an initiative – as opposed to posturing – depends on the degree to which the initiative does or does not serve these multiple objectives, one of which, obviously, may be staying in office. Therefore, the lack of "ownership" of a particular initiative by stakeholders whose support is needed by government leaders to stay in office frequently means that the leaders will not "own" it either. In addition, the policymakers' "ownership" will falter if they doubt the necessary compliance by stakeholders who have negative expectations regarding the initiative. In short, the failure to embrace ("own") an initiative on the part of these stakeholders can be doubly discouraging, in threatening policymakers' tenure in office and undermining the effectiveness of the initiative. One implication is policymakers' incentive and capacity to enact policies that are broadly favorable to society often requires support of a commensurately broad range of affected stakeholders. Bräutigam (2004, 656) argues, based on accumulated research, that "greater participation by affected social groups in policy formulation and implementation was likely to boost two elements found to be associated with successful management of economic policy: ownership and credibility."

---

[2] A broad definition of "ownership" is a policy preference that is desired independent of the incentives that are not directly related to the policy. Much of this political economy literature has been developed to address the lack of "ownership" on the part of government leaders of conditions required by international lenders, especially the International Monetary Fund (Drazen 2002; Boughton 2003). Thus Drazen (37), in relation to the external demands made by international financial institutions, defines "ownership" as the "extent to which a country is interested in pursuing reforms independently of any incentives provided by multilateral lenders." However, the logic holds for domestic interactions as well.

When policymakers are not sufficiently committed to their own initiatives, one fairly common tactic is "restriction by partial incorporation": adopting policies that seem to meet demands, but limiting the impact of the policies.[3] This may occur because demands are too strong for the reluctant government to ignore, but government leaders are unwilling to meet these demands fully. For initiatives involving programs or projects providing goods and services, this can be done by focusing on a limited set of targets for the initiatives, or limiting the resources devoted to them. For example, many governments have raised the age of compulsory education and have hired more teachers, but they have kept the compensation and training of teachers very low (Nordstrum 2015; Psacharopoulos 1989; UNESCO 2011), with the consequence that meaningful educational attainment has been weak.

For governance changes, restriction by partial incorporation is often found in decentralization efforts that reallocate responsibilities to subnational governments or community groups, but do not undertake the fiscal decentralization necessary either to transfer funds from the national government or to enhance the capacity of subnational governments to secure their own funds. Agrawal and Ribot (2006) conclude that this imbalanced decentralization has often stifled the capacity of these subnational governments. Thus, the labeling of an initiative may imply greater ambition than what is intended and will be enacted.[4]

For initiatives involving regulations, restriction by partial incorporation is often accomplished by reducing the administrative capacity to enforce them, building in loopholes to permit noncompliance, and so on. Environmental violations, tax non-compliance, and land takeovers are typical examples. Decentralization to levels of government dominated by interests that oppose the regulations is one tactic. Brazil's federal government has weakened the protection of the Amazonian forests "through decentralization of licensing and enforcement to levels of government that are more responsive to local entrepreneurial interests than to environmental concerns" (Fearnside 2016, 11). In China, pollution regulations have similarly been severely weakened through delegation of enforcement to the provinces (Lo, Fryxell, and Wong 2006).

One indicator of restriction by partial incorporation is the indirectness of the metrics and targets that the government presents. In the case of

---

[3] Lasswell and Kaplan 1950, 282–283.
[4] Turner and Hulme (1997, 151–174) argue that in general, decentralization is likely to be stronger in theory than in practice.

initiatives to improve education, a clear example is the metric of student retention through a particular grade, without taking into account the children who had never enrolled, or the irregularity of attendance.

For regulations, another indicator of partial incorporation is, paradoxically, unrealistically stringent regulations that have little hope of being consistently enforced. Pagés, Pierre, and Scarpetta (2009, 416) conclude that

developing countries often have detailed labor codes, which provide substantial protection – at least on paper. In practice, they generally protect a minority of workers in a subset of activities, often in the public sector, and are largely ignored by the majority of employers. At the same time, however, trying to enforce excessively stringent regulations may be costly for the public authorities and have a negative impact on labor market outcomes.

A political assessment might clarify how much government leaders need this policy to succeed; one indicator is the degree to which the policy pursues objectives important to both the government leaders' ideology and their core support. Of course, this has to be nuanced; government leaders are not all of the same mind, and one must take into account the additional need to keep disruption within bounds through compensatory policies for those who might suffer from the pursuit of the government's core objectives. In short, this assessment would be strengthened by understanding the government leaders' theory of how to remain politically successful while pursuing these core objectives.

A related assessment would focus on whether the government leaders demonstrate the willingness to take risks and make sacrifices. For example, in Ethiopia the overarching and controversial Agricultural Development-Led Industrialization program, begun in the mid-1990s and continuing with some modifications to the present, puts the government at risk because of its restrictions on urbanization (Broussard 2013; Lavers 2013), its reputation for favoring the rural sector, and the corresponding increase in urban unrest. Another indicator of the government's willingness to take risks is whether government leaders have been willing to punish lower-level government officials within their own group for not faithfully enacting the policy initiatives.

Another indication that government leaders are sufficiently committed to an initiative is taking available opportunities to embed the initiative within broader programs or agreements. Policymakers sometimes have the opportunity to increase the credibility of their commitment through decisions that would be difficult to reverse without high costs, which could convince both other governmental officials and stakeholders that the initiative will endure, and therefore compliance and participation are compelling. For example, they may create institutions, such as environmental ministries, that would be difficult to dismantle without antagonizing the personnel within them. Credibility often requires a strong enough symbolic commitment by political leaders that, if the initiative falters, would result in a political embarrassment, or devoting sufficient upfront resources, which, if wasted, also would be costly for the government. These forms of "self-hostaging" are typically apparent when they do occur; more in-depth analysis is required to determine whether such opportunities are ignored.

On the other hand, seemingly strong initiatives may be weakened by "goal displacement" that blunts the ambition of the initiative.[5] A fundamental goal, such as improving the health, education, and productivity of low-income families, may be supplanted, and indeed undermined, by efforts to achieve intermediate goals ostensibly directed to fulfill the ultimate goal. Consider a conditional cash transfer program, requiring poor families, eligible by meeting means tests, to keep their children in school and to provide them with appropriate healthcare. The intermediate goals may be to strengthen the capacities of the agency administering the program, register as many of the poor as possible, apply the eligibility criteria as accurately as possible, determine precisely which families meet the conditions to remain eligible, transfer the maximum volume of funds to the maximum number of families, or some combination of these. Program administrators may be evaluated on the basis of metrics related to these intermediate goals, depending on which goals within this internally contradictory set are emphasized in the performance evaluation. Yet registering as many families as possible may divert funds from the neediest, or from the families that would make the most progress in the ultimate goals of improved health, education, and productivity. Stringent determination of continued eligibility might sap the overall budget, and unnecessarily deny the opportunities to families with promising potential. The point is that pursuing these goals as if they were ends in themselves runs the strong risk of undermining more compelling goals. Another example is gender policy; Okafor and Abdulazeez (2007, 245) argue that removing obstacles to female activism is no substitute for much stronger imbedding of gender considerations within development initiatives. While in many countries, the governance system guarantees a quota for women to hold positions ranging from local councils to national legislatures, these provisions – often more symbolic than effective – may

---

[5] Introduced by Robert Michels (1915/1949), with reference to bureaucracies subverting the ultimate goals of their mandates.

distract attention away from initiatives that enhance the rights, prerogatives, and treatment of women.

The assessment of whether goal displacement is a serious problem depends on how distorting the intermediate goal may be. This can be assessed in terms of excessive effort to achieve the intermediate goal, the degree of neglect of other intermediate goals, and how much the progress toward meeting the intermediate goal differs from meeting the fundamental goal. For example, if the push to register beneficiaries of the cash transfer program is severely draining resources away from the expansion of services to meet the increased demand for healthcare or education, or if rewarding the personnel involved in signing up new beneficiaries dominates the assessment of how well the program is doing, it would be clear that goal displacement is a problem deserving of attention.

Overall, the question is whether the goal is still directed to providing the same valued outcomes as the original demands. One key to assessing the risk of goal displacement is to ask whether the initiative is framed in terms of the needs of stakeholders rather than the effectiveness or efficiency of providing the goods and services. Of course, effectiveness and efficiency are important; the question is whether the framing of the initiative runs the risk of elevating metrics related to intermediate goals that would supplant assessments of achieving more fundamental impacts.

Interpreting the interactions with international institutions can also be useful in assessing the seriousness of commitment, as an example of "hands-tying" – deliberate restriction of feasible options – though the analysis is complicated. As mentioned in Chapter 1, developing country governments sometimes agree to "conditionalities" (commitments to enact particular policies, sometimes including structural changes) with international organizations such as the International Monetary Fund, the World Bank, the regional development banks, and bilateral foreign assistance agencies, in order to secure loans or grants, and to benefit from broader collaboration. In some cases, government leaders are compelled, reluctantly, to make these agreements because of their precarious economic situation. The reluctance reflects the government leaders' belief that the policies are politically unpopular, reduce the power of government leaders, or are too costly to groups that the government wishes to favor.

However, in other circumstances the external commitments indicate a stronger commitment, if the policymakers voluntarily enter into these agreements. The motives may be to make the policy less vulnerable to opposition by raising the costs of abandoning the policy. These costs may be the cancellation of other agreements, economic sanctions, the withdrawal of foreign assistance, and so on. The agreements may also be intended to tie the hands of successors if need be, in addition to reinforcing their own effort with the collaboration of the external institutions.

POTENTIALS AND LIMITATIONS OF ASSESSING AND SHAPING INCENTIVES

Whether trying to gauge the seriousness of policy initiatives and the likelihood that various actors would alter the objectives, or devising strategies to motivate appropriate actions, it is obviously important to identify the types of incentives that would shape the behavior of involved individuals. With respect to reinforcing the commitment needed to propel sound policies and programs that development practitioners help design, they need to assess the degree to which the incentives built into the roles and rewards of leaders and staff must resonate with their incentive priorities. Just as importantly, development practitioners must be aware of the risk that extrinsic rewards would not undermine the intrinsic commitments of the leaders and staff. In some circumstances, providing external rewards can "crowd out" the intrinsic rewards that often bring people to public service (Festré and Garrouste 2015).

The two intuitive ways to infer incentive priorities are to examine individuals' behaviors for tradeoffs, noting the exchange of what is of lower priority to gain something of higher priority, and to assume that for people experiencing serious shortfalls in the typical level of rewards in that society would raise their priorities to overcome the shortfalls. However, these baseline approaches need to be augmented to overcome their static nature; past tradeoffs may not be relevant going forward, and perceptions of either shortfalls or threats to existing rewards may be highly volatile. Therefore, it is important to pay close attention to indicators of the current foci of attention, insofar as preferences are often "discovered" as much as they are "known" (Festré and Garrouste 2015, 1–2).

With respect to reducing the likelihood that sound initiatives would be diverted into less sound directions, the development practitioner also needs to anticipate when the implementers' incentives are inconsistent with the reward structures designed to motivate undistorted implementation (Eisenhardt 1989). This is the classic question of whether the "principle-agent relation" presents problems that may need to be addressed by greater monitoring, personnel changes, or altering the reward structures. If the interests of implementers and policy initiators are too much at odds, the development practitioner may have to decide that the prospects for the initiative are too bleak to be endorsed.

However, one should not assume that just because implementers faithfully carry out directives from higher-level policymakers, the initiatives are worth embracing. In some instances, top-level leaders delegate implementation in order to distance themselves from the harsh impacts of the initiatives. Hamman, Loewenstein, and Weber (2010, 1826) point out that

a principal may hire an agent to take self-interested or immoral actions that the principal would be reluctant to take more directly. The principal may feel more detached, and hence less responsible, for such an action if it is delegated, while the agent may feel that he or she was "just carrying out orders" or merely fulfilling the requirement of an employment contract. Through the use of agents, therefore, accountability for morally questionable behavior can become vertically diffused, with no individual taking responsibility.

DIVERGENT INTERESTS

The final broad concern is that an initiative that makes sense for the policymaker could run counter to the goals of the endorser due to differences in either risk tolerance or time horizon.

Risk Profile Differences. Potential endorsers who are not themselves policymakers also have to be aware of differences between their own risk profile (risk tolerance; how much is at stake) and that of government leaders. The costs – reputational, financial, or otherwise – that the endorser faces are likely to be quite different from those of the policymakers. This translates into different risk tolerance. The potential pitfall for the potential endorser is in trusting the policymakers' judgment on the advisability of an initiative if the policymakers' risk tolerance does not correspond to the endorser's risk tolerance. The analytical challenge is to gauge how much risk the policymakers are willing to take, both in the projects and programs they undertake, and in the adaptations they may or may not be willing to carry out if problems arise. Sometimes policymakers are willing to take on highly risky ventures because they have little to lose. Sometimes policymakers face what they regard as excessive risk if they were to alter a policy, even if that policy is at risk of disaster. For example, in Argentina the policy of setting the peso equivalent to the dollar was remarkably successful in choking off inflation when it began in 1991, but economic imbalances led to enormous economic and political turmoil in 1999–2002. The "peso-dollar convertibility" became untenable because of money laundering, Brazilian devaluations that increased Argentina's trade deficit, and other factors that had become increasingly apparent. Yet the Argentine governments were too politically fragile to wean the country off the policy when it became damaging. The International Monetary Fund, which had supported the plan, came in for severe criticism in the early 2000s when the policy unraveled, at great economic and human cost to the country (Daseking et al. 2004, 39–41).

Time Horizon Differences. Policies have short-, medium-, and long-term consequences; policymakers and potential endorsers often have different preferences and commitments regarding time horizons. Policymakers may select initiatives that are successful during the period most crucial to the policymakers, which may not be the same time period of greatest concern for the potential endorser. When elections are looming, government leaders often pump money into initiatives that will stimulate the economy in the short term, sometimes leading to higher inflation, or even bankruptcy in the longer run. The Argentine peso-dollar convertibility case is relevant here as well. The policy was effective for nearly a decade despite the lack of provisions for terminating the policy when necessary, providing short-term benefits that certainly bolstered Argentine governments through the 1990s, compared to the situation that would have held if high levels of inflation had endured. Yet from the perspective of the International Monetary Fund, the post-2000 debacle tarnished the organization's reputation in the long run.

HOW AND WHY WELL-INTENTIONED GOVERNMENT LEADERS LAUNCH ILL-FATED INITIATIVES

When government leaders are strongly committed with the intention of serving the common interest, it is useful to ask why anyone other than the formal policymakers should expect to be able to second-guess the wisdom of these policymakers. After all, they typically have access to technical expertise, both within their own governments and, if they wish, from other experts, both domestic and international; and presumably they have the political acumen to know what will fly politically.

However, even under these assumptions – political leaders' commitment and access to expertise – the likelihood of the success of the initiative needs to be assessed for two reasons. First, the government may not survive, but government leaders typically operate as if they will be able to continue even if the odds of being ousted are substantial. Therefore, even if the government leaders are realistic in their expectations of possibly leaving office, they may pursue the initiative even if others would be skeptical about their success. Of course, most government leaders would not signal their own doubts of survival; the development practitioner must seek political risk assessments to factor in this risk. It is important to keep in mind, though, that initiatives still may be blunted if government leaders come to believe that the particular initiative would increase the chances of being ousted.

The more common scenario of problematic policy initiatives by well-intentioned policymakers is that they have unrecognized biases. These biases can often be identified by others, by understanding that formal policymakers are often insulated from various forms of knowledge that would have led them to think twice about their policy initiatives. Being aware of these blind spots can reinforce the political risk assessment in determining whether the initiatives are less likely to succeed.

Because overconfidence may lie in overestimating the support or underestimating the opposition to an initiative, a broad diagnostic approach is to determine what information has come to the attention of policymakers who are expressing confidence that their initiatives will succeed in fairly undistorted form. One approach is to ask whether the policymakers have successfully identified the constraints that would limit the survival and effectiveness of the initiative. To accomplish this, it is important to identify why awareness may be lacking. Some stakeholders who would like to express their views on initiatives have limited capacity to do so; other stakeholders lack the incentive to make their true preferences known. It is common for government leaders to know less about the true feelings of the groups generally in opposition to that government, especially in authoritarian systems in which the fear of retribution increases the reluctance to provide information. Yet even without expressing opposition, stakeholders who dislike particular policies, projects, and programs can undermine these initiatives through techniques ranging from quiet boycotts and noncompliance to physical sabotage and insurrection.

Another limitation is that government analysts and policymakers are often unaware of the expectations of stakeholders as to the consequences of the initiative and what further initiatives might follow. Due to the general human tendency of people to think of themselves as more kindly and well-intentioned than others would, policymakers run the risk of incorrectly presuming that their expectation of fair outcomes for various stakeholders will be shared by those stakeholders. Stakeholders at greater distance from the policy deliberations are also less likely to know of the safety nets that planners and policymakers are prepared to enact if the damage to those stakeholders is too high. For example, planners and policymakers contemplating a hydroelectric dam project may feel fully committed to compensating downstream populations for any damage to the fisheries, but these populations have scant basis to be sure that this compensation will be forthcoming, especially given the uncertainties as to what the actual impact will prove to be.

In addition, analysts and policymakers may be fully preoccupied with assessing the substantive impacts of the initiatives that they are formulating and selecting. Yet, as mentioned in Chapter 1, some stakeholders may have longer-term expectations that if an initiative goes through, further initiatives would be more damaging to their interests. For example, if the initiative entails a new form of tax (as was the case of the first rural land tax enacted in Colombia in 1972), the affected stakeholders may worry that a modest initial tax rate will be increased substantially once the tax is in place. An important diagnostic tool is to assess the discrepancies between stakeholders' expectations and policymakers' beliefs about these expectations.

Another question is whether the champions of the initiative are underestimating the discretion, motivations, or limitations that downstream decision-makers have that would distort the initiative. Regarding discretion, those who make decisions as to which policy provisions should be applied to each specific case – the invocation decision – often have high degrees of flexibility, both in deciding which provisions to invoke and the nature and magnitude of benefits or sanctions. Those mandated to apply the selected rules often have their own discretion, or simply may not be able to enact the policy. The dilemma for policymakers is that a certain degree of flexibility is necessary in applying policies across different contexts, but too much discretion opens up room for implementers to undermine the initiative.

One might presume that government analysts would be able to anticipate these difficulties and convey them to policymakers. However, relying on in-house analysts has its own pitfalls. The analysts may feel compelled to engage in self-censorship for several reasons. The analysts may hide their private considerations for fear of antagonizing decision-makers, if these considerations reflect the possibility that decision-makers lack competence, commitment, or honesty. The analysts may feel compelled to disregard other aspects of uncertainty in the face of implicit pressure from policymakers to maintain optimism and morale for the pursuit of the government's overall "project."[6] The analysts may be fearful of suggesting an unpopular recommendation, such as modifying the brainchild of

---

[6] To be sure, analysts sometimes express more uncertainty than is justified, in order to reduce blame if projections prove to be inaccurate.

the policymaker, even if it reflects their best judgment. Comparing the analyses of intra-agency analysts to those of external analysts can often be a good diagnostic of these shortcomings.

An even thornier challenge arises when an initiative faces major, but low-probability, risks. Will an earthquake or hurricane destroy the key bridge in the highway expansion? Will the effort to induce shifts to other crops encounter unanticipated insect infestation? Will the implementation routines for conditional cash transfer programs break down? Will rumors of nefarious motives undermine immunization programs? It is very difficult to assign a probability to such low-probability, high-cost events. Simply to list such low-probability events may well imply greater risk than is reasonable. On the other hand, ignoring the possibility of such risks can bias the analysis in an overly optimistic way.[7] Analysts, whether or not within the government, typically can only warn policymakers about these risks, rather than venture probabilities or secure sufficient contingency funds to offset the potential damage. The reactions of the policymakers depend as much on their degree of optimism or pessimism as on the benefit-cost analysis details.

If an initiative is not enacted, the development practitioner faces a complicated diagnostic challenge. One possibility is that the personnel involved in determining whether the provisions of a policy ought to be applied, or the personnel directly involved in applying them, simply oppose the initiative and use whatever degree of discretion they have to blunt it. Delays, wasting available resources on peripheral tasks, invoking other prescriptions, and so on, are well-known tactics. Yet another possibility is that the initiative encounters so much resistance from stakeholders that those involved in the invocation and application functions, even if in favor, pull back from enacting the initiative. Moving people, taxing them, vaccinating them, or enlisting their labor in public works may entail either significant risks for the personnel who were supposed to enact these initiatives, or simply may be met with noncompliance.

It is also possible that the initiative simply cannot be applied effectively, either because of lack of administrative capacity or the physical impossibility of carrying out the provisions. For example, the plan to resettle people successfully may not be possible due to infrastructure deficits in that area. Larrousse, Mathur, and Saunders (2006, 12) note:

---

[7] Even if these low-probability occurrences result only in delays of the projects or programs, the rates of return decline as long as future cash flows are discounted. This is one reason why so many ex-post assessments of rates of return are more disappointing than the ex-ante rates of return.

The current population living in resettlement colonies in Delhi is 1.2 million, which represents 10.5 per cent of the capital city's entire population ... Despite the benefit of permanent homes, hardships remain following resettlement. Due to limited government attention and the resulting lack of civic amenities in these communities, living conditions remain similar to those found in slums. Further straining the inadequate infrastructure of these areas, slums and resettlement colonies get an influx of 150,000 migrants a year.

For the huge number of initiatives that require the cooperation of multiple agencies, planners and policymakers formulating the initiative often lack sufficient knowledge of the degree of commitment and capacity of other agencies. This frequently reflects the imbalance of information known within and outside of the other agencies. Therefore, the initiators are typically in a poor position to assess whether there has been a failure to enact necessary complementary policies under the jurisdiction of other ministries or agencies.

The lack of inter-agency cooperation can be examined systematically by noting the possible sources of opposition and conflict. Several sources of conflict are fairly common:

Mandate Conflicts. Different agencies have conflicts in the pursuit of their conflicting mandates. For example, Soetarto, Sitorus, and Napiri (2001, 26) note the problems of forest management in West Kalimantan, Indonesia:

The most prominent example of inter-agency conflict was between the forestry and industrial government administrative sectors. Forestry agencies commonly seek to impose limits on the growth of the wood processing industry, while industrial agencies' aims are to expand opportunities for new private sector investment in the district ... The issuance of location licenses for private sector timber plantation investment has also generated friction between the National Land Agency ... and the Plantations Branch Office.

Similarly, Gwynne and Cristobal (2014, 131) note that in Latin America the bureaucratic rivalries that pit agricultural and mining ministries against environmental agencies have undermined efforts to deter land invasions in protected areas.

This might seem to be resolvable through oversight above the involved agencies; in principle, government leaders at higher levels have the authority to direct the personnel of all involved to cooperate fully. Yet the information imbalance also holds in the advantage of lower-level officials who are closer to the realities involved in allocating resources and implementation. Lower-level officials can appear to comply, without really putting the resources into the effort. This is another instance of "restriction by partial incorporation."

At times, the conflicts over mandates translate into jurisdictional conflicts, as different agencies have formal claims to control a broad set of activities within the same area. In some countries, formal mandates of different agencies create conflicts over which agency ought to have jurisdiction over the same area or operations. The forestry ministry may designate land as "forest" according to its own land classification system – regardless of the density of trees – and therefore the ministry claims authority over residence and activities in the area. The agricultural ministry may invoke its own land classification system to make its counter-claim, as could the population resettlement agency. These conflicts among national-level agencies have been common in Brazil and Costa Rica (Ascher 1999, 116; 152–153). Land-use classifications employed by national governments and subnational governments may also conflict, as in Indonesia (Soetarto, Sitorus, and Napiri 2001, 1–2).

Ideological Conflicts. Even deeper conflicts of an ideological nature can divide agencies beyond their differences in mandates. New governments, even if dominated by a particular outlook or ideology, typically inherit personnel from previous administrations; these people may have quite different ideological commitments. Coalition governments, so prominent in parliamentary systems, frequently have ministers of different parties, with different priorities and often a need to differentiate themselves programmatically from other parties within the coalition.

Resource Competition. Even when the missions and outlooks do not clash, competition for funding is often present. The finite nature of the government's budget means that agencies compete for the resources they need to pursue their mandates. The perceived responsibility of a minister typically is to gain the largest possible budget, certainly not to press for more budget for other ministries aside from collaborative programs.

Leadership Rivalries. Cabinet members may be involved in personal competition for even higher position, particularly if they are party or faction leaders. Again, this may well be more pronounced if the leaders are of different political parties, ethnicities, or clans.

Conflicts among Government Levels. When initiatives are launched at one level of government but are to be implemented by another, differences in objectives and priorities may motivate the implementers to resist the initiative. The same holds when national and subnational policymakers need to coordinate if each is responsible for formulating and enacting provisions that ought to complement one another. This is especially problematic when the national and subnational leaders are political competitors motivated to undermine one another. For example, for extended periods since the mid-1990s, the national government of Thailand had been in the hands of the leftist-populist Thai Rak Thai Party,[8] while the centrist Democrat Party controlled the Bangkok Metropolitan Adminis-tration. The national government's decisions over transportation planning seriously undermined the land-use planning and regulation under the Bangkok Metropolitan Administration, contributing to the chaos of Bangkok's traffic and the vulnerability of developed areas to flooding.

Another analytical weakness can arise from the psychological dynamic of "groupthink," the tendency of people who work together to reach consensus uncritically.[9] The decisions emerging from deliberations reached this way are likely to seem more obvious than is warranted. Therefore, the alterna-tives that are likely to be formulated may not adequately reflect the appro-priate levels of uncertainty. If one is present at the deliberations, it may not be very difficult to determine whether groupthink is at work. However, it is more challenging to diagnose whether groupthink has been at play if one has not been present. One's own assessment of whether others are over-confident can be questioned, on the grounds that one's own level of uncer-tainty may be off-base. Therefore, gathering a broader range of judgments from analysts uninvolved in the deliberations would be a more robust approach, though obviously this would entail more effort. Short of that, the amount of time that the group devoted to reaching its decisions, and the definitiveness of the language used in putting forth the alternative, may be useful indications of overconfidence based on groupthink. One should also be more alert to the possibility of groupthink if the deliberations involved a dominant individual whose views would be difficult to oppose.

Another bias that often exaggerates policymakers' optimism rests on the spillover effect from the fact that they have succeeded in securing power. Overconfidence from such success, sometimes reinforced by the belief that reaching office has provided a strong mandate from the public, is often matched with the confidence that government as a whole will be both supportive and efficient in carrying out formal policies. One way to gauge the realism of this last form of overconfidence is to examine the elaborateness of policies, programs, and projects that the government launches (which often can be gauged by how many steps, how many elements, and how many agencies are required for the initiative to be successful). In many countries, painful experience demonstrates that more straightforward, less complicated measures are less likely to go off track.

Hedging for Development Practitioners. As participants in the policy process, development practitioners have to be aware of their own status

---

[8] This party took on several names, following bans, which followed military interventions.
[9] This term was coined by Janis 1972.

and roles, with respect to their standing with the policymakers and whatever organization they represent. As a defense against taking unwarranted blame for ill-fated initiatives, it is useful to note a possible hedging strategy that can reduce the costs of endorsing an initiative that does not pan out. Many policy endorsements ought to be cast in *conditional* terms: that they should be enacted and maintained only if particular conditions hold. For all who face the choice of whether to endorse an initiative, it is sensible to specify that if external conditions change sufficiently, the initiative should be aborted or at least changed substantially.

For those whose actions do not formally establish the policy, another conditional aspect of the endorsement ought to be that the government follows through with its commitments to the initiative. In many circumstances, government leaders have incentives to avoid following through with their commitments; these incentives range from the rising unpopularity of measures adopted in emergency situations, to the discovery that the measures undercut other economic or social objectives of the government leaders. However, by making continued support of the government contingent upon the government's commitment, outsiders may be able to reduce the discredit and other costs of having endorsed an initiative, while also increasing the likelihood of follow-through.

SUMMARY

Regarding the possibility that policymakers are not truly committed to the initiative, the budgetary commitment is the obvious first indicator to examine, to determine whether the policymakers are deliberately restricting the initiative despite their rhetoric, or the initiative's governmental champions simply lose out in the budget battle. Intelligence weaknesses on the part of government planners and policymakers, whether due to overconfidence, groupthink, or suppressed stakeholder intelligence, can lead to ill-considered initiatives. The likelihood that opposition will reduce the policymakers' initial commitment requires a more sophisticated analysis of the interests of stakeholders who believe that the initiative will affect them; this includes leaders and other personnel in the administrative agencies required to enact the initiative. The potential for resistance by implementing agencies must also be taken into account. The additional intelligence challenge for the development practitioners is to anticipate possible failures, in order to make their support (and accountability) for the initiative contingent on the government's commitment and its willingness to adapt when the initiative goes awry.

TABLE 3.1 *Core Problems, Causes, and Potential Indicators of Ill-Fated Initiatives*

Root problem	Causes	Potential indicators
Lack of commitment	Restriction by partial incorporation	Indirectness of metrics
		Unrealistically stringent regulations
		Inconsistency with policymakers' ideology and core support
		Unwillingness to punish lower-level officials for not enacting initiatives
		Unwillingness to embed the initiative within broader programs or agreements
		Unwillingness to enter into external commitments
Overly ambitious initiatives	Past political/policy success; leadership hubris	Discrepancy between government and external analysis of impacts
Intelligence deficits	Low intelligence capacity	"
	Government analysts compelled to over-optimism	"
Rejection of external input (see Table 4.1 for elaboration)	Psychological resistance; distrust	"
Stakeholder resistance	Stakeholder distrust and/or assessment of deprivation	Prevalence of demonstrations against government measures; noncompliance indicators
Intra-governmental opposition	Veto provisions in decision structures; decentralized authority	Many, or strong, actors with blocking power; prevalence of veto actions by other top-level government policymakers
	Sharp ideological differences	Pronouncements of different ideological perspectives
	Chief executive's lack of legislative majority	Legislative minority of chief executive's supporters
Inadequate/distorted implementation (see Table 6.1 for elaboration)	Inter-agency rivalry; dysfunctional agency isolation	Lack of inter-agency communication, degree of withheld information, failure to provide mandated inputs to other agencies

4

The Expert's Frustration: Rejection of Sound Knowledge or Recommendations

In 2012 the Independent Evaluation Group of the World Bank Group gave an "unsatisfactory" overall evaluation of the World Bank's efforts regarding the 2010 Tunisia Employment Development Policy Loan [DPL]:

The Bank team carried out ample analytical work to inform the design of the DPL. It would have also helped to have a solid political-economic analysis to better understand the constraints and frustrations of the workers and employers in Tunisia ... The team designed the DPL to support gradual reform steps to build up momentum for reforms. The Bank team pushed for a broader approach and inclusion of further sectors and ministries in the DPL, which was not an option for the borrower, leaving the Bank to either stay engaged with this DPL or dropping the operation ... The Bank underestimated the seriousness of the socio-economic, political, and governance situation in Tunisia and the lack of Government commitment to reforms, perhaps because access to information on the situation was very constrained, and the Minister of Cooperation was the main Bank counterpart. He was not from the establishment and remained in the interim Government ... The Macro risk was estimated as moderate during the global economic crisis; and the institutional risk as medium to high because of lengthy administrative procedures, insufficient cross-institution collaboration, and changes in high level staff, which could affect ownership. The ICR [Implementation Completion and Results Report] describes the Bank's risk analysis as less than fully adequate ... The political risk materialized and was triggered by the large number of underemployed low-skilled workers in the informal sector who were harassed by Government administrative procedures and through corruption. There were previous protests by students, however these were always suppressed and kept silent. Nobody was really fully informed about what was going on.

(World Bank Group 2012)

This case is a clear illustration of the frustration facing development practitioners when their technical knowledge and recommendations are disregarded or minimized. This is most painful when this intelligence would in fact dovetail with the objectives of the government leaders. In addition, one of the risks outlined in Chapter 3 is endorsing an initiative on the assumption that one's advice will be followed, only to find that quite different actions are taken. It is not uncommon for leaders seeking external support to imply that they will be delighted to accept the guidance of those who provide financial support; yet this implicit commitment is, especially if circumstances get difficult, often questionable.

Of course, it is possible that policymakers are not interested in developing policies based on inputs appropriate for the common good; these policies may not fit with the agendas of government leaders. As emphasized in the previous chapter, it is important to determine whether government leaders are exercising willful ignorance in order to push popular policies that would not stand up to scrutiny if additional knowledge were publicized.

However, *if* the policymakers are serious in their commitment, less obvious reasons why sound analysis may be rejected rest on differences in outlooks that require an assessment of potential incompatibilities among outlooks. Foreign development practitioners, in particular, are severely limited in identifying these incompatibilities, but it is still possible to identify the differences between one's analysis and those of others. Sometimes this problem is exacerbated by the fact that the development practitioner is interacting directly with like-minded planners and policymakers (for example, a free-trade, market-oriented outsider may be working with similarly oriented experts in the finance ministry), without direct contact with higher level policymakers with different orientations. It is also possible that development practitioners are bringing in their own biases. It is heartening that the World Bank, despite its technical reputation, has explicitly recognized the importance of taking into account the cognitive biases that may influence development practitioners. Its 2015 flagship *World Development Report* argues that:

Dedicated, well-meaning professionals in the field of development ... can fail to help, or even inadvertently harm, the very people they seek to assist if their choices are subtly and unconsciously influenced by their social environment, the mental models they have of the poor, and the limits of their cognitive bandwidth ...

The biases policy makers themselves may hold about the population they are intending to serve are also very important. When designing policies appropriate for a target group, policy makers must make some assumptions about this group. The biases policy makers themselves may hold about the population they are intending to serve are also very important. When designing policies appropriate for a target group, policy makers must make some assumptions about this group ... Most fundamentally, to take a policy stance, policy makers must have some knowledge about the decision context that exists in the population. In the absence of knowledge or objective interpretation of that knowledge, automatic thinking, as well as thinking unduly influenced by social context and cultural mental models, may prevail.

(World Bank 2015, 180, 186)

This chapter shares with Chapter 3 the diagnostics for determining whether the policymakers are not truly committed to the stated objectives of the initiative; the indicators that the Independent Evaluation Group critique outlined above point out that the warning signs of weak commitment were not heeded. However, assuming that policymakers are committed, and that the development practitioner's knowledge is indeed valid, the incompatibility may be due to limitations of the intelligence and appraisal functions upon which government planners and policymakers depend, differences in the objectives that different actors wish to promote, or limitations in the prescription, invocation, and application functions. The analytic limitations may be due to psychological rigidities in accepting conflicting information, the rejection of intelligence or appraisal that could be politically risky, differences in problem definitions, or uncertainty about which development approaches offered by ideologically competing international institutions ought to be heeded. Organizational conditions may block the incorporation of the development practitioner's contributions, whether from rigidities in changing policies or institutions, or from interagency rivalries and government leaders' priorities for control.

ANALYTIC LIMITATIONS: DIAGNOSING INTELLIGENCE AND APPRAISAL DEFICITS

The context that links development practitioners to government analysts and policymakers goes far beyond the content of the exchanges per se. The framework offered by Jones, Jones, and Shaxson (2012, chapter 2) encompasses the overall political context, the strength of individuals and institutions involved in knowledge production and policymaking, the relevance of different types of knowledge produced and sought, and the "processes of knowledge interaction." All of these have to be understood "to make sense of this complexity and draw out grounded, operational implications for action in a systematic way" (Jones et al. 2013, 2).

In terms of the strengths of the individuals and institutions on the government side, the analysts and policymakers one is trying to persuade to adopt sound policies may simply lack the knowledge base – both facts and theory – required to understand why the policies make more sense than the alternatives.[1] One challenge for the development practitioner, then, is that without being aware of the factual and theoretical understandings held by planners and policymakers, crafting communications to dispel their unsound assumptions is hit-or-miss. For example, in many countries the neglect of agriculture in favor of industrial development has been based on shaky assumptions that increases in agricultural productivity cannot be impressive, and that maintaining the strength of agriculture is unnecessary for industrial development and economic growth (De Janvry 2010; De Janvry and Sadoulet 2010). Unless one appreciates that these assumptions may underlie the lack of enthusiasm for one's advice to support agriculture, just stating that agriculture needs to be maintained would be talking past the analysts or policymakers who need to be convinced. Compelling arguments and examples are required to demonstrate that a solid agricultural sector can add to productivity and avoid bottlenecks to industrial growth.

Information Gaps

The first puzzle is why the offer to seek or provide information would be neglected, especially since developing countries tend to be information-poor. The fact that planners and policymakers within government often do not seek the factual information that development researchers could provide can arise from multiple sources, beginning with obvious practical constraints, but extending to cognitive limitations. The following facets of these two broad categories can be considered as a checklist of possible limitations to be explored.

Practical Constraints. While some developing country governments have very sophisticated analytical capabilities, others are severely challenged in the most basic capacities to collect, store, retrieve, and analyze information. One implication is that a development practitioner cannot simply assume that information can be "digested" effectively even if it is regarded as correct and valuable. Another implication, though, is that in many countries, it is worthwhile to help establish greater capabilities.

---

[1] It should be noted that development practitioners themselves may suffer from an intelligence failure in not understanding that the motives rather than intelligence failings of the policymaker may account for what the development practitioners see as the policymaker's analytic limitation.

Another common source of practical failure to seek or accept useful information is the haste to enact projects and programs. For example, the expert may be very leery about a resettlement scheme that would place farmers into areas known for mineral extraction; the expert understands that laterite soils make for poor farming. Yet the impatient government may skip the soil tests and rush into the resettlement program. Forty-five years ago, McNeil (1972, 591) warned about resettling populations for farming: "The southern Sudan and parts of Brazil have such laterite-tending soils, and the history of development projects in these areas exposes an almost complete disregard for the limits and conditions which such areas impose for productive development." Yet McLean and Straede (2003) document that people displaced from Nepal's Royal Chitwan National Park in the late 1990s were resettled to farm in areas of very poor soils, and Richter (2016) notes even more recently that the 2008–2015 resettlement of landless Cambodians through the Land Allocation for Social and Economic Development Project placed some settlers in degraded forest lands with poor soils. She notes that the biggest challenge of the program was the identification of suitable land; this was supposed to come from collaborations among multiple government ministries. The Cambodian government, to avoid losing grant money from the World Bank and the German development agency GIZ, proceeded with the project despite the limitations in identifying appropriate land, in part because of the conflicts among the relevant ministries. Richter (2016, 13) concludes that "[a]t the stage of land identification, a detailed Land Resource Assessment is required. In practice, land suitability and fertility with regard to farming is rarely sufficiently considered and assessed." Consequently, some of the sites have poor soils and low productivity (Richter 2016, 17).

Another practical constraint is that some information may be regarded as too politically damaging to be gathered and publicized. Program and project evaluations are often fraught with risks for the government if accomplishment falls short of targets. Also, surveys of income levels, health status, or educational attainment may aggravate inter-group conflicts. In fact, in some countries no general population census is undertaken: there has been no census in Lebanon since 1932, nor in Angola since 1970. Many countries neglect to include ethnic, religious, or linguistic categories in the censuses that they do undertake, even though this information can be of crucial socioeconomic and political importance.

Yet another practical constraint is the barrier that some agencies put up to avoid sharing information and analysis with other agencies, often due to bureaucratic rivalries mentioned previously. A development practitioner interacting with one agency may be disappointed to learn that their contributions are not widely shared with other planners or policymakers.

Cognitive Limitations. The fundamental premise behind straightforward cognitive limitations is that new information or theorizing is shaped by pre-existing beliefs. This occurs in interconnected ways. The *confirmation bias* seeks and favors information that is congruent with pre-existing beliefs. The *disconfirmation b*ias avoids and disfavors information that is incongruent with pre-existing beliefs (Edwards and Smith 1996; Taber and Lodge 2006); it frequently involves favoring particular key hypotheses that negate alternative knowledge (Nickerson 1998). This is often reinforced by overconfidence in existing beliefs, due to biased inferences (Dunning et al. 1990) that exaggerate the confidence of government leaders because of their success. *Selective exposure* entails the selection of sources that are congruent with pre-existing beliefs (Frey 1986; Taber and Lodge 2006); and *over-weighting* the instances that seem to confirm the pre-existing beliefs at the expense of new, different beliefs (Nickerson 1998).

In addition, because of the need for simplicity derived from the drive to comprehend, *attribute substitution* replaces complex, difficult-to-assess information or analysis with more graspable ones (Kahneman and Frederick 2002). The bias may be that the new information or recommendation is assessed not on its own terms, but rather in terms of the pre-existing impressions of the characteristics of the individual and his or her organization. If the development practitioner's organization is perceived as prone to furthering its own interests at the expense of the wellbeing of the country, the inference may be that the expert's input is also against the country's wellbeing. Government policymakers may be resistant to sound judgments out of a blanket dismissal of views of people perceived to be on the "other side" of broad policy debates. Government officials in conservation agencies typically share the polarization between agriculture and conservation. Scialabba and Williamson (2004, 4) note that

Due to the predominant agriculture's negative impact on biodiversity, conservation groups and protected area managers have historically viewed agricultural activities as being in conflict with stated conservation goals ... This view has often led to attempts by protected area managers at excluding agricultural and other productive activities from protected areas. Similarly, community members in and around protected areas have often viewed measures to conserve biodiversity (e.g. land takings or land and/or water use restrictions) as a threat to personal freedom, livelihoods and the economic viability of their agricultural enterprises. The imposition of such restrictions has often led to real conflicts between protected area managers and farmers.

Scialabba and Williamson (2004, 5) recognized at the time of their writing that "only recently have conservation biologists, protected area managers, agriculturalists and policy makers begun to recognize the biodiversity contribution and potential of agricultural landscapes and started working together in developing strategies to effectively integrate these two land-use activities which will increasingly occupy the same areas of land."

Other cognitive limitations are rooted in social psychology. The individuals and organizations on the same side of a policy debate come to share empirical and theoretical beliefs, often reinforced by commonly held normative commitments, to such a degree that they reject out of hand the information and argumentation supporting other positions (Sabatier 1988). This is frequently reinforced by the risk that accepting the expert's input would lead to ostracism from the group. Thus, *identity-protective cognition* tends to reject information that threatens individual's self-identifications (Kahan et al. 2007; Kahan, Jenkins-Smith, and Braman 2011); *value-expressive attitudes* (Katz 1960) express how people want to think of themselves and are thought of by others; and *social-adjustive attitudes* lead to the rejection of information that might challenge the individual's social, organizational, or professional standing (DeBono 1987). One does not have to be a cognitive psychologist to be aware of these obstacles, and to explore whether any of these rigidities is likely to hold in a particular context.

A deeper problem exists when government planners and policymakers have cognitive frameworks that do not recognize the importance of information that one deems to be quite relevant. For example, planners and policymakers considering redistributive initiatives may fasten on the national trends of quantitative indicators of income distribution, such as the Gini index,[2] as "solid" information, and neglect the "soft" information about the public's *perceptions* of the income distribution. Yet in fact, the public's perceptions of income distribution vary remarkably from the conventional indicators, in terms of where an individual stands within the income distribution, the shape of the distribution, and its trends (Gimpelson and Treisman 2011). Moreover, various segments of the population may base their reactions on perceptions of income-distribution

---

[2] The Gini index reflects the difference between the cumulative share of some asset – most typically income – beginning with the least privileged to the most privileged, and total equality; normalized such that complete equality is zero and complete inequality (i.e., the most privileged has all of the asset).

disparities across regions, ethnicities, or religions, rather than the overall national distribution for which data are readily available.

Other examples include the disinterest in studies of vulnerability to climate change by planners and policymakers who dismiss global warming (Brunner and Lynch 2010, chapter 1). Similarly, for highly state-oriented planners and policymakers, assessments of self-help capabilities of local communities, or NGO efforts to mobilize grassroots community action, may be of little interest. For example, Macdonald (1997; 2016) documents the limited access to most Central American governments that NGOs with such agendas have had, and the efforts of some Central American governments to channel other NGOs into executing state-funded programs.

Planners and policymakers may also neglect or reject analyses of what would happen if the government changes, or if a project or program is only partially enacted. If this analysis comes from staff within the government, it may be regarded as disloyal, or as an indication of lack of confidence that the project or program will succeed.

Competing Signals

The interactions of developing country governments with international assistance agencies provide the opportunity for many to provide their expertise, directly or indirectly. Yet no one's expertise can escape the competition from other individuals or institutions with different outlooks. For example, the institutions most closely affiliated with the United Nations (e.g., the UN Economic Commissions for each world region; the UN Conference on Trade and Development) take a far more state-interventionist approach (UN Conference on Trade and Development 2007) than the development banks and the International Monetary Fund, which typically take more market-oriented approaches.[3] Furthermore, high-profile conflicts occasionally have set the International Monetary Fund and the World Bank at loggerheads in their policy advice (the most highly publicized case being how these institutions dealt with the 1997 East Asian financial crisis). Much more recently, under Chinese leadership, the Asian Infrastructure Investment Bank (AIIB) has become a competitive source of loans (and therefore policy guidance, formally or informally) not only for Asia, but also for other developing regions. It is

---

[3] Utting (2006) has edited a collection of essays on the widely diverse efforts to define and disseminate the "development agenda," from the World Bank as the "knowledge bank" to the "policy autonomy" of the Global South.

quite likely that whatever conditionalities the AIIB might impose would be quite different from those of the International Monetary Fund and the World Bank.

Policymakers could easily feel cross-pressured, not only with respect to their own judgments opposed to external demands, but also the mixed messages of the external sources. Development practitioners would be well advised to find out who the "thought leaders" are in the minds of planners and policymakers; this can be done straightforwardly by asking, "What should I read to understand these issues?" Or asking, "Which organizations have the best approaches in dealing with these issues?"

Finally, government leaders may feel obligated to follow the advice of others out of loyalty or social relationships. These obligations also may stem from agreements that the nation has with other governments. For example, members of the Economic Community of West African States (ECOWAS) have commitments to the regional trade agreement that more liberal trade advice would question (Odularo 2009, 35).

POLITICAL INCOMPATIBILITY

The development practitioner's input may also be incompatible with the political interests of those to whom it is directed. This is relevant both to politics writ large and to inter-agency rivalries. This does not necessarily mean that the planners and policymakers who feel compelled by political considerations to ignore one's advice will explicitly state their opposition to it; they may congratulate the development practitioner for providing such enlightened input, but effectively ignore these inputs in formulating and enacting policy initiatives.

In terms of the public stances that government leaders must take, acting on some policy advice may be too politically damaging because it could undermine the unity of the political coalition supporting the leaders. Political coalitions, whether represented by a single or multiple parties or movements, may be glued together by a programmatic or ideological commitment that is simply different from the implications of one's advice. The advice may also be regarded by government leaders as politically damaging if there is a risk that acting on the advice would reduce their control over key aspects of the society. For example, national government leaders may reject sound advice to decentralize healthcare because they regard national control over the health system as programmatically or politically important. By the same token, more flexible regulations, even if advisable in terms of their effectiveness, may be seen by government leaders as reducing their capacity to control.

Inter-agency rivalries can underlie the rejection of sound advice if leaders of one or more agencies fear that acting on the advice would reduce the budget, jurisdiction, or general standing of their agencies. For example, the effort to replace conflicting land classification systems with a single coherent one is often likely to set off turf battles among the involved agencies, at least one of which is likely to fear that the advice would reduce its standing.

How can the development practitioner gauge the gravity of the inter-agency rivalries? One indicator is the withholding of important information on the part of an agency. This opportunity to deny information is greater if the monitoring and information gathering by the most central organs of the government (national statistical offices, accountability offices, inspectors general offices, and so on) entrusted with these functions are weak. Another indicator is the extent of lack of cooperation of one agency to provide mandated inputs needed by another – these can go beyond withholding information to encompass the withholding a wide variety of complementary inputs such as financing, physical infrastructure, goods and services, or community preparation. Establishing whether this is the case requires careful analysis of the progression of enactment.

An often equally undermining tactic is to delay cooperation, frequently with the excuse of limited administrative capacity, claiming that cumbersome processes are required to move forward. However, such an assessment must keep in mind that coordination indeed is often very difficult even when good will abounds. Sometimes acrimony itself can be detected. Outsiders may not be able to witness first-hand the acerbic exchanges between agency officials trying to maintain a public image of unity, but trusted insider informants often can be found. A subtler indicator requires assessing whether the pronouncements of agencies that are supposed to cooperate reveal different ideological perspectives. It is quite common for central banks, economic ministries, and planning agencies to be concerned about economic stability, free-market prices, and so on; the leaders of spending ministries are more likely to be led and staffed by sectoral specialists with greater concern for expanding the sectors they oversee. These differences are often reinforced by the fact that staff of the first set of agencies are more likely to be trained abroad, and are less likely to have close connections with stakeholders of particular sectors.

Distrust

Well-intentioned development practitioners are often surprised to learn that their contributions are dismissed because they are presumed to serve some ulterior motive. Experimental research reinforces the intuition that the attribution of motives of those who disagree with one's positions will tend to be negative (Malle 1999; Reeder et al. 2005). It is more comforting psychologically to assume that contrary opinions reflect negative traits than to accept that one's opinions are simply incorrect. This tendency to distrust not only positions that conflict with one's existing beliefs but also those who articulate them is reinforced by another tendency when the organization of the development practitioner is distrusted. Motives attributed to people viewed as belonging to a given "unit" are more likely to be attributed to all members of that "unit" (Heider 1958; Malle 1999). Many organizations involved in development assistance have been heavily criticized by ideological opponents, who frequently try to sharpen their critiques by impugning the motives of the leaders, staff, and overseers of these organizations. Does the advice coming from the bilateral development agency of a particular donor country cater to the commercial or geopolitical interests of that country? Is the assistance "tied aid," requiring that goods and services be purchased from that country?[4] Whether or not planners and policymakers accept these insinuations, it is likely that the information and advice will be greeted with doubt as to their motivation. Moreover, distrust, along with simple lack of familiarity, often can be attributed to lack of staffing continuity of the development practitioners outside of government.

Differences in Problem Definition

Policymakers also may disregard sound advice if they regard the information or recommendations as of low relevance to their own problem definitions. A problem definition[5] consists of prioritizing problems, along particular temporal and scope dimensions, for the wellbeing of particular

---

[4] Although Australia, Canada, Japan, New Zealand, South Korea, the United States, and the Western European governments have reached accords to severely limit the tied aid obligation to purchase goods and services from the donor country. Chinese concessional loans are tied aid, in that they require at least 20 percent of the funds (Organisation for Economic Development and Co-operation 2016, 156). Furthermore, the policymakers of the recipient country may harbor suspicions that the advice still is directed to tie the economy of the recipient country to importing from the donor country. Chinese concessional loans, in contrast, require "that at least 50 percent of the loan is tied to the purchase of Chinese goods" (Wolf, Wang, and Warner 2013, 7).

[5] Dery (2000, 37), surveying the literature, provides a generic definition: "Problem definition is concerned with the organization of a set of facts, beliefs, and perceptions – how people think about circumstances." This is too generic, however, for our purposes.

stakeholders (who thus "have standing"). Moreover, problem definitions vary in their theoretical assumptions, which in turn dictate assumptions about the most feasible approaches to the problems.

Examples include defining the problem of drug trafficking as criminality, with the implication that arresting or killing drug traffickers would be effective. It also may be viewed as ethically acceptable by those who do not regard the traffickers as deserving of standing – their wellbeing would not have to be taken into account. An alternative problem definition might be that hostile circumstances induce young men to form gangs for mutual protection; drug trafficking is a means of securing resources for that protection. This implies that a feasible approach would be to remove the threats that prompt people to join gangs. Yet another problem definition might identify drug use as the fundamental problem, along with the assumption that the supply will somehow be generated to meet the demand. The approaches implied by this problem definition may be either efforts to reduce drug consumption through education and treatment, or legalization of drug use.

One problem definition related to economic development strategy is that developing countries have been held back by illiberal policies (i.e., government distortions of the market economy) that have benefited the powerful and wealthy; the implication is that in the long run, these advantages will be reduced, resulting in greater equity and growth by reducing price subsidies, heavy regulation, international trade restrictions, and so on (Davis 2014). An alternative problem definition is that developing countries are held back by their positions within an unfair world economy. These two problem definitions may both reflect the normative commitment to the poor, but their theoretical underpinnings obviously call for very different approaches.

Differences in problem definition also reflect differences in the level of optimism. If government officials believe that the "infant industries" under trade protectionism will largely prosper, they are more likely to define the problem of economic underdevelopment as the lack of state-led industrial promotion. Definitions also vary in terms of time horizon. For example, forestry policy may be dominated by a problem definition that excludes long-term environmental consequences of rapid timber harvesting. Clearly, problem definition, theoretical assumptions, diagnosis, temperament, time horizons, and ideological orientations are closely linked.

Finding the appropriate analytic depth of a problem definition is challenging, for both psychological and political reasons. Often problems defined in superficial ways are accepted at face value, ignoring definitions that would suggest a more constructive policy approach (Schon 1979, 261; Bardach 1981; Dery 2000). This may reflect the psychological power of framing. It may be that many people presume that a problem framed in a particular way reflects how the bulk of others would frame it. It may be that people are most comfortable with simple explanations, which may also resonate more emotionally than complex definitions. For example, aggressive impulses may be triggered by defining the "gang problem" as the behavior of intrinsically bad people who need to be severely punished, even if this does not provide much leverage to counter gang recruitment. Certain simplistic problem definitions reduce anxiety or guilt – "the problem is due to others' actions, not our own." Politically, government leaders can often mobilize people more easily through simple problem identifications, and more direct action can be taken. Inflation may be defined as profiteering, legitimizing the direct approach of price ceilings and prosecution of sellers who raise prices and black-market money changers. Efforts to redefine the problem in more complex ways may be seen as an attempt to distract people from focusing on the government's failure to address the problem as the public would define it. The defined problem may also be more achievable, even if superficial, as in defining the education problem as too few teachers rather than poor or irrelevant education. This example demonstrates the close link between some simplistic problem definitions and the dynamics of goal displacement and restriction by partial incorporation presented in Chapter 3.

Often a problem definition becomes more useful in generating sound approaches by examining a more complete causal chain. Low productivity is due (among other things) to poor skill training; poor skill training is due to poor education; poor education is due to poor teachers; poor teachers are due to low teaching salaries and poor teacher education; low teaching salaries and poor teacher education are due to inadequate resources devoted to these needs. However, "deeper" problem definitions can also be paralyzing, or even used as a pretext for inaction. For example, for decades the politically attractive definition of the food insecurity problem in the Philippines has been the lack of food "self-sufficiency." Of course, if agricultural productivity in the Philippines were at a much higher and more sustainable level, domestic food production would reduce food insecurity. However, the protectionist policies against imported food have long exacerbated the food insecurity and poverty of low-income Filipinos (Cororaton and Corong 2009).

Problem definitions may also be simplistic in that they neglect other important goals. For example, a decentralization effort may provide greater responsiveness to public needs, but at the expense of the efficiency of the provision of services and the increased power of the local elite. Muhumuza (2008, 67) identifies such a case in Uganda: the dramatically increasing expenditures on Uganda's public administration that account for nearly a fifth of government expenditures.

[T]he proliferation of local government authorities has ended up consuming enormous financial resources that would otherwise be committed to development. Most of these local governments are small and unviable entities. Many of the new districts are not viable economically. They are created for patronage reasons as well as selfish political calculations to gain support, especially towards the period of presidential elections.

The differences between one's problem definitions, (assuming that they are sound and useful) and those of other planners and policymakers not only call for recognizing the discrepancies, but also for developing strategies to bring the problem definitions into convergence. The most fundamental approach is to ask how initiatives impact the full range of outcomes valued by stakeholders, and how to get the greatest purchase to maximize the achievement of these outcomes.

Psychological Predispositions

The lack of receptivity to sound input in general, and to more useful problem definitions, have some basis in the psychological predispositions of government planners and policymakers. Because it is rare that a development practitioner would be interacting solely with one counterpart, the analysis of individual personality or character is less useful than sensitivity to fairly common cognitive biases (already discussed above), prevailing moods that affect broad sets of planners or policymakers, and psychological reactions to the nature of the interactions with development practitioners of different backgrounds.

Climate and Mood

The receptivity to the development practitioner's input on the part of planners and policymakers is often sensitive to broadly shared moods influenced by broad economic, political, and social conditions. Policymakers, in particular, are not only susceptible to their own mood swings, but also must be sensitive to what they believe are the moods of various segments of the public. Just as problem definitions are shaped by the level of optimism, the reactions to recommendations that range from modest to highly ambitious also will vary according to this level. Some events trigger a general mood of euphoria. For example, Selway (2011, 184) attributes Thailand's Free Medical Services for the Poor Program of the early 1980s to the euphoria of the democratic opening, but notes that the overly ambitious program almost immediately ran out of funds.

The more common condition, however, is the advent of major crisis, which can have unpredictably contrary reactions: receptivity to new ideas ("Tell us what we can do to get out of this fix") or the hunkering down phenomenon of closing off external communications to concentrate on the crisis. A crisis often contracts the focus of attention to the immediate time period and the narrow scope of the threat. For example, Ismahan and Ozkan (2011) document the myopic policies of over-spending by the Turkish government in times of fiscal crisis, which have had the long-term effects of making fiscal crises endemic.

The "crisis mentality" often also leads to the policymakers' demand for more direct control of outcomes, even if subtler measures are more appropriate. For example, high levels of inflation frequently prompt direct price controls, alarming rates of deforestation provoke total formal exclusion of local inhabitants from forested areas, spikes in unemployment lead to state interventions to take over private firms shedding labor or at risk of bankruptcy.

Interpersonal/Intercultural Defensiveness

The knowledge and recommendations of development practitioners are often dismissed because of the defensiveness, whether or not it is consciously recognized, of planners and policymakers. This is especially a concern when development practitioners are of different nationality, ethnicity, or professional standing than the planners and policymakers with whom they interact. Local policymakers often presume that they are regarded as less sophisticated, as national-level development practitioners are presumed to be better educated, better paid, and more influential. In some cases, government officials react to outsiders from developed countries with what has been labeled a "subaltern mentality" (Bhadra 1988): an ambivalent mindset of submissiveness and resistance. The interactions with developed-country development practitioners based on this syndrome are marked by superficial agreement without serious commitment to pursue the recommendations.

THE DEVELOPMENT PRACTITIONER'S OWN COGNITIVE LIMITATIONS

Development practitioners may be unaware that their contributions are ignored because the policy implications are believed to be inconsistent with the demands and expectations of the planners and policymakers. To approach the assessment of whether this is the case, it is useful for the development practitioner to be sensitive to the interactions among identifications, demands, and expectations. Identifications are relevant because, as Lasswell and Kaplan (1950, 25) note, "[i]dentifications are both based upon and give rise to the sharing of demands." Because identifications entail how people regard and present themselves – to themselves and to others[6] – they establish the sense of belonging to groups, and, in many instances, the normative principles that individuals and groups follow.

Thus, in trying to infer the motives that drive policy choices, development practitioners unavoidably strive to deduce the relevant identifications of both policymakers and stakeholders outside of government. The problem is that identifications are multiple, and their content and relevance vary over time and according to who is involved. A common analytical mistake is to assume that for a particular societal role, whether ministry officials, low-income farmers, or bankers, one identification consistently dominates to the point of dictating the interests, and thus the demands, of those people. This can lead to caricaturing people in particular roles as pursuing only what seem to be the most obvious objectives, as if elected government officials only want to stay in office, businesspeople only want to maximize profit, and so on. Yet it is clear, from everyone's self-insight and from experience with other people, that individuals are more complex. Business executives may be more motivated to gain prestige than maximum profit; elected officials may have entered politics for programmatic reasons. In addition, opinion surveys show that priorities change over time (Simmons, Bickart, and Lynch 1993; Erikson 2007). When asked, "What is the most important problem of your country," respondents say very different things during a severe recession, or after a terrorist attack, or when corruption scandals emerge.

---

[6] Lasswell and McDougal (1992, 350) note that "Everyone makes use of symbols of thought or speech in referring to himself and others. These comprise a system of 'identifications' (or 'identities')."

Another dimension of identification that is centrally important in policy deliberations is the prioritization of group affiliations such as ethnicity, language, religion, and clan. The content and relative salience of these identities are also issue-dependent, but in ways that are difficult to predict because different components of identity may dictate different stances on particular issues. For example, the small-holder Sunni farmer may regard the general discrimination against Sunnis, affecting merchants and large-holder Sunnis as well, as far more important than farming issues, while in other countries the differences in economic roles and status may drive the positions that the small-holders would take. In Siberia, a new identification – *Sibiryak*[7]– has emerged among the ethnically mixed Siberians whose only ingroup identification is discontent with the "internal colonialism" by central authorities, viewed as responsible for the region's depressed state since the 1990s.[8] The risk to being ignored is that the policymakers would have different beliefs about how identifications would render the development practitioner's recommendations infeasible or counter-productive.

Finally, development practitioners may not realize that their recommendations would be ignored because of stakeholders' opposition that is invisible in the debate that the development practitioner can witness. Some government leaders may be aware of the views of these stakeholders, whose opposition is conveyed behind the scenes or is simply inferred by the government leaders. One might presume that the combination of a flowchart of the formal policy process through which a particular initiative seems headed, and an inventory of which groups have expressed preferences for different outcomes, would suffice. In fact, a rather common way to define "policy elites" is "those who have official positions in government and whose responsibilities include making or participating in making and implementing authoritative decisions for society" (Grindle and Thomas 1991, 59). Yet in many circumstances, the sources of informal influence do not even have to act; their expected negative reactions to particular aspects of the initiatives may discourage policymakers from including those aspects, even if those who were presumed to be in opposition have not been consulted. The classic "rule of anticipated reactions" (Friedrich 1941, 591–592) clarifies that other individuals and institutions may wield great influence in shaping the content

---

[7] *Sibiryak* – Russian for a person from Siberia.
[8] Anisimova and Echevskaya 2012. I am grateful to Natalia Mirovitskaya for bringing this to my attention.

and the success or failure of an initiative even if they do not take any action, formal or informal. The simple anticipation of their approval or disapproval may be enough to alter the nature of the initiative. For example, Naidoo and Maré (2015, 417–418) argue that the South African government's 1996 five–year Growth Employment and Redistribution plan was weakened because the government held back in seeking the endorsement of the multi-sectoral National Economic, Development and Labour Council, a concertation forum, out of anticipated opposition by the powerful labor unions. Similarly, Weyland (1996, 111–117) interprets Brazil's weak tax reform efforts of the early 1990s, despite fiscal crisis, as yielding to anticipated opposition. However, the fact that the rule of anticipated reactions means that some stakeholders may have influence without taking any action visible to the development practitioner does not make inferring influence a hopeless challenge. Frequently the development practitioner can ask trusted respondents what they believe the reactions to various policy initiatives would be. Even if this yields different predictions, these predictions themselves are enlightening in terms of understanding the policymakers' and planners' behavior due to *their* anticipations of the reactions of others.

PROCEDURAL AND CONTEXTUAL PROBLEMS

In some cases, the development practitioner's input is neglected due to rigidities in how the contributions could be used by planners or policymakers. Some existing policies are very difficult to change: some are embedded within the nation's constitution (such as the Brazilian constitution's guarantee of education funding, constraining other social-service expenditure); some are locked into the provisions of international agreements (such as the West African trade agreements mentioned above).

In other cases, the policy process is either so slow and cumbersome, or overwhelmed with immediate crisis, that uncertainty about the context when a policy could be enacted means that the policymakers simply are not receptive to advice. What advice on physical infrastructure or forestry would be useful for government leaders in the midst of the civil war in the Democratic Republic of the Congo?

In yet other cases the soundest policy recommendations are futile because of policy stalemates. This is different from the endorsement of ill-fated, enacted initiatives, but still undermines the effectiveness and efficiency of the development practitioner. Examples of these impasses abound. The policy stalemate over South African health insurance policy was mentioned in Chapter 1. In Argentina, the federal government in the crucial 2000–2001 crisis period was paralyzed, as "President Fernando De la Rúa of the UCR [Radical Civic Union] ... was unable to rule over provincial leaders and therefore faced nearly constant congressional stalemate from provincial delegations opposing measures contrary to local interests" (Benton 2009, 656). Stalemates occur even in countries of relatively strong governance. For example, despite a consensus in the 1990s that Chilean forestry-subsidy policies needed reform, Neira, Verscheure, and Revenga (2002, 28) noted that "the proposed piece of legislation, which was drafted ten years ago, has not been approved, mostly due to lack of consensus among the different stakeholders."

If other policies beyond the reach of the development practitioner's contributions are problematic, policymakers may feel compelled to ignore the development practitioner's recommendations, according to the logic of the "second best" approach of adopting a suboptimal policy to offset other suboptimal policies. For example, Rodrik[9] proposes that poorly functioning markets, institutional weakness, or both, justify undervalued currency exchange rates in developing countries where these problems are serious, going against the orthodox neoclassical doctrine of market-determined exchange rates. Two considerations make this scenario distinct from the situation of policymakers simply rejecting the development practitioner's input. First, the development practitioner may have the painful dilemma of maintaining the optimal advice, on the premises that it is important to convey best practice and to maintain the integrity of the development practitioner's institution, or to endorse an alternative that may be more consistent with prevailing policies but might make it appear that this suboptimal policy is more broadly acceptable. In other words, the policymakers may be sympathetic to the development practitioner's recommendations, but until the other policies are modified, the generally best-practice option may be ignored.

The causes of policy stalemates or gridlock, and approaches to overcome them, are presented in Chapter 5, but at this point it is useful to outline how the development practitioner could anticipate policy gridlock that may be too severe for the development practitioner to devote resources to the deliberations. One strong indicator of gridlock risk is

---

[9] Rodrik (2008, 5–6) argues that "tradables are special because they suffer disproportionately from the market failures that block structural transformation and economic diversification ... These market failures ... predominate in tradables ... tradables are special because they suffer disproportionately (compared to nontradables) from the institutional weakness and contracting incompleteness that characterize low-income environments ... In either case, there is a second-best role for subsidizing tradables. The reason currency undervaluation works is that it performs this subsidization function."

the presence of a perception by one or more groups central to the process that an agreement would expose the groups to further risk relative to the policy at issue or related policies. In other words, do some stakeholders view possible outcomes as setting broad precedents? Of course, transformative policies are sometimes enacted and highly successful, yet the development practitioner needs to be aware that stakeholders may see the policy issue in a much broader context. If the issue has already been on the policy agenda when the development practitioner is considering getting involved, the trends to that point can be useful indicators: Is the issue of growing symbolic importance, in ways that make compromise more difficult? Has the confrontational rhetoric been escalating? Have some leaders staked their reputations on winning without compromise?

On the positive side, the development practitioner's contributions can be rescued if these impasses can be overcome or circumvented. Therefore, we turn in our next chapter to analyze the causes of these impasses and strategies for overcoming them.

SUMMARY

The possibility of predicting whether the development practitioner's contributions will be heeded or ignored can be greatly increased if the practitioner can assess the congruence between policymakers' needs and their objectives, requiring analysis of political conditions going beyond the narrow confines of the initiative under consideration. Yet, the assessment also depends heavily on how to gauge the receptivity to the input from development practitioners outside of the government circle of planners and policymakers.

In diagnosing the analytic limitations, the chapter has outlined a cluster of psychological reactions to information that runs counter to pre-existing beliefs; assessing whether these reactions are at play requires either a deep analysis of the differences in the mindsets between the planners and policymakers on the one hand, and "outsiders" on the other, or the more straightforward approach of asking the planners and policymakers about their opinions of those beyond their circle. Even without these patterns of resisting inputs, the intelligence function may exclude the broad range of new considerations because of the contraction of attention in crisis situations. Fundamental differences in problem definition and time horizons also need to be identified. However, some intelligence weaknesses have been shown to come from organizational or political dynamics, such as inter-agency rivalries, truncating analysis to hasten implementation, and willful disregard of politically risky information.

Some of the dynamics relevant to understanding why development-practitioners' constructive contributions are ignored are in common with the challenges examined in Chapter 3: lack of policymakers' commitment, weak intelligence, and poor inter-agency cooperation, making the development practitioners' input off-target as well as difficult to heed. The new dynamics introduced in this chapter include the psychological resistance mechanisms; while their prevalence is important to note, their operation is difficult to detect. The development practitioner will have to rely on assessing whether attitudes and actions of planners and policymakers are at variance with outsiders' advice. A deeper analysis is required to assess whether the objectives, time horizons, and constraints of the policymakers and the development practitioners are compatible.

TABLE 4.1 *Root Problems, Causes, and Potential Indicators of Rejection of Knowledge or Recommendations*

Root problems	Causes	Potential indicators
Tenacity of pre-existing beliefs about policy effectiveness	Psychological resistance to challenging information	Discrepancies between governmental & external analyses
Distrust of motives of offering external advice	Potential of ulterior motives of development agencies	Discrepancies between governmental & external analyses; communications questioning development agencies' motives
Differing motivations	Mandate differences between policymakers and development practitioners	Discrepancies between goal articulations
Differing time horizons (see also Chapter 9 for elaboration)	Short-term pressures on policymakers	Differences among planning horizons
Differing problem definitions	Different ideological and disciplinary backgrounds	Discrepancies among levels/causes of problem definitions
Differing external advice	Multiplicity of international sources with different development doctrines	Discrepancies among advice from different external sources

5

Overcoming the Impasses That Block Sound Initiatives

This chapter explores why, in many situations, little progress is made in enacting policies to address problems that the bulk of stakeholders recognize can and should be addressed. This is a different scenario than the common situation in which a substantial set of stakeholders is content with the status quo. Instead, this chapter focuses on the scenario that is frustrating to all, or nearly all, concerned: general improvements are possible, but they have not been enacted over a considerable time period.

THE CASE OF MEXICO'S OIL SECTOR

This can be illustrated by summarizing the initial failure and later success of Mexico's oil-sector liberalization. Although reform of the notoriously inefficient, under-capitalized, and stagnant oil sector had been on the policy agenda for decades, President Felipe Calderón (2006–2012) of the center-right Partido Acción Nacional (PAN) was blocked in his oil privatization initiative, by both opposition parties, the centrist Partido Revolucionario Institucional (PRI) and the leftist Partido de la Revolución Democrático (PRD). Starr (2014, 53) reports that:

Calderón's energy reform proposal faced strong resistance, most notably to a provision permitting private investment in petroleum exploration and production undertaken by Pemex, Mexico's national oil company. This meant there were two ways this legislation could be approved: either by satisfying opposition demands on energy, which would inevitably result in a heavily watered-down reform; or by linking opposition concessions on energy with administration concessions on issues of great importance to the PRI and the PRD. The Calderón team hoped that the experience of working together to approve a significant (albeit limited) pension reform early in 2007 would generate the needed political trust, especially with the PRI, to enable an inter-temporal linking of political commitments. In the highly polarized political setting of 2007, however, this strategy failed to convince PRI lawmakers that their votes for energy reform would be reciprocated later with promised concessions on fiscal policy.

Starr attributes this, beyond the partisan jockeying, to Calderón's inability to provide credible assurances that commitments to follow through with the linked issues would be fulfilled. She observes (Starr 2014, 53) that "an unanticipated flaw in the sequencing strategy stands out: the parties' inability to make what political scientists call 'inter-temporal commitments.' These involve concessions made today in exchange for a promise to receive something in the future, and in the case of energy reform, linking compromises in one issue area to parallel concessions in another."

In addition, the partial privatization of the oil sector, even if Pemex continues to operate, is a highly symbolic, highly emotional issue. The 1938 expropriation of the foreign-dominated oil sector had been a matter of great pride, symbolizing the aspiration, clearly not fully realized, toward less dependence on the United States. As mentioned in Chapter 4, a high symbolic and emotional loading is often a telling indicator of stubborn, rigid positions that exacerbate destructive impasses.

However, Calderón's successor, the PRI President Enrique Peña Nieto, was able to make credible commitments, through a prominent pact with all three major parties, featuring a broad range of initiatives. Starr (2014, 53) adds that "the Peña Nieto administration worked hard to strengthen and sustain the trust and collaboration it created ... Peña Nieto front-loaded the legislative calendar with issues on which there seemed to be broad, tri-partisan agreement – reforms of labor markets, education, and telecommunications – to generate quick successes and solidify trust among the party leaders."

The struggles of Mexican leaders to break the Pemex monopoly, in the face of strong resistance by the powerful oil workers union, the highly politicized and symbolic status of this monopoly, and the acutely partisan positions of the three major parties, make this a classic case of the difficulties of overcoming a termination impasse. Yet the prescription function was managed by Peña Nieto to reduce the opposition by changing the incentives of the political parties, which required linking the policy sub-arenas involved with labor markets, education, and telecommunications.

This case illustrates that seemingly insurmountable impasses can be overcome. Although promising "win-win" initiatives may be stalemated for a host of reasons, in fact experience yields an impressive range of strategies to overcome these impasses. These strategies may entail altering the initiative to achieve a compromise that still preserves the soundness of the policies, perhaps by linking multiple issues, as in the Mexican case, or they may entail altering the channels through which the initiative is pursued. Yet, of course, different contexts and different dynamics may not be so amenable to clever strategies. To understand how to be clever in other situations, it is important to examine the variety of conditioning factors and decision-process malfunctions that policymakers confront.

VETO POWER OF KEY DECISION-MAKERS

The existing policy process for an initiative pursued through a particular channel may allow particular decision-makers to block the initiative. The political economy insight is that top government leaders need to cope with the veto power of lower-level officials, whether through formal vetoes, delays, or deliberate deviations in implementation (Drazen 2008, Tsebelis 2002). This literature demonstrates that the range of instruments available to block initiatives is quite broad.

Instruments Relying on Policy Choices. Vetoes may occur by keeping the policies from being formally authorized, invoked in specific cases, or applied. In the course of a given policy conflict, these functions may interact. The Chilean conflict over emergency contraception (EC) – the so-called "morning after pill" that may prevent pregnancy if taken within a few days of sex – is an instance worth examining at length. President Michelle Bachelet, having previously served as health minister, launched an effort to expand the recently instituted policy of making EC available to rape victims free of charge from municipal health clinics. In a comparison of Chilean and Argentine reproductive rights policy, Franceschet and Piscopo (2013, 135) note that

Bachelet appointed a health minister, María Soledad Barría, with links to reproductive rights advocacy groups ... In 2006, the MINSAL [the Health Ministry] released new fertility regulations that gave women over 14 years of age the right to access EC in the public sector without parental consent. The decree sparked immediate opposition from conservatives, and Chile's Constitutional Tribunal [TC] quickly ruled that the Health Ministry overstepped its authority. Bachelet responded by issuing a presidential decree, giving the EC regulation the force of law ...

Municipal variation appeared immediately, as conservative mayors from the opposition parties publicly declared their noncompliance, stating that they would not make EC available in their municipal clinics ... Thirty-six national legislators, mostly from the rightist parties, petitioned the TC to evaluate Bachelet's fertility regulations on the grounds that a policy mandating the public delivery of EC violated the state's duty to protect life. In April 2008, the TC sided with conservatives ... Since TC rulings cannot be appealed, the policy battle shifted once again to the municipal level. Now, however, progressive mayors from Bachelet's coalition were defying the (conservative) position of the TC by continuing to deliver EC in local clinics.

Subnational variation in EC accessibility demonstrates the ambiguities of decentralized authority for women's rights: When national policy was progressive, conservative local leaders defied the center; when the court blocked progressive policy, however, (mostly) left-leaning mayors defied central mandates. Most important, however, the recalcitrant mayors in each scenario framed the dispute by invoking municipal governments' autonomy over the health care sector.

It is important to note that the tribunal used two different rationales for blocking the initiative: the limits to the power of the ministry, and the unconstitutionality of the president's decree. However, the progressive mayors challenged the central government's authority even on constitutional matters, just as the conservative mayors were prepared to defy the president's order if it had stood. Yet the central government had another instrument to block the actions of the progressive mayors. Franceschet and Piscopo (2013, 136) go on to report:

These strategies [of the progressive mayors] were no longer viable after a ruling by the Comptroller General in June 2009 stated explicitly that any health clinic, public or private, that had contracts with the National System of Health Services was beneath the TC's jurisdiction, thus prohibiting the distribution of EC by the entire public sector. Following this decision, municipal variation decreased – but did not disappear – as some (but not all) mayors complied with the central government and ceased distributing EC.

The Comptroller General (Contraloría General de la República) is more than the accounting watchdog that the name implies – it is an autonomous entity with the power to declare the actions of both centralized and decentralized administrative actions illegal.[1] In short, the Chilean system goes beyond the equivalent of a Supreme Court in blocking initiatives deemed (albeit controversially) unconstitutional.

---

[1] Article 87 of the current (1980) Chilean Constitution states that: "An autonomous body known as the Office of the Comptroller General of the Republic, shall watch over the legality of the acts of the Administration ... and perform the other functions entrusted thereto by the respective constitutional organic law...." Article 88 states that "...In no case shall the Comptroller General allow decrees on expenditures exceeding the limit set forth in the Constitution..." (Republic of Chile 1980).

Franceschet and Piscopo contrast the Chilean experience with that of Argentina, in part to demonstrate that decentralization within this federal system has increased the financial responsibility of the provinces but has not liberated them from adhering to directives from the central government. They note (Franceschet and Piscopo 2013, 136) that

Whereas the Argentine Constitution gives provinces lawmaking powers that allow them to create, fund, and implement policies, decentralization has significantly expanded provincial responsibilities for managing the social welfare sector ... provinces became newly and wholly responsible for spending and administering in education and health ... [N]ow they must fund and administer these sectors in conformance with national directives (but without federal officials' direct involvement).

One important implication of the Franceschet and Piscopo contrast between the Chilean and Argentine experiences with reproductive rights policy is that formally unitary systems do not necessarily give the national government more control over subnational governments compared to federal systems. As long as subnational government leaders can act without the national government imposing effective sanctions, whether budgetary retaliation or prosecution for malfeasance, the subnational policymakers can pursue their own objectives, presumably reflecting some degree of responsiveness to the people within their jurisdiction.

In addition, although the bulk of countries are still formally unitary systems, some degree of devolution – transfer of authority that for all practical purposes is irreversible – is a highly pervasive trend among these systems. For Latin America in general, González (2008, 211) notes:

The immense majority of countries in Latin America, being federal or unitary, with relatively strong or weak subnational governments, have initiated some kind of decentralization process during the last two decades. In political terms, this means that where subnational officials were usually appointed, many Latin American countries are electing intermediate governments and the vast majority of them (in fact, all South American countries) have now elected local authorities.

Thus, the common presumption that unitary systems limit subnational governments' resistance to national policy initiatives to a greater degree than federal systems needs to be re-thought. Therefore, national policymakers in unitary systems must be equally vigilant in ensuring that sound guidelines will be followed by subnational governments' implementation. As Rodden (2002, 670) notes,

As experiences with federalism unfold, an abstract welfare economics literature emphasizing its efficiency advantages has given way to a more balanced political economy literature that draws attention to questions of institutional design. Much of this new literature points out that decentralization can be dangerous, especially in developing countries. Above all, skeptics point out the difficulties of macroeconomic management, adjustment, and reform in decentralized systems ... especially when they feature formally federal constitutions that empower states with veto authority over central government decisions.

Resistance Relying on the Intelligence and Appraisal Functions. It may even be that gathering and providing the information needed to invoke the policies is blocked. For example, Holzner (2006, 89–90) reports that in the late 1990s, neighborhood associations linked to Mexico's PRI Party withheld information about the opportunities offered by a program to provide land titles to squatters, reducing the number of families that invoked their rights to receive these titles.

Activists' policy initiatives may also be undermined because information is withheld. Stakeholders' initiatives to block major infrastructure projects, such as hydroelectric dams or highways, are frequently hobbled by the lack of information about the true cost of the projects that could scuttle the project. It is common for governments to permit private sector firms to keep the financial arrangements with the government secret, on the grounds that the arrangements are proprietary information. In Uganda, the 200-megawatt Bujagali Dam was approved, and received funding from both the World Bank and bilateral foreign aid agencies, before it was revealed that the arrangement with the U.S.-based power company, AES Corporation, meant that electricity costs would be relatively high. Leaving aside the corruption charges that later came to light, the initiative to block the dam would have been more effective if details of the agreement had been known. It is significant that the terms of the agreement were disclosed only after the Ugandan Supreme Court ruled in favor of lawsuits by Ugandan NGOs (Rich 2013, 69–70).

Appraisal (or evaluation) is often used to undermine the support for particular initiatives. Of course, in some cases this is fully justified. Yet in other cases, appraisals based on selective information about the outcomes of what seem to be similar initiatives can unfairly disparage sound initiatives. For example, the long-standing and pervasive debate over whether rural development initiatives should involve large-scale, multi-sectoral projects – so-called "integrated rural development" – has obvious political implications for both the intra-governmental rivalries among national-level agencies and relations between the national and subnational governments. The highly negative reputation of integrated rural development in many circles is easy to employ to attack such an initiative.

Yet Cohen (1987, chapters 1 and 7) clarifies that whether integrated rural development should be deemed a sound strategy depends on the variant adopted, the timeframe for evaluation, how much commitment the government demonstrates, and so on. With respect to the Ethiopian case, Cohen (1987, 120) concludes that:

Despite the rapid increase in participating farmers, rise in agricultural productivity, and expansion of area covered, a number of constraints prevented CADU [Chilalo Agricultural Development Unit – the coordinating entity] from reaching its full potential. Indeed, these constraints caused the project to have adverse effects on some of the tenants and small-scale landowners it sought to reach. By 1973 it was clear that they could not be removed without government implementation of progressive policy, administrative, and land tenure reforms. Yet, despite six years of effort, SIDA [the Swedish International Development Authority – the key international donor] and CADU were unable to obtain such government actions. As a result, the achievements of the project were overlooked and the negative consequences of its activities set [back] CADU's general reputation in the development community.

PARTISANSHIP AND REJECTION OF POLICY INITIATIVES

The intertwining of political competition for government office and the stances on policy initiatives frequently provoke opposition to initiatives. The success of policy initiatives is often seen as enhancing the political strength of political groups within government or otherwise championing the initiatives. Many impasses are motivated to deny policy victories to incumbent government officials. For example, Kantai (2003) attributes the opposition to Kenya's Masai Mara National Reserve, a carefully-planned wildlife conservation program, to the fact that it was an initiative of KANU party leaders. Similarly, Sinha (2014, 6) characterizes India's disinvestment policy as so highly politicized that "each new government formed has its own agenda and approach towards disinvestment," resulting in considerable policy inconsistency. The opposition to government initiatives to liberalize the Mexican oil sector will has been a blatantly partisan battlefield, as elaborated later in this chapter.

POLARIZATION OF ADHERENTS OF OPPOSING POSITIONS

Even if an initiative is not vetoed or otherwise formally blocked, policymakers may feel compelled to abort it due to insufficient support, whether or not the initiative is modified in search of a compromise. Thus, impasses arise when compromise is rejected; stakeholders' positions may become rigidly polarized even if all would gain from the compromise. The symptoms are obvious: rejection of the validity of opposing claims, lack of trust that opposing stakeholders will comply with whatever obligations the compromise requires of them, lack of trust that the government will maintain its commitments rather than favoring the other side, and skepticism as to whether the compromise will be sustained. The question is: What are the patterns behind polarization, which, if understood, could point to strategies for overcoming it? The roots of polarization are of three types: the consequences of strategy, the structural constraints of the institutions involved, and psychological dynamics.

Strategies of Escalation

Exaggerating the Intensity of Demands. One particularly potent source of polarization arises from the logic of exaggerating the intensity of demands. The logic is that a convincingly extreme position may induce the other side to yield more if a compromise is to be reached. The strategic logic of influencing policy agendas includes inducing greater attention to issues by adding the threat of disruption, thereby demonstrating the willingness to risk retaliation. In the extreme, the escalation results in physical attacks and sabotage, as in the case of some groups in Nigeria's Niger Delta region, this in an explicit effort to secure a larger proportion of the oil revenues (Obi 2007). Schelling (1980) points to the advantages of appearing to be irrational in risk-taking, on the grounds that the irrational risk taker may escalate conflict to the point of heavy damage on all sides of a conflict, inducing others to make greater concessions. However, one side's extreme stance may drive others to extreme positions as well, and leaders' extreme statements may bring followers to genuinely more extreme attitudes. This extremism may provoke opponents into more extreme positions themselves, making compromise even less likely. This strategy persists even though it can backfire; in some cases, concessions are forthcoming, but in other cases the provocateurs are mistaken in their expectations.

Discrediting Opponents' Positions. Another tactic that often contributes to polarization is for stakeholder leaders (or government leaders) to denigrate the arguments mounted by opponents. For example, the decades-old impasse over the reform of Mexico's oil and gas sector mentioned above was exacerbated by claims on both sides of the privatization debate that the other side was shortsighted, selfish, or even unpatriotic (Elizondo 2011). Although oil production and additions to reserves in the hydrocarbon sector had been declining for many years, the opponents of risk-sharing contracts and other sector-opening arrangements with private oil companies accused the proponents of these reforms of yielding Mexico's sovereignty to foreign interests, particularly from the United States, and abandoning the hallowed constitutional provisions that "in the nation is vested the direct ownership of oil."

Intra-governmental conflicts can also give rise to the tactic of disparaging the quality of rival agencies. For instance, the jurisdictional struggle over the Vietnamese water sector between the Ministry of Agriculture and Rural Development (MARD) and the Ministry of Natural Resources and Environment (MoNRE) led to sharp accusations of inappropriate objectives and incompetence. Molle and Hoanh (2009, 5) report that

MARD, on the one hand, was decried as being narrowly focused on irrigation and flood issues, heavily biased towards structural and engineering approaches . . . , and its involvement in regulation issues were contrary to the principle of separation of power between regulation and operation. MoNRE, on the other hand, was held as being technically weak . . . , without the competence needed to monitor and regulate water allocation, water quality, and environmental changes altogether.

Discrediting also can entail the use of misleading intelligence to refute the basis of opposing promotional appeals. The escalation of attacks and counterattacks using intelligence for promotional purposes can increase the overall uncertainty of people caught in the middle of controversies and greatly polarize policy debates. For example, the Kenyan debate on the status of environmental rights in the new Constitution has become even more contentious because of what the Commission for the Implementation of the Constitution (2011, 45) deemed "deliberate misinformation to members of the public by some members of both the executive and the legislature."

A much broader source of polarization arises in the ideologically heated debates over fiscal reform, which to a large degree revolve around the redistributive impacts of different policies. Estache and Leipziger (2009, 7) conclude that "in practice, much of the debate on fiscal policies boils down to the identification of the winners and losers . . . One major concern is the lack of independent studies that analyze the redistributive effects of a given policy, particularly in a world of sound bites, partisan lobbying, and frankly, considerable disinformation."

Structural Constraints

The complexity of governance, especially in democratic systems, means that the multiple governmental units, levels, and political entities almost inevitably come into conflict with one another. Differences in objectives and prerogatives among the highest-level units within government (e.g., in the executive, legislative, and judicial branches), among ministries or departments, and among different levels of government from the national to the very local, are only part of the picture. In addition, as has already been presented, the potential for conflict exists among the officials who select the formal rules, invoke them, and implement them. However, the potential for conflict does not necessarily mean polarization and impasse; other factors must be taken into account to explain why stalemates within government often occur.

Status Differences among Agencies. For one thing, it is quite common that the personnel of one government unit will be better trained and better financed than others. Most commonly, national-level units have this advantage over subnational units. At the same governmental level, ministerial offices often are more deeply staffed than legislative offices. The personnel of better-equipped offices may be tempted to dominate, and may express arrogance, whether conscious of it or not. The resulting animosity may exacerbate the conflicts and contribute to gridlock.

Different Constituencies. Different governmental units have different constituencies. This is most obvious for the contrast between national and subnational governments, given the narrower set of residents within the subnational unit's jurisdiction.

It is also common for agencies overseeing different sectors to serve different causes and the interests of different stakeholders: the agricultural ministry vs. the industry ministry; the spending ministries vs. the fiscal management agencies; and the environmental agency vs. a host of agencies promoting agriculture, industry, physical infrastructure, or resettlement programs. The question is why agencies pursuing different constituents' interests, or simply fulfilling their different mandates, sometimes cannot reach a compromise, or, in the case of different government levels, cannot establish straightforwardly which level has authority over particular decisions. Recognizing when rivalries may become destructive can be a first step in either mediating the conflicts or restructuring institutional arrangements. Therefore, withholding information, financing, physical infrastructure, goods and services, or community facilitation, which may occur because of weak monitoring and information gathering, could be identified and corrected by national statistical offices, accountability offices, inspector general offices, and so on.

As mentioned previously, another tactic is to delay cooperation by claiming weak administrative capacity, or by asserting that cumbersome procedures simply do not permit more rapid action. Such approaches are very difficult to dispute without detailed information about the inner workings of the agency and its capacities.

A potentially effective countermeasure is that leaders of agencies who need cooperation could inform whatever government accountability offices there are in the country that the foot-dragging agency is basically accusing itself of low competence.

Decentralization.[2] The impasses based on disputes as to which units have authority often reflect the fluid nature of governance arrangements, particularly decentralization trends. As the focus of the most prominent governance reform in many countries, decentralization is rarely a fully coherent, one-step transition. As a "work in progress" that is often conceived as a long process of governance reform, decentralization is typically characterized by uncertainty as to which agencies within the national and subnational governments have or will have authority, opening opportunities for conflicting jurisdictional assertions. The Development Partners Working Group on Decentralisation & Local Governance (2011, 27) summarizes some of decentralization's continually changing and potentially contentious aspects:

DLG [Decentralisation and Local Governance] is a dynamic process that involves gradual adjustments and readjustments of behaviour in changing environments. As public functions are constitutionally or legally decentralised, all of the central agencies involved experience a number of changes. Even in a modest decentralisation, there is by definition some de jure loss of control over their respective functions – for example, local governments typically assume revenue raising powers formerly controlled by the Ministry of Finance, public employment management functions formerly under the Civil Service Commission, and service delivery functions traditionally managed by the Ministry of Education, Health, Water, etc. There may also be some transfer of responsibilities across national ministries; for instance, a Ministry of Local Government may take over responsibility for monitoring local government fiscal activities formerly handled by the Ministry of Finance. In most cases, decentralisation fundamentally alters the roles that many central agencies play, with a movement away from direct decision-making and control of subnational actors to facilitation, support, and monitoring of them.

At the national level, Eaton, Kaiser, and Smoke (2011, 36) summarize the political economy consequences of the bureaucratic jurisdictional conflicts:

Perhaps the most central issue with respect to the bureaucratic dynamics of decentralization is the fact that national government agencies may have little or no desire to assume or divest responsibilities as envisioned under decentralization

---

[2] The best treatments of the decentralization issues can be found in Litvack, Ahmad, and Bird 1998; Litvack and Seddon 2002; Rondinelli 2006; and Cheema and Rondinelli 2007.

laws if they are not pressured to do so. In addition, they may have few incentives to work cooperatively with other agencies, even though coordination is normally seen as crucial for the "success" and sustainability of decentralization in terms of improved processes and outcomes. In some cases, powerful central agencies – and the departments and/or divisions within – may engage in direct competition for control of the decentralization agenda and the substantial internal and external resources that may be involved in its implementation. They may, if they have the power to do so, pursue policies and take actions that are inconsistent with the formal decentralization framework.

On the subnational level, change and ambiguity about both resource sharing and jurisdictions create parallel problems, both within a subnational government and among subnational governments. McGibbon (2004, 38) relates how the budgetary ambiguity following the radical decentralization in Indonesia exacerbates conflict across local governments in the Papuan province of Jayapura:

The lack of transparency in the provincial budget in fact created serious problems for the province – not least in triggering a conflict within local government ranks. Officials at the district level (kabupaten/kota) were dissatisfied with what they saw as a failure by Jayapura to distribute special autonomy funds evenly across the province. Local officials were particularly critical of the revenue-sharing formula offered by Jayapura in which the province received 60 percent and only 40 percent would go to all the districts combined. While this conflict was driven mainly by local competition over resources, it was also the result of the separate strategies that the government was pursuing through the decentralization and special autonomy laws respectively. The former law was designed to empower district elites (bypassing the provincial government); the latter devolved power and resources to the provincial elite.

The Indonesian case also exemplifies how rivalries among international donors can add to the ambiguity and jurisdictional conflicts among government agencies. Eaton, Kaiser, and Smoke (2011, 73) observe that:

A particularly powerful example [of poor development assistance coordination] is the Indonesian Decentralization Support Facility (DSF), a multi-donor partnership that drew inspiration from the Paris Declaration on Aid Effectiveness with the goal of creating more consistent and better-coordinated decentralization activities across government ministries and development partners. The structure of the DSF was initially highly donor-driven, however, and in the eyes of some critics dominated (although not primarily funded) by the World Bank. As a result, the DSF ended up reinforcing many long-standing competitive tensions among development partners and government agencies involved in decentralization.

Eaton, Kaiser, and Smoke (2011, 41) explain that the donor agencies themselves may be trapped into making inconsistent demands on the national or subnational governments:

In order to facilitate compliance with their own management and accountability requirements, for example, development partners may insist that the government adopt their preferred procedures and modalities, and in many cases they continue to work through separate implementation units or other parallel or semi-parallel mechanisms. Inconsistent procedures and separate mechanisms can inhibit the development of a unified public sector system and place a significant burden on government counterparts at the national and subnational level.

Divided Government. A structural feature of growing importance is "divided government," referring to a policy-selection process that involves decision-makers of different political parties, or other partisan political groups, collectively required to endorse an initiative for it to go forward. The strengthening of democracy in many countries has made top-level policymaking entities more likely to reflect multiple political parties or factions, to the point that the executive and legislative branches at a given level of government are dominated by different political parties (a variant of "divided government"), or, in parliamentary systems, the top leaders must form party coalitions to secure a majority. Some argue that divided government in presidential systems is more likely to lead to impasses (Linz 1990). It is certainly true that if one party controls both the presidency and the legislature, presidential initiatives are likely to be easier to enact. Nacif (2006a, 1) notes that

[t]he Mexican authoritarian regime had an enormous capacity to produce policy changes. Sometimes, the magnitude and speed of these changes took on a dramatic character, as when the government expropriated the oil industry in 1938 or the banking system in 1982. The presidency had the ability to deliver 'policy shocks' in response to critical situations. Under normal circumstances, the chief executive had the power to bring about substantive policy change even when this involved the amending of the Constitution.

However, Nacif (2006a; 2006b) points out that even though Mexico went from a long-standing one-party-dominant presidential system to divided government when the PRI party lost its hold over the presidency in 2000, the volume of legislation since then has not indicated stalemate, although the policy changes have been more incremental than radical. Even so, opening up the oil sector to private investment under the current administration has been a momentous change, accompanied by significant tax changes and electoral reforms (Starr 2014).

Psychology of Polarization

In some circumstances opportunities for cooperation are passed over out of straightforward antagonism and disdain arising from distorted stereotypes toward opposing stakeholder groups, or toward the government itself (Augoustinos and Walker 1998). Policymakers are frequently shocked at the vehemence of opposition to initiatives that the government leaders believe present minimal risk to stakeholders. Of course, some negative perceptions of others are richly deserved, but the circumstance in which negative attributes ascribed to others are greatly exaggerated provides an opportunity to overcome such stalemates, if the exaggerations can be identified and rectified. This requires an assessment of the psychology as well as the tactics to take advantage of the vulnerability to stereotyping.

The "unit" relationship mentioned in Chapter 4 as a reason why development practitioners of particular organizations are distrusted explains a far broader dynamic of stereotyping. According to Heider (1958, 176), regarding people within a category (e.g., an ethnic group, government officials, or in assistance agency) as all sharing a whole range of traits is a cognitive simplification that leads to stereotyping based on narrow experiences. For example, Dahana (1997, 70) flatly asserts that in Indonesia "the Chinese are always identified with the rich"; yet "most [Indonesian Chinese] earn a living by becoming shop-keepers, handicraft and furniture sellers, and even road sweepers and trishaw pullers in the poorer areas of Indonesia" (Dawis 2009, 189).

It is also an emotional simplification, inasmuch as holding positive and negative attitudes toward the same object can be psychologically painful. Thus, a negative experience with one government agency or an external development assistance agency, or a clash with members of a different ethnic group, may result in the conclusion that all officials of the current government, all development assistance agencies, or all members of that ethnic group deserve hostile reactions.

Heider's related contribution is that people tend to attribute their own failures to circumstances rather than to their own traits, while they attribute others' failures to the traits of these others. This implies that in any context in which development efforts have been disappointing, stakeholders are less likely to blame themselves, and more likely to blame others, whether for incompetence, ill will, or both. This dynamic may be bolstered by tendencies of particular groups to reinforce their own feelings of self-worth by thinking worse of other groups. Tajfel and Turner (1979, 40) posit that "Individuals strive to achieve or to maintain positive social identity ... Positive social identity is based to a large extent on favorable comparisons that can be made between the ingroup and some relevant out-groups." Al Ramiah, Hewstone, and Schmid (2011, 44) endorse this perspective by noting that "Group members are motivated to protect their self-esteem and achieve a positive and distinct social identity, and preference for one's own group is a way of achieving this."

However, an even more extreme dynamic is sometimes at play. Denson et al. (2006, 43) conclude that "[i]n many instances, lay people appear to believe that shared group membership with a wrongdoer is a basis for blame." The scope of blame establishes the scope of who is deserving of disdain and possibly punishment. In the extreme, Lickel et al. (2006, 372) assert that "vicarious retribution"

occurs when a member of a group commits an act of aggression toward the members of an outgroup for an assault or provocation that had no personal consequences for him or her but which did harm a fellow ingroup member. Furthermore, retribution is often directed at outgroup members who, themselves, were not the direct causal agents in the original attack against the person's ingroup.

As long as stakeholders are polarized to such a great degree, blocking their preferred initiatives may be motivated not only by the assumption that their gain would come at the ingroup's loss, but also by a more emotional antagonism toward "those horrible people." Frequently, stakeholder leaders will try to advance their own influence, or pursue the tactic of exaggerating demands, by demonizing opponents, whether in government or not. Insofar as followers are induced to accept such negative characterizations of others in the policy process, the polarization is even greater.

Personalized animosities also play an often highly divisive role in agency rivalries. Similar to clashes among stakeholder groups, interagency animosities are often worsened by the attribution of incompetence or ill will to the personnel of the other agency, when in fact differences in mandates, or structural problems, may be responsible to the lack of cooperation and coordination.

OVERCOMING THE OBSTACLES TO ISSUE
LINKAGE APPROACHES

The beginning of this chapter raised the possibility of making initiatives more acceptable to a broad range of stakeholders and even policymakers by linking more than one issue within the initiative. Often one issue has high priority among the top government leaders, putting the other issues into the category of potential policy concessions to the stakeholders whose opposition could scuttle the core initiative. A huge number of stalled initiatives would have been more viable if the government could have offered policy concessions more credibly. Identifying the obstacles to credible issue-linkage arrangements is the first step in understanding how to overcome them.

In general, overcoming impasses through issue linkage requires understanding the likely behaviors of not just the government policymakers, opposition political leaders, or top representatives of sectoral groups, but also the government's main supporters and the supporters of opposition leaders or stakeholders represented by sectoral leaders. Government policymakers must have access to sufficiently sophisticated intelligence to identify viable linkages and linkage strategies. Recall that top government officials, especially when they are newly installed in office, frequently are prone to exaggerated assessments of their own power and breadth of support that their initiatives can muster. Issue linkage requires top government leaders to yield on some issues. The same holds for the supporters of the main initiative; they may balk at making the concessions on other issues.

Here it is important to distinguish two scenarios as to the types of groups involved. In some situations, political parties dominate the contention over policy initiatives; in other situations, sectoral organizations, such as labor unions or business associations, are more directly involved. When political parties are the major contestants, even if they have their bases in different sectoral groups, both the opposition leaders and their supporters typically view the policy conflict in terms of their party's strength as much as, or even more than, the policy outcomes. The risk for opposition leaders is losing ground in the partisan political competition, and appearing weak to the party loyalists, insofar as acceding to the policy main initiative is seen as a political victory for the government. Therefore, for opposition leaders, trading their opportunity to weaken the government politically in exchange for policy gains (i.e., concessions on other issues) may be quite unattractive. Indeed, in some contexts, the followers of opposition politicians may care more about the partisan political struggle than the issue outcomes. For example, Ezrow (2011, 7) provides the Lebanese example of the separation between party support and issue preference: "Parties in Lebanon are not well rooted in society. 'Ideological' linkages, i.e., policy linkages, are non-existent and links are based on personalism and patron-clientelism." Opposition party leaders may scuttle promising policy concessions in order to inflict a political loss on the government, where party followers have so little interest in the policies per se.

When the issue-linkage consultations more directly involve the government's interactions with sectoral organizations, the partisan political competition may be less central, but it is even more important that these stakeholders are sufficiently confident that the compensatory measures would materialize. This is one reason why broad concertation efforts, as outlined in Chapter 2, are undertaken.

Obviously, the success of broad pacts depends on perceptions of the credibility of the policymakers' commitments and, for that matter, the loyalty of the stakeholders' representatives. These representatives may not be faithful to their supporters' interests, and press for their own prominence or other rewards (Harstad 2008). Just as opposition party leaders sometimes switch their party allegiance to the party in power, or join the governing coalition, some sectoral leaders may be co-opted by the government. Madrid (2003, 63) notes the opportunity for Latin American governments to co-opt union leaders by rewarding them with government posts.

In summary, the development practitioner can utilize his or her understanding of the dynamics of issue linkage to assess the likelihood of overcoming policy impasses through such linkages, and – depending on the development practitioner's resources – even may be able to play a brokering role in forging some linkage agreements. Clearly, strong intelligence gathering and analysis would help to identify the kinds of issue linkages that would be sufficiently compelling. Willingness to negotiate with political archrivals is necessary within the scenario of political parties playing the major role in considering whether to accept linkage agreement.

The willingness of government leaders to engage in some degree of hands-tying would increase the credibility of inter-temporal commitments, whether these commitments come from highly publicized pacts with political parties or sectoral organizations, binding agreements with external organizations, or embedding the commitments in fundamental laws or constitutional provisions that are difficult to reverse. Development practitioners representing international institutions may be able to help forge these agreements. For example, the World Bank has assisted in Bolivia's complex process of linking decentralization, overall fiscal resources, and the distribution of hydrocarbon resources, by providing analysis and recommendations (Frank 2010; Aresti 2016). Even for the development practitioner without a role in the selection of strategies, awareness of whether the strategies are available, and top policymakers are willing to undertake them, would be helpful in determining whether the impasse can be overcome.

ARENA STRATEGIES

"She was wise, subtle, and knew more than one way to skin a cat."
  –Mark Twain, *A Connecticut Yankee in King Arthur's Court*, 1899

One way to look at an impasse is that an initiative being pursued through particular channels, involving particular institutions, does not have sufficient support or capacity for compromise to succeed in reasonably intact shape. This perspective points to the possibility of shifting to different channels and either engaging different institutions or altering the institutions already involved. The set of institutions and processes in which an initiative is deliberated, selected, and enacted, or the "policy arena," sometimes can be changed to increase the likelihood of overcoming the impasses.

The strategy of arena selection or "venue shifting" goes beyond overcoming impasses. The champion of any initiative may consider whether different channels would pose fewer roadblocks and enhance the effectiveness of the resources that the champion can muster. Therefore, much of what follows is enlightening with respect to the generic case. However, the challenges to overcoming impasses call for additional considerations in selecting or modifying the channels.

Selecting an Existing Venue

Because of the multiple dimensions of government, the conceivable possibilities of arena selection are extremely broad. The first cut comprises the formally distinct decision-making entities within the national government that have some degree of autonomy. Here it is useful to inventory the institutions related to the decision functions. The prescription function is dominated by the top executive leadership and the legislature, whether separated, as in most presidential systems, or joined in parliamentary systems in which ministers are parliamentary members. Yet other rule-making formal institutions with some degree of autonomy are widespread: regulatory commissions whose commissioners are guaranteed to serve out their terms; central bank officials insulated from executive or legislative pressure; and even courts, which regularly create rules in order to manage issues that have come under judicial control.

On a more fine-grained level, initiatives may have an easier or harder time navigating through the legislative process depending on the committees through which they are channeled (Jones, Baumgartner, and Talbert

1993). The same is true of the options among several executive agencies to pursue approximately the same initiative. A resettlement agency can provide agricultural inputs to resettled populations just as an agricultural ministry can. State enterprises can take on functions previously reserved for core ministries. For instance, in Venezuela many of the community-development and social-welfare functions that had been performed by mainline executive agencies are now performed by the state-owned oil company, PDVSA. Brazil has seen a proliferation of so-called "arm's-length bodies" of various degrees of autonomy from the core executive ministries (Pacheco 2013).

In carrying out their administrative functions, many of these bodies, such as the "social organizations" that provide public services, including health and cultural facility management, develop standards and therefore are involved in the prescription function, even if they do not fit the conventional image of creating policy the way the top executive and legislative bodies do.

Although the invocation function is conventionally seen as the province of the court system, regulatory agencies (including some of Brazil's "arm's length bodies") also engage in the invocation function, insofar as they determine whether actions by private entities violate laws or regulations and therefore ought to be subject to negative sanctions. Other "watchdog agencies" serve the invocation function; as mentioned above, Chile's Contraloría General de la República (Comptroller General) can intervene to negate executive decrees even when the Constitutional Tribunal cannot.

This proliferation is repeated on the subnational levels. In many countries, the diversity of institutions at the various subnational levels is remarkable. In addition to the conventional constitutionally formalized jurisdictions (provinces, states, departments, counties, districts, communes, municipalities, etc.), special-purpose entities such as watershed councils or transportation authorities cut across the conventional jurisdictions. Thus, venue shifting may encompass not only the choice of level, but also institutions and processes of each of the relevant subnational governments.

Initiatives also can be channeled through international bodies that, in turn, can alter the direction and incentives of the domestic policy process. These international bodies can further the initiative through intelligence, persuasion, funding, conditionalities, brokering domestic agreements, and so on. For example, the World Bank brokered an accord among Ghanaian NGOs, micro-enterprise institutions, government regulators, and the Danish International Development Agency to resolve conflicting laws regulating micro-enterprise finance (Muntemba and Amuah 2000, 31).

However, the intervention of international bodies often runs the risk of negative reactions fueled by nationalist sentiment.

Matching Arenas and Resources. One fundamental consideration in channeling initiatives to an arena is the match between the resources at the disposal of the champions of the initiative, and the likely effectiveness of deploying those resources in particular venues. This consideration is relevant whether the initiative is so new that the choice of the original channel is yet to be made, or a "venue switch" is advisable because the current channel is less effective in using the resources at one's disposal. An unexamined presumption often exists that a particular channel is the "natural," "obvious," or "legitimate" approach to pursuing the policy objectives. Sometimes it is important to overcome this presumption, which may require forceful promotional tactics. In addition, it must be recognized that the effectiveness of resources when policies are contested depends not simply on the strength of one's resources, but also whether resources of that type are stronger than resources of the same type held by policy opponents. For example, the capacity to mobilize thousands of people to take to the streets would be less effective if policy opponents have the same capacity.

Applying the matching logic is extremely complicated, in that the potential resources encompass multiple "welfare assets," such as wealth, skill, wellbeing (which ranges from physical attractiveness to the ability to ensure safety or health), and enlightenment (in the sense of knowledge, insight and information regarding personal and cultural interactions). But there are also "deference assets" (power, affection, respect, and rectitude (in the sense of righteousness).[3] The following are simply illustrative of some of the possibilities:

- If the champions of an initiative have an advantage in technical expertise, channeling the initiative through highly technical processes may be more successful in accomplishing the same goals as the same or similar initiatives run through different channels. One prime example is the ability to persuade the central bank to increase the money supply to stimulate the economy (if the budget office does not permit more government spending). Another is the ability to help a bureaucratic agency fashion new guidelines for its interpretation of laws, in lieu of new legislation. In Chile, for instance, crucial aspects of the labor law are effectively established by the Labor Directorate ("DT"). Marzán (2009, 504) explains

---

[3] Based on Lasswell and Kaplan 1950; Lasswell 1971.

that the Director of the DT can determine the meaning and scope of labor legislation in the country ... so that its career servants can uniformly implement the law across the different regions of the country ... This type of administrative interpretation of the law is accomplished in Chile through a procedure known as *dictamen* – an opinion or report issued by the director of a specific administrative agency ... A *dictamen* directly binds all the officers of the administrative agency ... It also indirectly binds private parties regulated by the law, as they must adapt their behavior to the *dictamen* if they want to reduce their chances of being fined or otherwise penalized by the government agency.

- If the supporters of the initiative have strong interpersonal ties with subnational authorities, the advantages of respect, affection, or both may direct the initiative toward subnational governments, even if this strategy does not initially have the broad scope of national policies or programs.
- If the initiative's supporters can mobilize citizens to express their support for the initiative, to a greater extent than their opponents can, the channels that are more directly in the public eye may be more promising. Of course, public demonstrations run the risk of getting out of hand, which could lead to a backlash against the initiative.
- If the initiative's supporters have an advantage in financial resources, they also may be able to use channels in the public eye, and, through publicity, financing studies, and employing teams of people to convince stakeholders to support the initiative actively.
- If at least some of the supporters of the initiative are regarded as having high levels of rectitude (i.e., moral righteousness), they also may be able to make a public appeal if the initiative is channeled through institutions of relatively high public visibility. Nelson Mandela obviously had enormous moral influence on the post-apartheid policy process in South Africa, in addition to his influence ending apartheid.

Creating or Modifying a Venue

Modifying the Process with Existing Institutions. Some development practitioners have enough formal authority, negotiating advantage, or informal influence to contribute by substantially modifying existing formal policymaking institutions or creating new policymaking venues. Changing policymaking procedures without creating new institutions is extraordinarily common – agencies are shuffled from one ministry to another, jurisdictions are re-assigned. In the case of the Vietnamese

MARD and the MoNRE mentioned above, the top government leadership changed the roles and relative power of the ministries several times during the 2000s (Molle and Hoanh 2009, 4–7).

Creating New Formal Institutions. As mentioned in Chapter 3, when a new agency is established, a set of vested interests arises, involving the personnel in the agency, the stakeholders receiving its goods and services, and the stakeholders providing goods and services to the agency for its programs and other activities. In many cases, these constituencies can pressure top policymakers to expand, or at least maintain, the activities of the agency, providing a basis for strengthening an initiative as well as expanding the opportunities for issue linkage. The establishment of Latin American environmental ministries, also mentioned in Chapter 3, has changed the power balance in the contest between economic expansion and conservation (Gwynne and Cristobal 2014, 131).

In addition, the existence of the agency's mandate confers some degree of responsibility, whether legal or political, for the government to fulfill those mandates. This is particularly strong in the case, albeit rare, that private citizens have the right to sue the government for nonfeasance (i.e., for the nonfulfillment of a responsibility) going beyond simply avoiding damage on the part of governmental actions. In Brazil, the 1988 Constitution provided this right through the *ação popular* (popular legal action). Findley (1988, 40) explains that:

> The *ação popular* is a constitutionally authorized proceeding by which any citizen may seek judicial invalidation of public administrative acts injurious to the public patrimony of the federal, state, or local government. The statute that regulates the constitutional provision provides that public patrimony includes "property and rights of economic, artistic, aesthetic, historic or touristic value." In addition, the National Environmental Policy Law of 1981 mandates "governmental action to maintain ecological equilibrium, considering the environment as a public patrimony to be necessarily secured and protected, taking into account its collective use." The *ação popular* can be directed at administrative nonfeasance as well as misfeasance. Before enjoining or compelling administrative action, the court only need find that its intervention is necessary to prevent injury to the public patrimony, not that the administrative action or inaction, absent judicial intervention, would violate any specific law.

Another fundamental consideration is the political power balance, as well as resource effectiveness, at the subnational level compared to higher levels. Recognizing that decentralized decision-making does not eliminate politics, but rather alters its site, the question of whether decentralization will permit a sound initiative to proceed depends on contextual specifics. One advantage that decentralized efforts do have, however, lies in the

potential to enact an initiative in a limited number of subnational jurisdictions where the context is welcoming, and which, if the initiative is
successful, might be replicated elsewhere. Thus, Lai, Catacutan, and
Mercado (2016) enumerate successful local agro-forestry initiatives in
Indonesia, Laos, the Philippines, and Vietnam that have demonstrated
their potential for scaling up to broader coverage. Tantivess and Walt
(2008) report that successful public-private programs offering antiretroviral therapy programs in two Thai provinces were scaled up across the
country.

Considerations Specific to Overcoming Impasses

The additional venue considerations related specifically to overcoming an
impasse will be highly context-sensitive, but in general would begin with
trying to identify arenas that provide potentially vulnerable stakeholders
more confidence that all commitments would be honored. To reinforce
this, some venues involve deliberations over both policies with uncertain
impacts and policies that would provide safety net guarantees for vulnerable groups. In other words, this would call for venues that facilitate
credible damage-minimizing measures.

In many contexts, this confidence would be enhanced if the venue
involves multiple stakeholder groups, political parties, or both, negotiating over a fairly broad range of issues, such that government reneging on
commitments would risk the unraveling of the whole pact. Again, sometimes this can be accomplished through concertation, outlined in Chapter 2, if government leaders can organize the consultations so that they are
seen as sufficiently inclusive by relevant stakeholders. Highly public
venues may deter reneging, insofar as it would be widely known.
A decision-making process that clarifies how the government leaders
benefit from the full set of policies could also enhance confidence. Some
policy processes permit the enactment of policies within the timeframe of
that government's tenure in office, reinforcing the confidence that government commitments could be honored. Venues that are relatively insulated
from severe short-term shocks may also be advisable.

Finally, the option of amending or even fully rewriting the constitution
can serve as a venue focus, to enact a substantive policy outcome, or to
change the policymaking structure so that processes below the constitutional level could be more effective. For those who view a constitution
as simply a combination of procedural rules and guarantees of rights, it
may come as a surprise to learn that some constitutions include

substantive policy commitments. The Brazilian Constitution enshrines not only budgetary commitments to education, as mentioned before, but also commitments to the social security system (De Oliveira, Barreto, and Beltrão 2001). Amendments to the Mexican Constitution have changed the policies on communal versus private landholdings (Muñoz-Piña, De Janvry, and Sadoulet 2003). The post-independence Indian Constitution required affirmative action for *dalits* ("out-castes") and *adivasi* ("tribals"), and this policy is still in force, despite enormous controversy over its fairness especially after the inclusion of a huge number of other groups) and its effectiveness (Bagde, Epple, and Taylor 2016).

Unless a constitution is simply imposed by highly authoritarian leaders ignoring most stakeholder groups, a constitutional conference or convention is a broad-based negotiation that must encompass multiple issues. Therefore, it is an opportunity to establish issue linkage, on both the substantive and process levels. The post-apartheid Constitution of South Africa reflects complex negotiations over affirmative action for Blacks and guaranteed land rights for large land owners (Pieterse and Van Donk 2002; Herbst 2005, 99).

SUMMARY

The capacity to impose an impasse rests in part of the capacity to veto actions formally, or to balk at implementation. In accounting for motivations to resist impasse-resolving impasses, this chapter posits that impasses may emerge from polarization, whether inter-group, inter-agency, ideological, or partisan, as indicated by denigrating or punitive communications. Additional warning signs that impasses are emerging, or will continue, are jurisdictional uncertainty, inter-agency conflict, and exaggeratedly negative appraisals. The prospects for overcoming impasses rest on the willingness and capacity of government leaders either to force the enactment of the initiative, or to induce cooperation by credibly offering concessions on other issues.

Thus, this chapter has emphasized the breadth of factors that the development practitioner must take into account to identify and understand the risks of policy impasses, and to recommend strategies to overcome them. This requires understanding the social psychology of intergroup relations and the political logic of issue linkage as much as the structures of policymaking that permit impasses to be effected by officials from the top levels to the bureaucracy.

TABLE 5.1 *Core Problems, Causes, and Potential Indicators of Impasses That Block Sound Initiatives*

Root problem	Causes	Potential indicators
Insurmountable differences among stakeholders required to acquiesce	Stakeholder negotiating brinksmanship strategy	More extreme positions than what emerged from prior agreements
	Inter-group polarization	Disparagement of groups against other groups
	Divergence of stakeholders' perceived interests	Extent of conflict among group interests
	Divergence of stakeholder expectations	Divergence of communications regarding likely outcomes
Effective resistance by stakeholder or political groups	Resistance due to high symbolic and/or emotional importance	Communications conveying high symbolic and/or emotional importance
	Stakeholder perception that agreement sets dangerous precedents	Communications projecting fears of future initiatives due to passage of the current initiative
	Stakeholder rejection of policymaking procedures	Stakeholder communications denouncing the policymaking constitutive arrangements
Non-compromising leadership	Leaders staking reputations on winning without compromise	Leaders' communications emphasizing their toughmindedness
Inability/unwillingness to shift venues	Procedural inertia; constitutive rigidity	Continuing efforts in arenas that lead to distorted enactment
Stakeholder unwillingness to accept any initiative	Intrinsic uncertainty	Discrepancies in analyses and projections available to stakeholders
Lack of possibilities to link issues	Non-integrated policy venues; lack of leadership credibility	Isolation of policymaking on linkable issues

6

Inconsistent or Incomplete Enactment of Initiatives

This chapter focuses more specifically on how to account for what appear to be implementation failures. Of course, this overlaps with the challenge of identifying ill-fated initiatives, as addressed in Chapter 3, but a more in-depth analysis of apparent distortions arising as initiatives are implemented can illuminate the more specific causes. In addition, this chapter examines approaches to minimize the deviations from stated policy objectives. The chapter demonstrates how tortuous the enactment of even the seemingly most straightforward policies can be.

More than any other chapter, this chapter also demonstrates the dependence of implementation's success on the quality of intelligence, prescriptions, and appraisal. When seemingly sound initiatives fail to be enacted, or are enacted in ways that deviate seriously from the intent of the initiative, the conventional explanation is that the bureaucracy is weak, corrupt, or incompetent. Certainly, this is sometimes true, but a useful diagnosis must consider a much wider range of possibilities, and the prevalence of combined causes. Thus, Mahannop (2004, 213), accounting for deforestation in Thailand, argues that

a number of conflicts arose among the different state organizations regarding the utilization of forest lands. The situation was further aggravated by unstable and vague policies, poor law enforcement, forest encroachment by poor as well as influential people, strong opposition to forest plantation development by non-governmental organizations (NGOs) and poor administration by government organizations.

VAGUE POLICIES

Many policies have failed to provide sufficient specificity to avoid unsound interpretations of what can be enacted. Yet before accounting for avoidable vagueness, it is important to note that a tradeoff frequently exists between flexibility, recognizing the need to adapt to specific contexts, and avoiding unsound interpretations of broad instructions. Sometimes the open-ended nature of flexibly-interpretable policies is necessary even if it risks perverse outcomes.

Motivations

Motives behind vague policies are associated with each of the decision functions. This mapping is useful for identifying how to reduce unnecessary vagueness.

Weak intelligence makes it difficult to anticipate both the true needs in specific contexts and the problems confronting implementation. Policymakers who recognize this may try to incorporate different treatments and contingencies, but future conditions obviously cannot be fully anticipated, and weak intelligence also often entails greater difficulty in anticipating the consequences of policies even if no surprising contextual circumstances arise. Once policymakers become aware of failures arising from highly specific policies, they are likely to build more flexibility into the policies.

Promotional advantages of vague policies begin with the consideration that appearing to broaden the range of possible beneficiaries often makes an initiative more attractive. The stated beneficiaries of projects and programs may exceed the available financial resources, prompting the government to be vague about the magnitude of benefits for each stakeholder group or the process of allocating the benefits. For example, Ahsan (2003, 268) highlights the remarkable discrepancy between the funds earmarked for education spending by the Pakistani government in the Eighth Five-Year Development Plan (1993–98) and the actual spending: "With regard to financial achievements, an amount of Rs. 69.0 billion was earmarked but only Rs. 32.5 billion were allocated, out of which Rs. 24.8 billion were utilized."[1]

---

[1] Over this period, the Pakistani rupee ranged from Rs. 40 per dollar to roughly Rs. 50 per dollar

Government leaders face an even more awkward situation with respect to emotionally charged issues of rights, morality, and identity. When policymakers feel compelled to formulate policies regarding issues that cannot avoid tradeoffs between opposing goals (e.g., linguistic diversity vs. sociocultural unity, reproductive rights vs. "right to life"), vagueness about the tilt of the policy is an obvious option. Some initiatives address what seem to be obviously virtuous goals, such as eliminating child labor, but are weakly enforced because of the realities of the families involved (Bharadwaj, Lakdawala, and Li 2013). In addition, the promotional advantages gained by appealing either to raw impulses or conscience, rather than instrumental appeals, typically would de-emphasize practical matters.[2] Some policies are essentially "value expressive"(Katz 1960), keeping the message bold by keeping it broad.

Prescription approaches relying on vagueness may be designed to paper over impasses or to avert open confrontations as a means of coping with conflicts of objectives. For instance, Vian et al. (2012, 52), assessing the causes of weak and inconsistent efforts to root out corruption in the Vietnamese health sector, note that a "[c]losed and centralised policy process produces vague policies that give appearance of unity and allow party insiders discretionary power to interpret as they like." Vagueness in laws, regulations, or resource-allocation criteria thus opens opportunities for favoritism. Leaf (2002, 27), also assessing the discretion of Vietnamese public officials, attributes the "regulatory vagueness" of land appropriation to the fact that "guarantees of tenure rights are secured through personalistic ties to local authorities, rather than through proper administrative procedures." Similarly, in China, Jingyan (2013, 7) concludes "[t]he vague policies and regulations regarding rural public goods provision by local level governments have nurtured the growth of guanxi [favoritism through personal connections]."

Vagueness, whether through inconsistent precedents, or straightforward ambiguity, may be used to provide the flexibility to avoid reducing benefits for stakeholders whose reactions would be too costly for government policymakers. The *terminations* that do not follow specified procedures or criteria undermine certainty in all aspects of the sector in which

---

[2] Sometimes the combined appeal to raw impulse, conscience, and rationality (what Lasswell [1932] labeled the "triple appeal principle," based on Freud's id-ego-superego distinction) is a potent combination However, the triple-appeal principle does not necessarily call for appeals that evoke all three components. The appeal to conscience may be undermined by the expectation of personal gain, just as evoking raw impulses such as punitiveness may seem hypocritical if complicated by considerations of personal gain.

apparently arbitrary terminations occur. Contreras-Hermosilla (2003, 3), addressing the inconsistent treatment of Honduran forestry rights, notes:

In Honduras even agreements between government and communities are subject to arbitrary change and are therefore not trusted by the parties involved. For example, harvesting rights are not secure and provisions for change are unclear. Thus, the government can unilaterally repeal them for reasons that are not necessarily understandable to the communities affected. Naturally, communities tend to view these agreements as transitory and subject to arbitrary termination by government. In these conditions, long-term legal commitments to forest management are dismissed in favour of the more immediate, but illegal, capture of benefits from forest use.

Invocation and application procedures may exacerbate vagueness insofar as the officials in invocation roles, ranging from judges to street-level personnel such as inspectors and police officers, apply rules inconsistently as a means of maintaining a broad, mixed scope of precedents to permit discretion in future cases. If every firm violating an environmental regulation had been fined, it would be riskier for the inspector to ignore a violation by a favored firm. Inconsistent enforcement of borderline infractions of health and safety regulations provides inspectors with the option to impose the penalties for violations or to look the other way. In this manner, the invocation process adds to the breadth of possible interpretations, and thus increases the vagueness of effective policy.

Appraisal tactics can increase vagueness if they involve leaving targets and timing imprecise or ambiguous, which can serve to reduce accountability. Tate-Campbell (2010, 8), assessing how the Thai government has hedged on its commitment to provide HIV and AIDS education to both Thai citizens and migrants, notes that the "ambiguous targets could make monitoring, evaluation and holding the RTG [Royal Thai Government] accountable difficult."

STARVING THE ENACTMENT BUDGET

Underfunding of policies, programs, and projects often limits implementation. Furthermore, starving enactment not only reduces overall impact, but also risks inconsistent application when resources cannot be allocated wherever the policy ought to be invoked. Of course, drastic economic downturns may leave the government budget short of covering planned initiatives that would have been feasible under normal circumstances. Yet initiatives are frequently underfunded despite the fact the resources could be available. This section reviews explanations beyond major budget shocks.

Motivations in Formulating the Initiatives

Seeking Credit Without the Commitment. As mentioned in Chapter 3, overly ambitious formal commitments are often politically attractive, leading to new programs or agencies and ambitious targets even when top government leaders are ultimately unwilling to devote the requisite volume of resources. What can be added here is that the accountability for failing to accomplish overly ambitious initiatives is often passed on to administrators or service providers who are denied the resources to enact the programs. As Chapter 3 notes, when underfunded education initiatives fail to meet enrollment or graduation targets, teachers are often blamed. Under-resourced forestry departments are blamed for deforestation, subnational officials are blamed for weak implementation after national authorities fail to provide sufficient fiscal decentralization (i.e., tax transfers or taxing capacity) to fund decentralized services, and so on.

Backing off of Commitments. The strategy of restriction by partial incorporation (see, again, Chapter 3) may be pursued by maintaining formal institutions but underfunding them as well, a way of reducing the impact of a policy without the political cost of dismantling the institutions. Argentine President Carlos Menem used this approach to reduce the impact of the government-funded National Women's Council (Consejo Nacional de la Mujer or CNM), which had been vigorously pursuing a reproductive rights agenda. Franceschet (2010, 12) notes: "Although Menem did not downgrade the agency in institutional terms, he did reduce its resources. The conflict emerged when Menem sought to ally himself with conservative Catholics while the CNM . . . was taking a more progressive stance on gender issues."

WHEN PROBLEMS DO LIE WITH THE IMPLEMENTERS (BUT OFTEN WITH ROOTS ELSEWHERE)

Shifting now from causes associated with the origins of the initiative to the causes related to the actions of officials entrusted with enactment, the more conventional explanations of bureaucratic noncompliance, self-serving actions, and low competence arise. The most useful diagnostic questions are why implementers would wish to depart from directives of higher-level policymakers, why and how the decision process permits the implementers this latitude, and how the process can permit sufficient enactment flexibility without risking undermining the soundness of initiatives through excessive discretion. This chapter has already argued that desirable flexibility can degenerate into excessive vagueness that permits unsound applications. Three other causes are added here: the obvious point that administrative weaknesses of all sorts can undermine sound initiatives, the factors that motivate the implementers to alter the thrusts of initiatives, and the capacity of "downstream" processes of invocation and application to modify the effective policies, including the special case of decentralization.

Administrative Weaknesses

For the poorest countries, the public administration may be weak simply because of the difficulty of recruiting people with enough relevant education, particularly in contexts where the private sector or the political party apparatuses siphon off the most qualified. In some poor and not-so-poor countries, administrative posts are handed out through political patronage to unqualified individuals. One useful diagnostic indicator of patronage appointments is the degree of turnover of civil service staff following changes in the party leading the government.

However, weak capabilities of the public administration often also rest on low administrative salaries. While this is most commonly conveyed as a source of corruption, it is also a reason why highly qualified individuals do not enter the public administration in many countries. Government leaders often have a huge political challenge in raising the salaries of public servants: the fact that underpaid bureaucrats often feel compelled to demand bribes obviously contributes to the public perception that bureaucrats are corrupt; this undermines support for increasing their salaries. The widespread perception that many bureaucracies are bloated is an additional obstacle to bringing salaries to an optimal level.

When bureaucratic agencies are unwilling or incapable of working together, whether out of rivalry or low capability, the separate "siloes" of each agency are likely to make it more difficult to deliver complex services effectively and efficiently. The indicators of siloed agencies include a history of failures to complete multiagency projects; the thinness of constructive information flowing among agencies; and expressions of hostility, as shown by the acrimonious exchanges among Vietnamese water agencies.

Decentralization often worsens administrative capabilities. Central governments typically are more attractive for the most highly qualified individuals seeking positions in public administration. On top of that, as mentioned in Chapter 3, decentralization of responsibilities without matching fiscal decentralization typically leaves subnational bureaucracies weaker than national ones.

Partisan Political Capture. Hiring through patronage not only can lead to unqualified personnel in bureaucratic positions, but also to loyalty to a political party or faction that could color the administrative decisions. Mousseau (2006, 306) recounts that in Turkey, "virtually all political parties in power and coalition governments between 1973 and 1980 attempted to replace state bureaucrats and civil servants with their own partisan bureaucrats." Beh (2007, 215) concludes that in China, administrative weakness in the rural sector reflected the fact that the bureaucracy "had traditionally been under the purview of the party organization rather than the state bureaucracy." It is appropriate for cabinet and other very high-level officials to be political appointees to ensure loyalty to the policy agenda of the government leaders; in democratic systems, their decisions generally can be observed by stakeholders and thereby the government can be held accountable for their decisions. The problem occurs when the public administration is captured by a political party or faction to the degree that the invocation and application decisions are made to gain political advantage for the party or faction, at lower levels that cannot be observed by stakeholders to keep the government accountable. It may also be the case that partisan bureaucrats "left over" from previous administrations will persist in actions that undermine the initiatives of current government leaders.

Interest Group Capture. As mentioned in Chapter 2, agencies may also be "captured" by interest groups. The obvious consequence is favoritism in the invocation and application functions toward those groups. A less obvious consequence is that different agencies may be captured by different interest groups – yet another source of inter-agency conflict. It is difficult for an agricultural agency captured by, say, large land owners, to work effectively with a land reform agency serving the landless rural population.

Staff Attrition. In assessing administrative weaknesses, as well as the possibility to overcome them, the development practitioner must take account of staff turnover – not only of implementers within the target government, but also of external development practitioners. For example, a detailed evaluation of a major Dutch initiative by the International Cooperation Agency of the Association of Netherlands Municipalities (VNG International) to support local government capacity building in developing regions through "twinning" with Dutch local government officials and experts revealed serious obstacles due to staff turnover in both the targeted agencies and their Dutch counterparts. Baud et al. (2010, 35–36) report:

High staff turnover is however a reality in most countries and poses a real threat for the sustainability in projects. One of the main challenges of MIC [Municipal International Cooperation] is therefore the institutionalization of the projects. Some municipalities have incorporated part of the programs in their own plans and budgets as a first step to become less dependent of external support. But a real area of concern is the extent of institutionalization of new knowledge. In many cases only a few people are in control of technical programs, which makes programs vulnerable to changes. In case of a slim organization possibilities to involve more people are however limited (This applies amongst others to projects on citizen registration projects in Benin, GIS training in Govan Mbeki and Buffalo City in South Africa).

... Finally, sustainability also concerns the Dutch local governments and related organisations. Staff turnover of Dutch experts, both within local governments and at VNG International can seriously slow down processes. And like the Southern municipalities, in many of the Dutch municipalities only some civil servants are involved in international exchange.

Attrition can be a huge problem even if at any point in time a planning or implementing agency seems to be at full staff – the understandings among different units, the experience with what works and what does not work, and the levels of commitment can erode seriously as staff depart. Cornell (2014, 210) notes that:

The high staff turnover rates that exist in the public administrations of many aid-receiving countries seem to be problematic for the execution of aid programs financed by development cooperation. The prospects of implementing future development cooperation projects with public sector institutions may depend on the extent to which donors and recipients are able to address these high turnover rates and their causes.

Staff turnover may be aggravated by a host of conditions. Low salaries and poor working conditions are obvious sources, but a more complicated source is the attempt by government leaders in some countries to replace existing personnel to make way for patronage and bring in loyalists more likely to support new initiatives. The turnover may be extreme; Akhtari, Moreira, and Trucco (2015, 2) note that: "political control over the bureaucracy can extend beyond the highest levels of the bureaucracy. In the country we study, Brazil, the president, state governors, and mayors all appoint tens of thousands of people to the federal, state, and local bureaucracy, respectively, once they enter office (anywhere from 15,000 to 105,000)."

To understand why implementers may resist directives from higher-level policymakers, it is important to emphasize that bureaucrats, whether staffing government offices or in front-line positions interacting with the public, can have a wide variety of orientations, goals, and insecurities. The stereotype of the bureaucrat as simply a risk-averse individual concerned only with job security does not do justice with the range of motivations that may be at play.

Bureaucratic Orientations. It is useful to identify four broad orientations that arise out of combinations of priorities held by government officials:

- A *careerist* orientation prioritizes individual advancement within the organization, often reflecting the priorities of personal power, respect, and wealth in the prospect of keeping one's job, or promotion. Of course, striving for recognition and promotion is hardly objectionable; problems arise if career-climbing comes at the expense of the sound initiatives. In some circumstances, the careerist orientation induces strong risk aversion. For instance, Hu (2006, 236) explains the Hong Kong's lack of proactive science and technology promotion not on policy but on the aversion of the bureaucracy to intervene:

  Non-interventionism may no longer be government policy but non-interventionist thinking is still widespread among government officials. For the bureaucrats, noninterventionism is a good excuse for non-action, which minimizes the risk of making mistakes. Especially for the generalist who lacks specialist knowledge, non-interventionism is the safest approach. Hong Kong people have for many years been used to making proposals within the confines of non-interventionism; they find it difficult to think out of the box, even now that the restrictions have been officially lifted.

  In other circumstances, ambitious administrators at all levels may be willing to take risks in order to stand out as dynamic, and to seek promotion. The obvious implication is that whatever conditions increase or decrease the levels of insecurity within the bureaucracy will have a major impact on adaptability.

- An *organizational-loyalist* orientation prioritizes greater standing of individuals' agency or sub-agency, often reflecting the priorities of affection and respect within the organization, and possibly the expectation that the organization's strength will redound to the benefit of the individuals as well. As mentioned earlier, this orientation fuels the "bureaucratic politics" that pits one agency against another in the rivalry for resources and expanded jurisdiction. However, it also serves to protect job security and remuneration of the individuals within the agency. For example, (Giacchino 2003, 205) argues that the initiative in Malta to reform a weak financial management system failed because:

  Responsibility for the policy was entrusted to senior management at the Ministry of Finance but, because they felt threatened by aspects of the policy, they did not act upon it or allow it to be acted upon by other officers of their organization. Had the policy involved senior managers from other Ministries and Departments who were equally affected by the policy, but who might have had more to gain from it than to lose, responsibility would have been spread and enough pressure might have been leveraged to generate a momentum for the policy.

- A *programmatic orientation* entails a commitment to policy-relevant objectives. These may be the primary goals of the organization; individuals dedicated to building the transportation infrastructure may gravitate to the transportation ministry. Yet the goals may not be the primary objectives of the organization, but rather potentially in conflict – a crusading programmatic orientation to bring other priorities to the agency. The environmentalist who joins the transportation ministry is a case in point. Yet, whether committed to the primary mission of the agency or another mission, the substantive outcomes of the individual's contributions are the priority, often reflecting the rectitude of pursuing that mission. For example, Silva (1996, 24) recounts how the pro-environmental personnel of Chile's Ministry of National Properties, which had not been very active on conservation issues beyond managing state-owned land, had pressed the ministry to become far more active in conservation activities, and had lobbied (ultimately successfully) for the establishment of an environmental ministry.

- A *professionalist orientation* prioritizes individuals' obligations to, and standing within, their profession, often reflecting a combination of seeking professional respect and the rectitude of adhering to professional norms. The professionalist orientation has strong potential to clash with initiatives of their agencies insofar as these initiatives are regarded as violating the ethical standards of the profession. For example, civil engineers may defy leaders' orders to design inexpensive and therefore dangerous physical infrastructure; the professionalists may prevail if agency leaders are concerned about their vulnerability to accusations of shoddy construction.

Of course, hybrid orientations are not only possible, but also common. The desire to have a stronger agency may be motivated by the programmatic desire to strengthen the agency's programs. Some professionalist orientations are supplemented by organizational loyalty when the organization itself is dedicated to upholding professional standards. Regulatory agencies and inspectorates are likely examples. Careerists may be loyal to their organizations, insofar as the success of the organization elevates the careerists within it.

Bureaucratic Insulation. Whereas in some cases, bureaucratic agencies are deliberately and appropriately structured to insulate the officials from external influences, the form of bureaucratic insulation relevant here concerns actions by civil servants to reduce their need to comply with directives coming from other sources within the government. Particularly when government leaders have engaged in a series of administrative reforms, presumably as a popular measure to cater to the public perception that the bureaucracy is corrupt and inefficient, bureaucrats understandably become defensive. This defensiveness may prompt actions to insulate the bureaucracy beyond the rationale of guarding against undue political pressure. For example, this may involve denying information to other governmental entities mandated to monitor the agency's actions, employing esoteric methods and terminology beyond the ken of non-experts, stalling implementation of institutionally-threatening reforms, putting up barriers to interactions with stakeholders, appealing to legislative allies to fend off administrative reforms, and so on. Shirley and Xu (1998) found that state enterprise managers in Senegal, India, Ghana, and the Philippines were successful in reducing governmental oversight over performance contracts through delays, providing incomplete information, and involving higher-level, more technically expert managers in the negotiations with governmental oversight institutions. Eaton (2003, 36) reports that Argentine tax bureaucrats successfully tabled some of the government's reform efforts. Suhardiman et al. (2014, 458) note the resistance of Mexican and Philippine irrigation administrators to the reforms that threatened the reduction in bureaucratic staffing.

Impacts on Stakeholder Participation. Citizen involvement at the grassroots level can be crucial not only to convey needs and wants up to the highest policymaking levels, but also to hold implementers accountable to enact sound initiatives. However, this involvement certainly faces major challenges. Andrews and Shah (2003, 6.2, 6.29) list the primary impediments to "citizen-centered governance":

- low capacity (both personnel and systems)
- organizational centralization and top-down governance
- "social insulation" and non-transparent management of the bureaucracy
- monopolization of service provision, precluding more efficient sources of services
- permanence [rigid structure] and non-innovation
- process orientation rather than an explicit results orientation to improve effectiveness
- internally biased and non-responsive incentive structure
- poor organizational and accountability mechanisms; weak internal evaluation mechanisms; few external evaluation mechanisms

The "social insulation" problem – isolating the bureaucrats from the stakeholders – identified by the Andrews and Shah assessment is a crucial point that goes beyond insulation from higher levels of government. The decentralization strategy of "deconcentration" – deploying central government officials throughout the country (Rondinelli 1981) – typically reduces the likelihood that bureaucrats will have ethnic similarities as a basis for social interaction and understanding. The most prominent case is India's approach of posting Indian Administrative Service personnel in areas far from their home region, and rotating them regularly. This approach does reduce the risk that bureaucrats would be biased in favor of their own group, or "captured" by local elites, yet it does entail the tradeoff of social isolation.

Capacity for Deliberate Policy Changes by Implementers. What are the circumstances in which neither hierarchical discipline nor the threat to withhold financial resources can prevent implementers from altering even rather specific initiatives from top-level policymakers? For one thing, top-level policymakers may presume that their authority to issue directives alleviates the need to enforce them. Enforcement can be expensive; it can erode the solidarity among public officials. Furthermore, to punish noncompliance requires knowing when directives are being ignored or distorted, and – as mentioned above – the informational advantage that implementers have over the policymakers can be large. Deconcentration thus involves another tradeoff: gaining more knowledge of the local areas, but greater difficulty for higher-level government officials to monitor the actions of locally-based bureaucrats. Robbins (2000) documents how forest guards in Rajasthan can receive bribes for entrance into protected areas with little fear of punishment by higher-level authorities. Much of the literature on such noncompliance focuses on corruption, but it also pertains to officials adapting policies in order to manage political pressures. For example, designating some families as ineligible for conditional cash transfer benefits because the means test puts them just over the eligibility requirements, while slightly poorer neighbors are deemed eligible, could arouse not only hostility among neighbors, but also toward the individuals making these eligibility decisions.

In addition, the officials involved in the invocation and application functions may have the formal authority to change the initiative. Chapter 5 notes that formal veto power can be found at several levels, including courts, regulatory commissions, watchdog agencies, state enterprises, and lower-level governments with devolved authority. Whereas Chapter 5 presents the power of these entities as a potential source of impasse, in many cases their formal authority also can be wielded to alter the initiative. Regulatory commissions' interpretations of laws may diverge sharply from legislative intent. When courts find fault with laws, regulations, or executive orders, their authority to dictate remedies transforms the initiative. For example, the 2005 Thai Supreme Administrative Court ruled against the government's attempt to privatize the state-owned public utility, the Electricity Generating Authority of Thailand (Dressel 2010, 677), changing the policy context for privatization efforts thereafter.

PREMATURE TERMINATION OR EMASCULATION

One way that initiatives become ill-faded has little to do with the quality of the policies, programs, or projects but rather results from the termination of the initiative before it has had enough time to demonstrate its effectiveness. Highways, port facilities, pipelines, and so on, are left unfinished; curricular reforms are abandoned (sometimes leaving inconsistencies across schools and regions), clinics are built but unstaffed, and so on.

Premature termination may occur because of:

- *Government Change.* Newly empowered top policymakers may have other priorities, in terms of sectors, regions, content, and so on. Obviously, these policymakers typically wish to gain credit for their own programs. In some instances, however, this temptation can be offset by relabeling existing programs, often with modifications, including expansions. For example, Mexico's prominent conditional cash transfer program, *Progresa*, begun in 1997, became *Oportunidades* in 2002, and was renamed *Prospera* in 2014. While the differences are not trivial, the continuities are striking. Martínez Valle (2016, f.n.1), of the Mexican Ministry of Health, acknowledges "that [t]hese name changes have been principally because of different political parties being in power. The essential characteristics of a conditional cash transfer program have remained unchanged."
- *Policymaking and Administrative Restructuring.* Reshuffling can leave agencies under-staffed, or even orphaned. Restructuring, which often follows a change in top leadership, is frequently defended as necessary to reduce bureaucratic bloat, or to reorient governmental priorities. Yet, even if unintended, prior initiatives may stall because of the delays in gearing up the new units and the potential confusion over jurisdictions. The development practitioner has to look beyond the positive spin that government leaders will often put on these changes, to ask whether substantial restructuring will undermine even existing initiatives that top leaders wish to continue.

- *Deliberate or Unintentionally Negative or Premature Evaluations.*
  Taking action when initiatives are going off track, whether or not the
  implementers are deliberately distorting them, often faces a major
  challenge in knowing whether these problems indeed are occurring.
  Conversely, initiatives may be disparaged by misleadingly negative
  assessments, and therefore run the risk of being abandoned or distorted, even if their actual impacts are positive. Moreover, implementers may undermine the intent of an initiative through actions that
  provide high scores on the prevailing performance metrics, at the
  expense of the overall quality of what is implemented. In short, even
  if the problems of poor monitoring and withheld information can be
  overcome and relevant information is available, the evaluation or
  appraisal function may be weak and can distort the implementation
  of the initiative.

Premature terminations may be less likely for initiatives that involve
commitments to both international and subnational entities, insofar as
termination or emasculation would entail higher political costs to the
government leaders, increasing the likelihood that initiatives would be
continued unless they are plausibly regarded as failures deserving termination before the pre-specified term of the policy, program, or project. For
example, the Corazon Aquino government in the Philippines fended off
strong pressure to terminate international loan commitments incurred
during the Marcos administration, by declaring its commitment to the
international monetary fund and the World Bank to pay the loans
(Tadem 2009, 228).

TECHNICAL CHALLENGES OF APPRAISAL

Gauging Success Comprehensively

Appraisal is remarkably complicated, because of the multiple dimensions
of what can be evaluated. The dimensions covered by an appraisal effort
can vary widely, because of both the goals that motivate whoever directs
the appraisal and the views of what can be evaluated reliably.

The time period covered by an appraisal can also impart dramatically
different impressions even without data inconsistencies. In summarizing
evaluations of the effectiveness of value added taxation initiatives in many
developing countries, Bird and Gendron (2006, 13) note that "[a]ll such
calculations are very sensitive to the period and data used."

Sensitivity to Baselines. To gauge changes over time, the evaluator has to select a starting date and use a method to link the relevant series. Rodríguez (2006, 503) notes that for Venezuela, "the choice of base year and linking techniques is crucial for the diagnosis of economic growth"; and demonstrates how this fundamentally alters the assessment of Venezuela's performance:

> Suppose you are asked to write on Venezuelan economic growth during the 1970s and you know nothing about it. You might decide that the first logical step would be to look at the data from the Venezuelan Central Bank on constant price GDP. If you did that, you would conclude that Venezuela did okay during the 1970s with an annual per capita growth rate of 0.62%. It would not seem to be a star economy, but you might say that at least it was growing. Now instead suppose that you were informed by a colleague about the existence of [the Penn World Tables] and their crosscountry comparable data on GDP growth. If you used that data, you would conclude that Venezuela's annual per capita GDP growth rate was −2.79% during that decade; that is, you would find a country that experienced a dramatic growth collapse. (Rodríguez 2006, 504)

If this much ambiguity exists among professional economists and statisticians, one can imagine how much uncertainty about trends exists among policymakers and the public.

Balancing Qualitative and Quantitative Measures. Despite such examples of the ambiguity of quantitative assessment, a major challenge to sound evaluation is the greater weight typically given to "hard" quantitative information over "soft" qualitative information. This is one reason why economic indicators are often favored over social and political indicators. The legitimate unwillingness to use quantitative indicators, even if they are misleading, may be taken by others as a tactic to evade specificity, putting greater pressure on evaluators to emphasize quantitative indicators.

Confounding of Effects. As mentioned in Chapter 2, assessing a policy's success is thornier in developing countries with frequent policy changes and greater socio-political and economic volatility. The lingering effects of earlier policies are difficult to discount, as are external shocks. Consider the reactions to Brazil's rosy growth projections prior to the dramatic cutback of Chinese demand for Brazil's raw products. Perhaps the Brazilian planners could have anticipated some reduction in export demand, but the magnitude of the Chinese contraction was virtually impossible to predict.

Incomplete Coverage of Input, Output, and Outcome Measures. Both the evaluative criteria built into the assessment criteria and ad hoc measures in implementation reports frequently fail to include a balance of input, output, and outcome measures. The discretion in selecting different types of metrics gives policymakers and implementers the ability to manipulate the reported evaluation. One dimension is the magnitude of resources devoted to an effort (inputs), direct results of the effort (outputs), and consequences of these outputs (outcomes). At first glance, outcome evaluation might seem like the gold standard of evaluation, but positive outcome evaluations – which simply may reflect fortuitous circumstances – could lead to neglect of sustainably high levels of inputs and outputs. While outcomes seem to be progressing well, hidden risks may be lurking in the neglect of important inputs. The most striking examples are the positive safety records of major infrastructure projects that thus far have not suffered from tunnel cave-ins, wall collapses, river contaminations, etc., even though safety provisions, ranging from the use of correct materials to the conduct of safety expectations, have been skimped. It is all too common that in the aftermath of physical infrastructure catastrophes, the inputs are revealed as inadequate, and their inadequacy had evaded attention.

Overlap of Policy Evaluation and Personnel Performance Evaluation. A negative evaluation of policies, projects, and programs typically influences how implementers are judged, whether the weaknesses are in the initiative, changes in the context, or poor implementation. One possible reaction is that implementers will alter the initiative to reduce their own vulnerability. Referring to joint forestry management initiatives in the Indian state of West Bengal, Joshi (1999, 10) found that

front-line workers were motivated to support any policy that would improve their work situation; in other words make their [forest] protection work easier and safer. They were facing dual pressures – on the one hand they were facing potential violence from villagers making their work increasingly dangerous; on the other hand, front-line foresters were often held responsible for rapid forest degradation by the senior officials and sometimes punished for 'negligence of duty.'

This does not mean that the forestry officials and guards were simply "risk-averse bureaucrats." Joshi (1999, 15) adds that

forest officers and front line workers demonstrated their commitment by using their official powers and resources in a discretionary fashion to help villagers overcome difficulties created by initial protection, at some risk to themselves. They promised the villagers some ultimate benefit from the protection activities and were willing to provide it at their own risk.

Unrealistic Targets. The comparison between the performance of a policy, project, or program and the explicit targets established at the launch of the initiative often colors the evaluation. Therefore, unrealistic targets can be seriously distorting. They may be unrealistic at the outset, because of intelligence failures; they may prove to be unrealistic due to unpredictable changes in the overall context. The point is that predictive uncertainty exposes any target to the possibility of error, but it is also true that the range of plausible targets may be quite broad.

Political Manipulation of Evaluation

The varieties, uncertainties, and ambiguities of evaluation outlined above provide the basis for manipulating the appraisal function. This conforms to the broader principle that technical ambiguity provides the space for politically-motivated interpretations.

Explicit targets may be set deliberately low, to increase the chance that they will be easily met. They may be ambiguous to reduce accountability, as illustrated by the case of the Thai HIV/AIDS program mentioned above. Or they may be confined to dimensions that the policymakers believe will do well. Conversely, targets may be exaggerated deliberately for several reasons: to exhort greater effort, to enhance the government's popularity, or even to make the implementers more vulnerable.

The pressures to express ambitious plans are exemplified by the South African government's effort to shore up support by exaggerating its capacity to boost the agricultural advantages of Black South Africans. Ortman (2005, 291–92) argues:

Following President Mbeki's "State of the Nation" address early in 2004, in which he requested that a concept document for the implementation of BEE [Black Economic Empowerment] in agriculture be compiled, the Minister of Agriculture and Land Affairs, Ms Thoko Didiza, released a draft AgriBEE document ... Amongst other proposals, this document recommended that 30% of commercial agricultural land be owned by blacks by 2014, an additional 20% be leased by blacks by 2014, 10% of existing farmland be set aside for farm workers for their own production, that farm workers achieve a 10% ownership stake in all farm enterprises by 2008, and that illiteracy among farm workers be eliminated by 2010 ... These proposals have attracted considerable criticism, particularly from organised agriculture in South Africa, due to the lack of clarity on definitions, the perceived 'impossible' targets set for transformation, and because the document was produced without consulting major stakeholders.

Similarly, in Malaysia, the targets stated in the 10th Malaysia Plan (2011–2015), which reflected policies of state domination and continued pro-Malay affirmative action – both widely believed to discourage investment – were seen as exaggerated from the beginning. O'Shannassy (2011, 179–180) notes:

Domestic critics complained that the government, by neglecting to deal with the serious structural problems identified by both programs, had set unrealistic targets for the [10th Malaysia Plan]. For example, the Malaysian economy was required to grow by 6% annually, a projection based in part on the assumption that private investment would grow at an annual rate of 12.8%. However, from 2006–09, the annual private investment growth rate was only 2%, and in the absence of meaningful reform it seemed unlikely that private investment would reach this target.

In fact, economic growth over the five-year period was mildly disappointing at 5.3 percent, but the overall investment rate at 8.4 percent was very disappointing.[3]

The range of evaluation issues demonstrates the numerous ways that aspects of the appraisal function can lead to altering or rejecting initiatives. Combined with administrative deficiencies, policymakers' reluctance to follow through on apparent commitments, and the tendencies toward vagueness, these problems also provide insights into approaches for addressing these shortcomings. Common threads include greater understanding of policymakers' motivations, stronger intelligence regarding both the impacts of initiatives and balanced evaluation, greater transparency of political leaders' true commitments, greater accountability of policymakers' responsibility to provide adequate resources for their initiatives, and appreciating how each of the decision functions can be analyzed – and possibly strengthened – to reduce unnecessary vagueness.

SUMMARY

The dynamics introduced in this chapter encompass both the relationships between the top policymakers and implementers, and the relationships between implementers and society as a whole. Top policymakers sometimes handcuff implementation in the face of unanticipated conditions; sometimes excessive flexibility permits implementers to indulge their biases. Thus, the problems of enactment are not necessarily to be laid at the feet of the typically much maligned bureaucracy. On the other hand, some implementers do take advantage of their discretion, often based on their informational advantages, to pursue their own interests. The development practitioner needs to be alert to the indicators of such deviations from the intent of initiatives.

---

[3] Focus Economics: Malaysia Economic Outlook, www.focus-economics.com/countries/malaysia.

TABLE 6.1 *Core Problems, Causes, and Potential Indicators of Inconsistent or Incomplete Enactment of Initiatives*

Root problem	Causes	Potential indicators
Low administrative capacity	Inadequate administrative budgets; corruption due to low salaries; patronage appointments; siloed agencies	Discrepancies between overall administrative budgets and benchmarked administrative budgetary needs; high civil service turnover; history of multiagency project failures
Inter-agency conflict	Conflicting/overlapping mandates	History of multiagency project failures; degree of withheld information; failure to provide inputs needed by other agencies; pronouncements of different ideological perspectives
	Representation of different constituents	"
	Clashes among agencies established by different regimes	Establishment and staffing by different administrations; acrimony in inter-agency exchanges
	Extreme budgetary competition	Volatility of budget allocations among agencies
Administrative restriction through partial incorporation	Administrators' disagreement with initiatives' goals &/or consequences	Extent of failures to enact feasible provisions of initiatives
Administrative vetoes	Administrative veto provisions in the formal decision-making structures	Frequency of initiatives blocked by decisions of lower level administrators
Vague prescriptions	Policymakers' avoidance of accountability	Breadth and multiplicity of interpretation of prescriptions
Overly rigid prescriptions	Policymakers' concern over administrative discretion	Excessive rigidity of policymakers' formal initiatives

7

Inadequate Accommodation for Excessive Deprivation

This chapter takes up the chronic problem of policy initiatives that fail to take adequate account of the damage that the initiatives may impose on stakeholders, particularly those who are most vulnerable. Even if government leaders are willing to impose deprivations on particular stakeholders, other development practitioners may regard the deprivations as unacceptable; such initiatives would be "ill-fated" as discussed in Chapter 3. Excessive deprivation also has obvious implications for the challenge that will be faced in Chapter 8: how to minimize destructive conflict. The chapter illustrates the utility of the decision process model in highlighting the potential for adverse consequences of a weak intelligence function, particularly with respect to the informal sector, and a promotion function that deceptively understates deprivations in order to reduce opposition. The prescription-function problem of weak participation by vulnerable groups often exacerbates the risks, and some initiatives may entail harsh program termination. Yet, some policy approaches can guard against excessive damage. The lack of specificity of many initiatives runs the risk of permitting implementers to act punitively.

Cases do exist in which governments willfully adopt policies in full knowledge that certain stakeholder groups will suffer more than is necessary; sometimes for reasons that the government regards as politically compelling. However, this chapter primarily addresses the more promising context in which government leaders wish to minimize unnecessary deprivations, or even to avoid any deprivation for anyone, especially the most vulnerable.

It is important to note that it is a rare policy indeed that harms no one. An exception is an initiative that changes an existing policy that otherwise would result in so much destructive conflict that everyone would suffer, but far more common are initiatives that harm some stakeholders. Policies that alter the economy will affect the competitive advantages of different industries and firms. New programs and projects financed from the government's budget draw funds that could be applied to other purposes. Administrative reforms that enhance efficiency by "doing more with less" come at the expense of whoever's goods or services are reduced. Stronger regulation may protect stakeholders from nuisance or greater harm, but it infringes upon the opportunities of those whose actions are limited by the regulatory restrictions.

However, many such initiatives incur unnecessary, gratuitous harm. Here it is important to be clear about definitions. "Gratuitous harm" is a deprivation that could be avoided without reducing the benefits to others. Some policies do *nearly* gratuitous harm: altering the policy would reduce the costs to harmed groups, but the benefits to those favored by the policy would be lowered only modestly. In many circumstances, beneficiaries of an initiative would be willing to sacrifice some of their potential gain as "side payments" to mitigate the losses of others – if only to increase the likelihood of enactment and to reduce the likelihood of future conflicts.

POLICIES PRONE TO EXCESSIVE HARM

Excessive harm can occur across a very broad range of policy categories. Several of these are economic measures. Tax-rate increases can impose severe deprivations on individuals and firms, or reduce the tax advantages of particular activities in which they have invested to the point where they are unprofitable. Cutbacks of government social-service budgets can decrease the healthcare, nutrition, educational opportunities, or other social services; or increase the costs to purchase these services from other providers. Conversely, inflationary government spending can erode the purchasing power of incomes and savings. Increased fees for goods or services provided by government or state enterprises (especially if they had been subsidized) can reduce access to these goods and services or reduce their purchasing power for other goods or services. The same is true for privately-provided goods or services set at higher fees by government policy. Minimum wage policies, while benefiting employees who retain their jobs, can discourage future hiring and provoke dismissals.

Other policies are regulatory, with both economic and sociopolitical effects. More stringent regulations can reduce the opportunities to earn or retain income. Yet, elimination of exclusionary regulations can expose previously favored stakeholders to competition against which they have no chance of succeeding. Environmental regulations can make manufacturing unprofitable, lead to the expulsion of populations from their ancestral rural areas to make way for conservation reserves, or lead to the bulldozing of informal urban settlements.

Education policies that change the language of instruction can severely disadvantage the families that use the former languages of instruction. The shift from French to English in Rwandan primary schools privileges the Tutsis whose families were exposed to English as refugees in Uganda (King 2013, 145–146). Changes in the language or languages used in government agencies can exclude people who are not fluent in the relevant language. The Kazakh government excluded many ethnic Russians (and some ethnic Kazakhs who spoke only Russian) from positions in the public administration.

Ownership policies can have the most severe impacts. This includes outright expropriation of real property or businesses, and land reform that takes rural land without adequate compensation. Government ownership changes can also have highly adverse impacts, as privatization of state enterprises can result in worker dismissals and higher prices for goods and services. Property rights and user-rights changes resulting from resettlement programs, whether motivated to reduce over-crowding, promote regional development, separate antagonistic groups, change the ethnic or political composition in the target area, or accommodate people displaced by government projects, can adversely affect both the resettled people and the people of the target area.

Finally, political reforms can create open-ended disadvantages for particular groups. Changes in electoral rules, or, more broadly, the institutions of political competition, can undermine the influence of formerly influential groups. Decentralization policies can change the power relations to the disadvantage of groups that had stronger positions when the national government had more authority.

DIAGNOSING DECISION-FUNCTION CHALLENGES
TO REDUCING UNNECESSARY DEPRIVATION

As with the diagnosis of incomplete or inconsistent enactment in Chapter 5, mapping out the causes of gratuitous damage to stakeholders can be aided by identifying challenges arising from each of the decision functions.

Intelligence Weaknesses

As noted in Chapter 4, policymakers often proceed with inadequate information. In some cases, the prevailing socioeconomic conditions simply limit the government's intelligence, particularly with respect to low-income stakeholders. Insofar as stakeholders fear that providing information would increase their vulnerability, they may engage in willful withholding of information. For example, in Ghana the Livelihood Empowerment against Poverty conditional cash transfer program receives poor information because district leaders hide information about families that no longer formally qualify for transfers. Oduro (2015,34) writes:

To expose noncomplying beneficiaries so that they lost their entitlement was to run the risk that the district would be excluded from future social intervention programmes. The CLIC [Community Livelihood Empowerment against Poverty Implementation Committee] members therefore concealed negative information from the district social welfare unit in order to ensure that they would continue to benefit from future social programmes.

Similarly, although Zambia's market liberalization has made it more important that agricultural price information is widely shared, Chomba et al. (2002, 4) point to the difficulty that the government has in collecting market information from commodity traders. These traders may well fear that providing accurate information would benefit their competitors.

By the same token, although the Indian state government of Meghalaya has a strong interest in knowing the population strengths of the tribal groups within the state in order to address land issues, some groups conceal their ethnic identity. Haokip (2014, 309) argues that:

Owing to their constant insecurity as a result of their minority status in the state, the Biates have been perpetually hiding their identity. They are unable to exert their identity openly due to fear of being tormented, subdued and even their properties (both movable and immovable) being seized by the majority community. Indeed, such incidents have occurred a couple of times in the recent past.

Inadvertent damage is often due to ineffective consultation with stakeholders, whose current circumstances therefore are not well understood. For India, Hanstad et al. (2009, 258) note that:

India's first-generation land reforms suffered in their effectiveness because they failed to take into account the vulnerability of the tenants and sharecroppers on the land. Legislation that successfully abolished intermediary interests in land unintentionally caused the eviction and resulting landlessness of some of those most dependent on the land. If policy makers had possessed greater knowledge of the rural realities and likely responses of all groups to the new legislation, governments could have designed protections for these populations, such as the protections West Bengal gave its bargadars [sharecroppers].

This case also demonstrates the difficulty of anticipating second-order consequences. The analytic limitations, whether or not initially hobbled by inadequate information, may fail to anticipate long-term adverse impacts. Loevinsohn (2013, 2) cites the unanticipated rise in deaths from insecticide use in the Philippines, linked to subsidized credit that had been made available to Philippine farmers for, among other things, the purchase of highly toxic pesticides.

This case is also a reminder that it is easy to neglect some of the dimensions of impact of policies that are designed to address quite different dimensions. The analysis of the consequences of providing subsidized credit may have been confined to economic considerations, without sufficient attention to health. The analysis of housing policy options, even if it successfully identifies how to secure safer housing, may neglect the impact of separating nuclear families from their extended families. Resettlement programs had become notorious in their neglect of noneconomic dimensions of impact. Cernea (2003, 40), based on probably the most comprehensive reviews of infrastructure-related resettlement through the early 2000's, concluded:

Resettlers' losses in income, assets, rights, are multi-sided – economic, social, cultural, in cash and in kind, in opportunities, in power. Resettlers lose not only natural or man-made physical capital but also human and social capital, through the unraveling of patterns of social organization and of mutual help networks. The income lost is not only cash income, but also wealth that is psychological in nature including culture, status, and identity.

However, as true as this is, identifying and assessing the magnitudes of these losses remains a daunting intelligence challenge. Certainly, having anthropologists and sociologists involved in the analytic effort is helpful, but some of the uncertainty is inevitable. This limitation in the intelligence function calls for both adaptability to be built into the initiative and a strong appraisal effort to guide adaptations to address excessive harm.

The intelligence function applied to selecting policy initiatives inevitably relies to some degree on the cumulative wisdom of development theory, doctrine, and practice. However, some "conventional wisdom" assumptions about the benign nature of certain policy initiatives may blind planners and policymakers to risks of harm. For example, microfinance (providing small loans to low income entrepreneurs) is widely, and, in many circumstances, deservedly a promising approach. However, Islam (2016, ch. 1) notes that under some circumstances, even microfinance initiatives can hurt the poor, because of their inability to repay their debts.

Promotional Challenges

When policy advocates use the promotional tactic of making exaggerated claims about the virtues of their favored initiatives, they may be neglecting the vulnerability of various stakeholders. For example, the promotional efforts to gain support for very expensive large-scale infrastructure projects, such as hydroelectric dams, major highways, airports, and seaports, commonly have exaggerated estimates of benefits and inadequate accounting for potential harms. For example, Prado et al. (2016, 1134) note the exaggerated claims of the Brazilian government regarding the energy needs that proposed hydroelectric dams would fulfill. Flyvbjerg, Holm, and Buhl (2005, 131), assessing 210 rail and highway projects in 14 developed and developing countries, report that:

The study shows with very high statistical significance that forecasters generally do a poor job of estimating the demand for transportation infrastructure projects. For 9 out of 10 projects, passenger forecasts are overestimated; the average overestimation is 106%. For half of all road projects, the difference between actual and forecasted traffic is more than ±20%. The result is substantial financial risks, which are typically ignored or downplayed by planners and decision makers to the detriment of social and economic welfare.

Flyvbjerg, Garbuio, and Lovallo (2009) argue that physical infrastructure projects' net benefits (which, of course, need to take into account the negative impacts as costs) are exaggerated not only because of the wishful thinking but also because promoters often practice deception to gain the financing for these projects.

Promotional tactics of obscuring negative consequences may even extend to neglecting intelligence gathering that could reveal the potential harm to various stakeholders. Chapter 4 recounts several instances of resettlement programs undertaken before research on the suitability of the resettlement areas was undertaken. This is another example of promotional tactics operating through the intelligence function.

Particularly aggressive promotional efforts may rely on denouncing a particular stakeholder group that would be harmed by an initiative, in order to reduce the regret for the deprivations that that policy would impose upon that group. Outright property expropriations have long been accompanied by disparagement of the targets of expropriation, whether people of South Asian or Arab extraction in Zanzibar (Killian 2008) or people of European extraction in Venezuela, all denounced as parasitic exploiters.

Prescription Challenges

The challenges to the prescription function to reduce unnecessary harm encompass both the processes of rule-making and the content of the initiatives.

Prescription Processes. Initiatives that result in unnecessary harm are often traceable to the limitations in the participation of relevant stakeholders. In addition to the government's intelligence limitations that arise when particular groups are out of the loop, these groups are more vulnerable insofar as they are excluded from direct input in early involvement in formulating initiatives, in opportunities to react to initiatives before enactment proceeds, and in capacity to appeal damaging treatment.

Multiple reasons can account for why some stakeholders are so limited in their participation. Perhaps the most obvious reason is that they lack the resources to participate: remoteness from points of contact, lack of education, lack of communication capability, or beliefs that pressing demands is inappropriate or dangerous. This is a widespread problem for stakeholders in the informal sector. Keene-Mugerwa (2011, 162) assesses that in Uganda:

workers in the informal sector lack safety net mechanisms in case of job loss, injury, sickness and death. The absence of organized and recognized interest groups, such as unions and business associations, to negotiate with government agencies to solve the problems affecting the sector have further exacerbated the lack of voice of informal sector workers in decision making and implementation processes.

More subtly, exclusion may be due to policymakers' attitudes that these groups do not deserve to be heard. Anyaegbunam, Mefalopulos, and Moetsabi (2004, 48), describing the biases in soliciting input from rural villagers in Ethiopia, Malawi, Namibia, Swaziland, Zambia, and Zimbabwe, note:

the tendency for rural researchers to visit and talk with villagers who have already adopted and are using the new ideas or practices promoted by a development agency. In many communities these groups often ensure that the researchers easily notice them through such distinguishing things as club T-shirts, badges or caps.

Those who have not adopted the offered solutions are not interviewed to find out why they have not done so. Instead the researchers see them as laggards who do not deserve to participate in the study.

Yet, even within communities, some stakeholders may not be deemed worthy of participation. Heffernan and Misturelli (2000, 77), assessing community deliberations on livestock issues in Kenya, conclude that in community meetings "individuals who are believed to be responsible for their own poverty are excluded from the process. Thus, the community may intentionally or unintentionally misrepresent the voices of the poor. At community meetings, it is unlikely that the 'undeserving' poor will be present or that the truly poor will be heard."

More complicated patterns involve the polarization that could push government leaders into punitive or retaliatory motives. An important diagnostic indicator is the degree of policymakers' antagonism toward the stakeholders who stand to lose. Of course, this requires sufficient sophistication to discount any exaggerated rhetoric, whether overly favorable or unfavorable toward these stakeholders.

However, policies with deliberately adverse impacts on particular stakeholders may reflect a less vindictive motive: the concern that a group's power and capacity to oppose the government needs to be reduced by reducing that group's wealth, organizational capability, respect, and so on. For example, according to Wood (2006) and Bradley (2007), the Iranian government has discriminated against the Arab population in the Arab-majority province of Khuzestan. Bradley (2007, 184) reports that:

Local ethnic Arabs complained that, as a result of their divided loyalties during the Iran-Iraq war, they are now viewed more than ever by the clerical regime in Tehran is a potential fifth column and suffer under an official policy of discrimination ... The men said that Farsi is the only language taught in their village school, although all the students are Arab, and that no Arabic-language newspapers are allowed to be published in the province. They said they also suffer much higher levels of unemployment and poverty than Persians. 'The government says we are traitors,' added another man.

In addition, the government has been resettling Persians in Khuzestan in order to undermine the electoral strength of the Arab population (Wood 2006).

Sometimes the processes requiring multiple agencies make it difficult to bring ameliorating policies along with the major thrust of an initiative. Programs to assist populations harmed by new initiatives typically take time to formulate, authorize, and fund. Matli (2005, 42–43), assessing the consequences of the dam that was the centerpiece of the Lesotho Highlands Water Project, reports that:

Ha Sepinare villagers accounted that several houses, and in some cases the property inside, had been damaged or lost from road works vibrations or dam earth tremors. In Ha Theko, a demolished primary school building had not been rebuilt. These damages had repeatedly been reported to LHDA [the Lesotho Highlands Development Authority] and the government in writing three years ago but all in vain. Some similar damages that occurred during the Ha Mohale road and dam construction phases had also not been repaired ... some people have had their houses repaired or rebuilt to their satisfaction despite delays of up to ten years in some cases.

As mentioned above, the informal sector is particularly difficult to protect, because of the government's limited potential to provide safety-net protections through the conventional employment, insurance, and pension provisions. This means that rather than having funds generated from contributions by employees or employers, funding would have to come from the budget, making the support vulnerable to taxpayer resistance. Some efforts have been made to induce self-insurance and savings by informal sector workers, such as Thailand's community-savings-based "one baht a day" program (Petchmark, Boonyabancha, and Hosaka 2011), but these face the limitations of the low incomes of the contributors.

Venue Shifting. As policymakers select the channels through which to direct their initiatives, venue shifting may result in either more extreme initiatives or more limited opportunities to reduce harm (for examples of venue shifting, in Chile and Vietnam, see Chapter 5). When part of the venue shifting involves triggering street protests, in order to pressure the government, the mobilization is likely to require promoting rather extreme demands. Insofar as the willingness of people to take the risks of confronting others with policy demands that require high expected rewards, mobilizing stakeholders in contexts of potential retaliation polarize not only attitudes, but also the demands.

If, in contrast, initiatives are pursued through the more esoteric venues, such as the legal system or regulatory bodies, the deprived stakeholders may lack the resources to seek recourse. Less educated, less organized stakeholders who lack connections with high-expertise NGOs are obviously more vulnerable.

Content of Initiatives. The most straightforward way to reduce the damage to stakeholders is to identify policy modifications that leave most of the expected benefits intact but modify the impacts on negatively impacted stakeholders. Compensation for families displaced by major infrastructure projects ought to be resettled with greater care than has typically been the case. One of the most common efforts to reduce the harm to affected stakeholders is to engage local people as guides or other service providers for areas newly established as conservation reserves. In other realms, shifting the language of instruction to either the national language or to a more widely used language such as English or French can be accompanied by a stronger effort to prepare children with less exposure to this language. Land tenuring that reduces the routes for pastoralists can be accompanied by establishing other routes supported by provision of resources, or buffering their risks; for example, with livestock insurance in Kenya (van Ginkel et al. 2013).

Another approach is to offset the damage to particular stakeholders by linking the initiative to other policy initiatives that otherwise would not be undertaken. Some policies may not cost other stakeholders beyond prioritizing the compensatory initiative. For example, the Lebanese government could make a concerted effort to reform the obsolete regulations governing micro- and small-scale enterprises (Hamdan 2005).

Another way to reduce the harm to particular stakeholders is to provide "side payments," defined as transfers of part of the benefit that would have gone to policy beneficiaries, to those who otherwise would not benefit from the policy or would suffer harm from it. Often it is possible to reduce the harm through side payments that leave everyone better off, but this reduces the benefits to the favored stakeholders. It is understandable that policymakers intent on maintaining or increasing the support of stakeholders favored by the initiative may not be willing to yield that much to potential losers. Therefore, although in principle, side payments could leave every one better off, the lack of motivation to reduce the benefits of favored stakeholders is common, in addition to the practical challenges of accomplishing side payments.

In order to account for unanticipated harm, initiatives may incorporate provisions for compensating for the damage. To insulate these provisions from the risk that the budget commitments will not be met, in some instances it would make sense for special funds to be established. This is, in a sense, equivalent to a bond posted by a private firm to cover damages incurred on others. Sometimes a special quasi-governmental authority is established to oversee the construction and operation of major infrastructure projects; this provides the opportunity for a concerted effort to identify and redress such harm. These authorities have been fairly common for major water projects: India's pioneering Damodar Valley Corporation, Brazil's São Francisco River Valley Authority (restructured as the São Francisco River Valley Development Company), Jordan's Jordan Valley Authority, and so on.

The perennial challenge is to secure sufficient commitment to provide redress if it proves to be necessary. In the cases of lost resources for which the immediate compensation may not be able to take into account future problems, it may be possible to provide continuous income streams for people for whom initial compensation (akin to a severance payment) proves to be insufficient. An early example is the rent scheme created for families displaced by the construction of three dams in Japan. The power company Hokuriku Denryoku agreed in the early 1950s to pay rent indefinitely to farmers in Jintsu-gawa whose land was submerged by three small dams (Nakayama and Furuyashiki 2009, 434–437). Cernea (2007, 1038) has elaborated a broad set of benefit-sharing mechanisms for people forcibly resettled for income-generating infrastructure projects, as well as the communities that in the posting the resettled populations:

(i) Direct transfers of a share of the revenue streams, to finance specific post-relocation development schemes; (ii) Establishment of revolving development funds through fixed allocations; while the principal of those funds is being saved and preserved, the interest generated from saving the principal is used for post-resettlement development; (iii) Equity sharing in the new, project-created enterprises (and other productive potentials) through various forms of co-ownership; (iv) Special taxes paid to regional and local governments, additional to the general tax system, to supplement local development programmes with added initiatives; (v) Allocations of electrical power, on a regular and legally mandated basis; (vi) Granting of preferential electricity cost rates-or, for example, lower water fees, or other forms of access to in-kind benefits.

Similarly, a superior strategy to severance pay for dismissed formal-sector workers is to provide pensions for "early retirement" in order to provide a continual stream of "compensation." Auer and Popova (2003, 34), in their survey of Turkish labor policies, conclude that "early retirement is in fact the instrument giving the best protection to workers and contributes most to the acceptance of restructuring. Therefore, Turkish policies are quite well in line with those that have been enacted by the European countries that faced restructuring and privatization."

Regardless of the provisions for mitigating excessive harm, the policy-content challenge is to protect these provisions from eroding over time. If they address economic deprivations, they may be vulnerable to the ravages of inflation, budget cutbacks, or second-order harm (e.g., the collapse of fish stocks for fishing-dependent populations relocated below a dam). The power-sharing arrangements that may have been worked out as part of a decentralization initiative may erode as the majority group within the subnational jurisdiction consolidates its power. The promises that minority-language children will receive special attention so that they can prosper when a different language replaces their own may evaporate in the face of budget cutbacks.

Invocation and Application Problems

The ways that initiatives are enacted can worsen or alleviate the risk of excessive harm, depending on the capacities and motivations of the implementers. Within the bounds of how explicit the initiatives are, and the policymakers' capacity to enforce them, implementers can be lenient or harsh in interpreting policies, deciding in which cases they should be applied, and calibrating the rewards or punishments. As mentioned in Chapter 6, the vagueness of policies creates the flexibility for implement-ers to apply regulations harshly when they are so moved. For instance, contrary to conventional understandings outside of the Islamic world, the meaning of the term *hejab* (or *hijab*) is not "headscarf," but rather proper appearance of Muslim women. Regulations, such as those in Iran, requir-ing that women dress in conformity to *hejab*, raised the possibility of harsh invocation and application. Nandi (2015, 9) reports on both the ambiguity as to when violations of hejab dress will be invoked, as well as the range of punishments that could be applied:

Hejab is a generic term for proper Islamic dress and improper hejab is often interpreted to include hair not fully covered by hejab, tight-fitting clothes, and even the use of makeup. Article 638 of the Islamic Penal Code prescribes that women who appear in public without proper hejab can be sentenced from 10 days to 2 months or fined between 50,000 to 500,000 riyals. It also accommodates the judges to sentence the accused to 74 lashes.[1]

Government leaders' exaggerated disparagement targeted against par-ticular groups may be taken by implementers as a valid basis for harsh treatment in enacting the initiative, or as a convenient defense for harsh treatment arising from other motivations. The threat of harsh implementation in fact may be convenient for demanding bribes. In their investigation of detention centers for drug users in Cambodia, China, Laos, and Vietnam, Amon et al. (2013) have documented the practices of

---

[1] The maximum fine is equivalent to US$16.00; the harassment, and obviously the lashes, are likely to be harsher. The references embedded in the quotation have been deleted to ease reading.

demanding bribes to avoid incarceration in these extremely punitive centers, and the forced labor in Cambodian, Chinese, and Vietnamese centers, that in some instances was devoted to constructing homes for the center's staff.

Forestry officials, as illustrated by the case of Rajastani forest reserves cited in Chapter 6, may be acting out of a mix of motives ranging from lack of resources to opportunities for corruption. Typically, the more stringent the regulation, the greater the pressure on stakeholders dependent on the restricted behavior to resort to bribes. This problem may well be worse in cases where ethnicity-based rivalries are present. Pierce-Colfer et al. (2007,12) recount the Ugandan experience with the Benet (a small ethnic group numbering fewer than 10,000 people) ejected from ancestral lands for the sake of expanding the national park, revealing both the harsher treatment due to the shift of enforcement agency to the more narrowly-mandated wildlife conservation agency, and corruption reflecting ethnic discrimination:

In 1993, the Government of Uganda again changed the designation of the protected area to Mt. Elgon National Park, shifting management from the Forest Department to the Uganda Wildlife Authority, or UWA. This led to tighter restrictions on protected area access by local people, and relations between the Benet and the government deteriorated quickly as a result of harsh enforcement of exclusion policies. Livestock grazing and cultivation of Irish potatoes in the moorlands were prohibited and any remaining Benet homes inside the protected area were burned. In addition to livelihood consequences, exclusion policies were seen by the Benet to have negative consequences to conservation through increased corruption among park rangers, who encouraged bribes from local elites (mostly non-Benet) for access to forest resources.

In some cases, the mitigating provisions embedded in the initiatives as formulated by higher-level policymakers are ignored by the implementers. For policy initiatives that institute or increase fees for government-provided services but provide exemptions to buffer the poorest families, implementers may balk by taking advantage of the bureaucratic discretion outlined in Chapter 6. Kivumbi and Kintu (2002) document that in Uganda, where all-too-meager decentralized healthcare budgets depend on healthcare fees, some local officials have defied the central government's requirement of fee waivers for the poorest families.

Termination Challenges

Of the long list of policies that risk causing excessive harm, four broad scenarios entail the termination of benefits:

- elimination or reduction of expensive subsidies, as a central facet of liberalization;
- reform of regulations that protect or privilege particular stakeholders;
- cutbacks or elimination of projects and programs due to budget short-falls or changed priorities; and
- shedding of government personnel or state enterprises.

When termination arouses strong mobilization, the relations between the adversely affected stakeholders in the government may become so polarized that government leaders may conclude that mitigating the impacts would be politically futile. In short, a vicious cycle frequently arises through which kind benefits or opportunities provokes high levels of hostility, which then lead to punitive actions on the part of the government.

A general point is the typically low adaptability to termination by the populations with the weakest assets, when these changes entail the withdrawal of opportunities for which they devoted scarce resources. This pattern is frequently reinforced by the fact that when government leaders feel compelled to cut back on spending, they are typically less likely to target the programs or projects that benefit the politically powerful.

Cutting Subsidies. The most distressing complication of cutting wasteful and distorting subsidies lies in the fact that the poorest beneficiaries, who can least afford increases in non-discretionary costs, typically find reduction in subsidies for the purchase of fuels, water, transportation, healthcare, or food to be more painful than for other beneficiaries, even though these other beneficiaries may gain more by maintaining the subsidies. For instance, eliminating fuel subsidies would benefit a country in general, because of increased government spending opportunities, foreign-exchange savings through reduced fuel imports, and reduced pollution. Yet, the impact on the very poor can be substantial, even if much greater quantities of fuels are consumed by wealthier people. The most efficient means of addressing the higher energy costs for low income people is with cash transfers, but if that is not politically or administratively feasible, exempting a fuel used predominantly by the poor, usually kerosene, could mitigate the impact. Although maintaining kerosene subsidies in countries where the poor rely heavily on that fuel is not as efficient as the cash-transfer option, eliminating kerosene subsidies often has a regressive impact in terms of income distribution (Del Granado et al. 2012). Similarly, in Egypt and the Philippines, bread and rice, respectively, have been subsidized heavily at various times, with considerable "leakage" of the benefits to the non-poor. In Egypt, the potential impact on the poor in such a politically explosive context has blocked the reform (James 2015, 10), but in the Philippines cutting the rice subsidy at times has been successful, with the poor buffered by having government outlets selling a corn-rice mixture, which limits the leakage in so far as the mixture is an "inferior good" (i.e., a good that is less demanded as purchasers' incomes rise).

In addition, the reduction of subsidies can be accomplished with less harm to the poor by "block" or "tiered" pricing that charges at lower rates for more modest consumption (for example, for electricity or water), or employs different rates in different locations. Colombia has long had such a block pricing scheme for electricity (Maddock, Castaño, and Vella 1992); Tunisia for residential water (Zekri and Dinar 2003); and many others. The Dominican Republic established a program of lower electricity rates for poorer areas in 2001 (Regalia and Robles 2005).

Reform of Regulations. People protected by regulations that exclude potential competitors are vulnerable to regulatory changes that open up opportunities for others, often with lower compensation. For instance, in many developing countries, the regulations that qualify individuals to serve as teachers have been dramatically relaxed to hire "contract teachers"[2] who are less qualified, less organized, and typically far less paid than regular teachers. This has undermined the status, security, and compensation of regular-rank teachers in many countries. For instance, for Benin, Fyfe (2007, 13) concludes:

Analysis of teacher identity and status in Benin demonstrated how the policy of salary freezes and increased recruitment of lesser-paid contract teachers had led to a more embittered teaching force. The use of contract teachers was seen as undermining one of the basic elements of teacher identity in Benin: that of being a respected civil servant with a decent steady salary, job security and high social status. Teachers felt betrayed by the State and as a consequence engaged in a host of negative behaviours such as absenteeism and moonlighting.

More generally, several types of employees are vulnerable to dismissal due to liberalization reforms, even if they benefit the country as a whole.

---

[2] Fyfe (2007, vii) defines "contract teachers" as follows: "Many different types of teachers fall under the label of 'contract teachers,' including volunteers, community teachers and para-teachers. However, everywhere, the salaries and conditions of contract teachers are far inferior to those of regular civil service teachers. Contract teachers are typically hired for one year at a salary of one-half to one-quarter of that of a regular teacher and few belong to a trade union."

Private sector employers in many countries gain greater flexibility to dismiss workers; Kus (2014, 283) notes that labor liberalization in Turkey meant that "[m]any legal obstacles to firing workers were removed, and limitations were imposed on severance payment amounts, annual vacations, and the financial liability of employers." Trade-regulation reform has had very broad, sector-wide impacts. Reducing import tariffs and non-tariff barriers, though opening up opportunities to expand the workforce in export-oriented industries, increases the vulnerability of workers in previously protected industries.

Program or Project Cutbacks. It is easy to overlook the fact that policies, programs, and projects that promised benefits to particular stakeholders very often require the stakeholders to undertake investments and risks that make them vulnerable to terminations, cutbacks, or simply inadequate support despite explicit or implicit government promises. People who migrate in the hopes of taking advantage of new opportunities may be stranded in their new locations, without the support needed for viable livelihoods. Borras and Franco (2010, 20–21) elaborate on the plight of Brazilian migrants to the Amazon, stimulated by government programs:

> João Pedro Stedile ... leader of the Movement of the Landless Workers or MST, explains that in recent years under the Lula administration the government settled 380,000 families, but 64 per cent of these families were sent to the Amazon, which avoided any expropriation of private land owners. "The families are now completely out of the class struggle ... Our people are stranded in the Amazon, lost in a hostile environment. Not even a small market for their produce is available there."

Shedding Employees. As noted above, dismissing government staff of terminated or reduced programs and projects, privatization, vulnerability of less protected industries, more relaxed regulations on private-sector dismissals, and general bureaucratic streamlining all contribute to the risks of unemployment. This is not confined to the formal sector; governments frequently support programs for low income individuals in the informal sector, ranging from forest guides and conservation areas to people repairing rural roads. Losing these jobs may mean less of an absolute reduction in income, but even a small reduction carries more weight for the very poor.

For any of these scenarios, the terminations can be less damaging if policy makers are careful to clarify the likelihood that a policy, program, or project may be terminated, either through an explicit "sunset" provision (i.e., an explicit end date, though possibly subject to renewal), or by clarifying the conditions under which cutbacks would be likely. The logic is that stakeholders will be mindful of the likelihood of termination, and therefore will not over-invest in the opportunities offered by the initiative.

When policymakers do choose to terminate the program, it is likely to be less harmful if there is a lag between the announcement and the ending of the program, or if the program is phased out gradually. For employees of a terminated government program, severance pay or pensions will obviously reduce the deprivation. However, these must be calibrated, keeping in mind that the resources required for this transition may deter appropriate reductions in government employment and draw resources away from more compelling government spending.

Appraisal Challenges

The inevitable uncertainty that limits the intelligence function in anticipating potentially excessive harm to some stakeholders puts a crucial burden on the appraisal function. Insofar as unanticipated harm can be identified, attributed to particular policy measures, and brought to the attention of policymakers, it is possible to mitigate the damage. In addition, accurate appraisal is important for triggering whatever compensation has been built into the policies prior to enactment.

The standard problems of appraisal are present for evaluating unanticipated harm: poor information, whether or not reflecting deliberate manipulation; the difficulties of separating out the impact of the initiative from other policies and external trends; basic disagreements on aspects deserving to be taken into account; and conveying this information to the relevant planners and policymakers.

However, two challenges stand out regarding excessive harm. First, when people are set adrift from their positions, home areas, or sociopolitical status, their circumstances may be much more difficult to track. The transitions from formal-sector to informal-sector work, from residing in villages submerged by reservoirs to being swallowed up in large cities, or from regular interaction with the national government as prominent individuals to political non-entities vis-a-vis the newly-dominant subnational government, restrict the information available to gauge the degree of harm that they may be experiencing. An International Regional Information Network (2011) report on the plight of people displaced by the Kenyan violence, triggered, in large part, by the land distribution policies of the Kikuyu-dominated government, asserts:

Thousands of Kenyans displaced to Nyanza province during post-election violence in 2008 have yet to receive full payouts under a government compensation scheme, say officials ... According to the government's Ministry of Special Programmes, there are almost 25,000 households of internally displaced persons (IDPs) in Nyanza province ... A total of 78,254 houses were destroyed countrywide while 350,000 IDPs sought refuge in 118 camps and 313,192 others were "integrated" among various communities, according to the Ministry of Special Programmes ... William ole Naremo, the district commissioner for Rachuonyo North ... told IRIN [International Regional Information Network] the challenge administrators faced in the province was getting accurate numbers of IDPs who returned in 2008 and those who were displaced earlier in the 1990s. 'Only a few of the IDPs have formed groups and listed the genuine cases, the problem is that the majority of the IDPs are in urban areas living with relatives or have rented houses on their own and since they are often on the move, establishing their exact numbers has been difficult,' Naremo said.

If compensatory measures could provide modest incentives for affected people to report on their status, government policymakers could at least partially overcome this limitation. For instance, periodic small payments for people who renew their registration at regular intervals would keep the government informed.

Second, policymakers and planners may, consciously or not, turn a blind eye on negative information about the circumstances of people adversely affected by policies, programs, or projects. The previous point, namely that the government's contact with many of the adversely-impacted stakeholders becomes tenuous, makes it easier to interpret the inevitably incomplete information about negatively impacted stakeholders as idiosyncratic and therefore not decisive.

ANTICIPATING LIKELY HARM

Policymakers, and the planners who support them, must be able to diagnose the pitfalls posed by the patterns explored in this chapter. Other development practitioners, in order to decide whether to endorse or oppose an initiative, must assess whether the motives and actions of the policymakers themselves may produce excessive harm. Thus, all concerned need to be sensitive to the diagnostics that would indicate the problems reflected by each decision function. This concluding section, therefore, summarizes how the insights about malfunctions can generate useful diagnostic indicators.

The obvious intelligence malfunction indicator is the thinness of information about potential impacts. An especially telling indicator, as mentioned earlier in the chapter, is any sign of willing ignorance about potential harm. Another intelligence function indicator is a gap between the government's projections of impacts and the projections by analysts outside of government, as long as the true expectations can be separated from the rhetoric.

However, as a promotional tactic, extreme government rhetoric itself is a relevant indicator of the willingness to impose hardship – as well as the willingness of implementers to do the same. Other promotion malfunctions may be indicated by the degree of mobilization in favor of the initiative, which can reinforce the expectation that the initiative is to be implemented stringently, without the leniency that might otherwise be granted to hardship cases, and by the polarization that could provoke government leaders to opt for harsh enactment to undermine the capacity of opponents to challenge the government.

The degree to which potentially impacted stakeholders are excluded from participation in the prescription function is often an indicator of the risk that the formulation and approval of initiatives could lead to excessive harm. The exclusion per se indicates either low concern by policymakers, or polarization that reduces the likelihood that the policymakers would be motivated to accommodate these groups. In addition, as outlined earlier in the chapter, this goes beyond simply trying to gather information from or about the stakeholders; the degree to which relevant stakeholders are unwilling to share information and express their preferences is a potent indicator of their feelings of vulnerability.

The problems of invocation and application can be better identified by paying attention to the inconsistency of enactment, as examined in Chapter 6. This can be reinforced by gauging the degree of inter-ethnic amity or animosity between implementers and the stakeholders affected by the enactment. Estimates of the incidence of corruption also may be regarded as a possible sign of harsh regulations or their implementation to compel bribes to avoid enforcement.

One indicator of potential problems with termination as a design challenge is the paucity of analysis or contingencies for mitigating, delaying, or compensating in case of unanticipated harm. Another indicator is whether policymakers have the capacity to mitigate or compensate (recall that the contingencies may not be able to reach some of the vulnerable stakeholders). For existing initiatives, indicators of the likelihood that excessive harm from the termination will go unrecognized or unattended include the weakness of feedback and the degree of ethnic-based animosity.

Just as the scarcity of information in formulating an initiative suffers is an indicator of policymakers' indifference or even desire to deprive particular stakeholders, the neglect of easily obtainable information about harm of an existing initiative is an indicator of an appraisal malfunction. As mentioned previously, some of this information may not be easily obtainable, but when it is, it is worth asking whether government leaders do not want to make it known.

SUMMARY

A very wide range of policies can wreak excessive harm unless the initiatives are carefully designed, with challenges posed in every decision function. The risk of gratuitous damage to particular groups begins with inadequate intelligence about the likelihood of harm, which can be traced to a range of factors, including poor information on the informal sector; uncertainties of the impacts of complex policies such as tax changes and changes in language policy, especially in the long term; and poor communication with stakeholders. The promotion function may be abused by deliberately downplaying likely damage, sometimes through willful disregard of information. Alternatively, government leaders may promote excessive harm by denouncing the target groups to arouse hostility in order to build support for punitive policies. Reducing unnecessary harm may be hampered by prescription processes marked by inadequate stakeholder participation. This inadequate participation may be due to intergroup polarization that results from sociopolitical discrimination or particularly provocative or exclusionary venues. It may also be due to lack of coordination among government agencies that could otherwise minimize damage. Yet the content of prescriptions can reduce gratuitous harm through issue linkage, or side payments,

The invocation and application functions are hampered in reducing avoidable deprivation by problems on both ends of the continuum from vagueness, which may permit the implementers to discriminate punitively, to rigidity, which limits accommodation to relieve excessive harm. The termination of policies, whether through reform, austerity, or government personnel reduction, entails the termination of benefits that frequently lack redress. Finally, inappropriate terminations may be provoked by premature appraisals prompted by uncertainty of future benefits or political maneuvering.

TABLE 7.1 *Core Problems, Causes, and Potential Indicators of Excessive Deprivation*

Root problem	Causes	Potential indicators
Inadvertent harm	Weak intelligence	Thinness of information about impacts
	Exclusion of stakeholders in the prescription function	Discrepancy between government and external analysis of impacts
	Administrators' social isolation	Ethnic differences between administrators and local stakeholders; narrowness of contact with local stakeholders
	Unwillingness of stakeholders to express preferences	Sparse communication of stakeholder preferences; degree of failure to transmit stakeholder input to higher policymaking levels
Lack of capacity to mitigate or compensate through side payments/ issue linkage	Lack of side-payment mechanisms	Narrow scope of policy provisions of potentially multi-issue initiatives
	Non-integrated policy venues	Isolation of policymaking on linkable issues
Policymakers' antagonism toward deprived stakeholders	Polarization between government leaders and stakeholders	Hostile government rhetoric against stakeholder groups
	Stakeholders' antagonism toward government as unfair	Stakeholder accusations of government favoritism toward other groups

8

Reducing Avoidable Conflict

The avoidance of initiatives that pose a substantial risk of triggering destructive conflict is an obvious development objective – perhaps best labeled "conflict-sensitive development" – that has generated enormous attention from governments, aid organizations, NGOs, and researchers.[1] The connections with previous chapters are also clear: the need to avoid endorsing an initiative that is ill-fated because it would trigger violence; the polarization that is often behind policy impasses also is frequently associated with destructive conflict; and avoidable harm is likely to provoke resentment that also could provoke violence.

However, important differences should be noted. Chapters 3 through 7 focus on the consequences or likely consequences of the initiative's provisions; this chapter is as much about the reactions to the mere fact that the initiative has been launched. Chapters 3 and 7 basically focus on the direct consequences that initiatives could or do produce; this chapter also alerts the development practitioner to long-term, indirect consequences. These include changes in:

- the relative economic, social, or political standing of different groups;
- the economic roles played by group members;
- elevated perceptions of threat;
- the evolution of group stereotypes;
- perceptions of exploitation or dominance;

---

[1] For relevant writings, see Ascher and Mirovitskaya 2015; Bercovitch, Kremenyuk, and Zartmant 2009; Broussard 2013; Brown, Stewart, and Langer 2007; Lund 2009; Muscat 2002; Norden 2012; Stewart 2005.

- beliefs that government favors another group, or that the group manipulates or even controls the government; and, ultimately,
- inter-group animosity.

Just as the decision-process framework assists in suggesting possible empirical patterns (e.g., malfunctions of any of the decision functions) even if the framework per se has no empirical content of its own, the distinctive contribution of this chapter is the use of a more specific framework to generate context-sensitive empirical propositions. Thus, it is useful to outline four clusters of conditioning factors to link policy initiatives to the levels of destructive conflict:

- predispositions to engage in aggressive behavior
- opportunities to engage in such behavior
- incitement of others to engage in such behaviors
- deterrence efforts or circumstances to prevent or reduce violence

The connections are straightforward. Initiatives, whether existing, newly launched, or just announced, can intensify or dampen the *predispositions* to violent confrontation. These may have been heightened by the *opportunities* for confrontations: groups coming into proximity with one another, insults or accidents that escalate into violent confrontations, government or group actions that may prompt preemptive violence or openings to gain from violence, communication channels that permit provocateurs to be more effective, and so on. The provocateurs' actions, or spontaneous outbreaks, constitute *incitement*. Yet predispositions, opportunities, and incitement may be blunted by *deterrence* actions that reduce the impetus for violent confrontations or deters it by posing costly consequences.

Predispositions. The fear, animosity, punitiveness, or opportunism that predisposes individuals to violent confrontations can have many causes, some unconnected to government policies. The willingness to attack others, or to engage in aggressive confrontations that may lead to violence, arises from the desire to gain, to defend, or to punish. What circumstances generated by a policy initiative would predispose people to take advantage of the initiative through hostile confrontation or direct attacks?

The possible causes are arrayed all across the temporal dimension. Immediate reactions to the announcement of initiatives can instill fear of damage that may compel a potentially violent confrontation to try to block enactment. The announcement may also lead people to conclude that the government is planning further actions, whether simply to extract resources from that group, or to marginalize it in order to reduce its influence.

A crucial though often overlooked pattern creating predispositions toward violence connects perceptions of government policies to the attitudes toward groups believed to be in league with the government. Intergroup hostility is likely to be elevated if members of a group believe that they are, or will be, harmed by policies that another group has influenced the government to adopt.

Opportunities. Opportunities also contribute to the likelihood of violence by placing people in proximity such that conflicts over rights, concerns over exploitation, exposure to disdained beliefs and practices, or person-on-person offenses could unleash violent confrontations. Policies, programs, and policies also create opportunities for gains that some stakeholders believe could be increased through combative acts.

Incitement. Many development initiatives are involved with acts of provocation, or of aggressive confrontations that lead to violence even if it is not intended by those provoking confrontations. Development initiatives can reduce or increase the incentives for incitement, quite directly due to opposition to the initiative, or indirectly by the longer-term effects of the resources held by various stakeholders, animosities toward other groups or the government, or by creating incentives and resources for provocateurs. Contextual factors can be captured by *opportunities* dynamics, that range from the proximity of groups to their resources to attack one another.

Deterrence. Some dynamics encompass the factors that could dissuade stakeholders from engaging in confrontations or outright deliberate attacks. Potentially violent confrontations sometimes can be averted through the initiative per se, but also through norms, institutions, and actions preexisting the initiative. Some policies, programs, and projects include preemptive provisions that reduce the incentives or compulsion to engage in potentially violent confrontations. These simply may be credible punishments for using violence to take advantage of the main thrust of the initiative. Initiatives can also include positive incentives to keep peaceful relations with others in order to prosper economically or otherwise. The deterrence actions distinct from an initiative's provisions may include general strengthening of the state's capacity to intervene early in confrontations. The actions may also involve creating the general conditions for people to believe that peaceful interactions are in their interest, so as not to risk the benefits by initiating aggressive behavior or retaliating to perceived provocations. In some contexts, it is also possible to strengthen norms against engaging in violence, by demonstrating the overall negative consequences.

INTELLIGENCE

Here it is necessary only to bring up aspects of the intelligence function that are specific to the challenge of minimizing destructive conflict; obviously, many of the intelligence issues involved with ill-fated initiatives, impasses, and excessive harm are relevant to avoiding destructive conflict. For example, Chapter 3 raises the possibility that stakeholders may exaggerate the harm that current or future policies may impose upon them. Similarly, Chapter 5 covers the importance of identifying the likely sources of impasses that can lead stakeholders to resort to hostile confrontations, toward the government, other groups, or both. Therefore, it is useful to begin by identifying what *additional* information one would need, ranging from the perceptions of stakeholders who may be prone to violent confrontations, to the identifications that stakeholders hold in understanding competition and cooperation.

First, it is important to know how stakeholders define "ingroups" and "outgroups," on the premise that much of the predisposition to conflict rests on the impulse to defend other members of the "ingroup" and, in some contexts, to punish members of the "outgroup." The very thorny complication is that the definition of groups is a "social construct" – a subjective rather than objective matter that can change over time and from one policy arena to another. President Fernando Henrique Cardoso's 2001 launch of the affirmative action policy for Afro-Brazilians raised the salience of race. In Venezuela, President Hugo Chavez's rhetoric attributing the poverty of Venezuelans of Indian and African ancestry to the "European" elite reinforced ethnic polarization (Norden 2012).

An important aspect of perceptions of other groups is how strongly each group is perceived to be uniform in characteristics. As noted in Chapter 5, the "unit relation" (Heider 1958) represents the tendency to regard somewhat similar people as even more similar than they really are. Here it is important to understand that the degree of this stereotyping may be crucial in predicting whether aggressive actions will be targeted broadly toward people perceived as members of a specific outgroup, somehow holding them all responsible for offenses, or all responsible for threatening behavior. This is clearly relevant for anticipating the likelihood that members of one group would be predisposed to punish members of another group indiscriminately.

Second, antagonism of one group toward another frequently hinges on whether the other group is seen as in league with government leaders, whether controlling them or simply being favored by them. It is striking, in light of the fact that most stakeholders in most countries are only dimly aware of the inner workings of policymaking, and have limited knowledge of the distribution of benefits and burdens of policies, that beliefs about control and favoritism are often strongly held despite this lack of information. In Kenya, it is "common knowledge" that successive governments have been "dominated" by one ethnic group or another. For example, Hodler and Knight (2011, 67) asserted in 2011 that: "In Kenya ... there has long been fierce political competition along ethnic lines, and numerous members of the Kalenjin-dominated government around Daniel arap Moi, who was president from 1978 to 2002, and the Kikuyu-dominated government around Mwai Kibaki, who has been president ever since ... [i.e., 2002–2011]." However, the ETH Zürich (2016) analysis of Kenyan ethnic groups and political dominance concludes of the period of coalition government – hardly a Kikuyu-dominated government:

This period starts in February 2008, when the parties reached an agreement (brokered by former U.N. Secretary Kofi Annan) on a PNU-ODM coalition government with Kibaki as president, Odinga as prime minister, and an equally shared cabinet reflecting Kenya's ethnic diversity ... In the words of Chege "the political tools used to ... end the conflict ... include a 'grand coalition government' of all major parties and leaders; 'powersharing' between ethnic-based factions; and allocation of executive positions so that all major groups are fairly represented" ... According to BBC ... the cabinet is fifty percent Kibaki appointed ministers and ... fifty percent Odinga appointed ministers, which reflects a carefully balanced ethnic coalition ... The grand coalition continued its existence until elections in 2013.

The question is not which perceptions are more accurate, but rather how important they are believed to be in accounting for the degree of favoritism of government policies toward various groups. The presumptions of different stakeholder groups as to winners and losers, even if based on distorted information, are typically more important in accounting for levels of conflict. Therefore, an intelligence malfunction exists when analysts neglect the potential impacts on *beliefs* about government favoritism.

The beliefs that a particular group dominates the government go beyond the fairly obvious presumption that in countries with hyper-mobilized ethnic divisions – like Kenya – a government elected by an ethnically-defined party is likely to favor the interests of that ethnic group. A much broader pattern is the rise of beliefs that governments are dominated by economic groups, which in turn are believed to be comprised of particular ethnicities. In Botswana, Darkoh and Mbaiwa (2002, 156) asserted that "The cattleowning and political elite dominates the government and administration"; the cattle owners are predominantly of the Tswana ethnic group.

On a more micro level, James (2000, 11), assessing a land tenure conflict in the South African province of Mpumalanga, notes the relevance of the perception that the provincial government is beholden to ethnic groups, even if the precise nature of the dominant group is ambiguous:

As a background to this fierce contestation, in which the importance of ethnic separateness is inextricably interwoven with notions of entitlement on the basis of descent from particular ancestors, regionally-patterned ethnic power bases are emerging. Some locals perceive the Mpumalanga provincial government as dominated by ethnic interests opposed to those of the Pedi – whether these be the culturally and linguistically proximate "Mapulana" as one opinion has it, "the Swazi" as it is represented in another view, or more broadly "the Nguni" which incorporates the Swazis but primarily highlights Ndebele language, culture and economic power.

This case exemplifies how difficult it is to identify how the outgroup is defined. Ethnically-related people are members of broader ethnic designations, and perhaps are seen as belonging to even broader ethnicities. Knowing who is regarded as the "other" in policy struggles is by no means simple, and cannot be assessed fully by the technical analysis of winners and losers likely from a particular policy option.

The opportunities for deterrence bring up the question of whether the intelligence function employed by government planners and policymakers can integrate the considerations behind the initiative with the considerations of preempting conflict that might otherwise result from the initiative. Often the planners and policymakers involved in such initiatives as altering natural-resource rights, promoting resettlement, changing educational guidelines, or raising commodity prices are operating in isolation from the government agencies entrusted with maintaining peace. This is less a case of inter-agency rivalries as it is a more straightforward case of siloed decision processes. Thus, the planners and policymakers formulating the initiative may be unaware of the potential of other agencies to deter violent confrontations, and these other agencies may be unprepared for the need to do so if the initiative goes forward.

PROMOTION

In addition to the promotional tactics presented in Chapter 5 that increase polarization, the approaches that are particularly inimical to maintaining peaceful relations begin with government efforts to make an initiative more attractive overall by denying or minimizing the harm to particular stakeholders. The cynicism that emerges when harm does occur can fuel the resentment against the government and any groups that the harmed groups believe are in league with the government.

Development practitioners associated with foreign assistance need to pay special attention to the disparagement, not only to consider whether sanctions to deter unfair and provocative behavior are appropriate, but also to adjust expectations as to the likelihood that the initiatives they are asked to fund will be problematic because of the disruption that hostile rhetoric might provoke.

The analytic challenge for the outsider is to gauge what aspects of government rhetoric will contribute the negative stereotypes, in light of the fact that the impact of rhetoric on attitudes may be subtly associated with specific cultural understandings. Clearly negative disparagement may or may not add to negative stereotypes, depending on how strong they had been before and how the rhetoric is interpreted. Even seemingly positive characterizations, such as "clever" (perhaps interpretable as capable of taking advantage to exploit others), "loyal to their families" (perhaps interpretable as clannish or even disloyal to the rest of the nation), and so on.

However, promotional tactics can contribute to peace. Emphasizing the policies, programs, and projects that genuinely provide benefits in a balanced way is worthwhile, as long as it is credible in the context of policies in general and the associated perceptions. In addition, highlighting genuine information that the negative stereotypes are inaccurate can reduce animosities, such as those that associate the role of Chinese merchants in much of Southeast Asia with greed and exploitation. Most overseas Chinese in Southeast Asia are not merchants; not all Southeast Asian merchants are Chinese.

Similarly, government leaders and others can promote the advantages of maintaining cooperative relations among groups, economic sectors, and ethno-cultural entities such as religious institutions and private language schools. Varshney (2003) emphasizes the importance of joint Hindu-Muslim civic associations in Indian cities as a way to reduce communal violence; these associations involve Hindu and Muslim businesspeople with much to lose if communal riots break out.

PRESCRIPTION

While initiatives that risk direct harm (see Chapter 7) obviously have the potential to trigger violence, the overlap of considerations and diagnostics between excessive harm and the risk of violence is by no means complete. For the potential for violence, perceptions arising from initiatives play an enormous role, whether or not excessive harm would occur. In addition, as mentioned earlier in this chapter, long-term effects that stakeholders may not even recognize can have consequences that set groups against one another. Important effects include:

- Greater relative resources for a group that might be more willing to attack another group – or these greater resources may be assumed by others as presaging an attack, which may provoke a preemptive attack by others.
- Loss of benefits and resources of one or more groups due to decentralization, either because the decentralization involves the transfer of fewer budgetary resources, or because subnational authorities deny resources to those groups. The weakness of fiscal decentralization ranges from Latin American infrastructure (Bardhan, 2002; Cheikrouhou et al. 2007, 62) and natural-resource management (Andersson, Gibson, and Lehoucq 2004) to urban services in Sub-Saharan Africa and Asia (Ebel and Vaillancourt 2001; Basdeo and Sibanda 2013)
- Weaker social services that result from secondary consequences of initiatives (e.g., reductions of subsidies) that may push people into the arms of radical, criminal, or otherwise potentially violent groups. For example, neighborhoods in countries ranging from Brazil and Colombia to Nigeria and South Africa are effectively controlled by gangs that depend not only on coercion, but also on the services that they provide. Shaw (2004,7) notes of the gangs in Colombia: "The gang provides services, but does so without cutting the organic tie to the community, which means services come without the stigmas of charity or 'assistance' that are associated with benefits from the State or the Church." Flanigan and O'Brien (2015, 622) note that "[a]rmed non-state actors, such as Hezbollah and Hamas, are visibly engaged in providing social welfare in addition to participating in violence."
- Potentially conflictual populations placed into proximity due to resettlement programs, leading to struggles over property rights, political power, social status, language dominance, and so on. These resettlement episodes are especially violence prone when the policies

or programs skimp on the resources needed to accommodate greater population density and the more complicated governance challenges of a more diverse population.

- Property rights struggles that emerge as secondary consequences of policies that have much more limited direct impacts on property rights. Chile's brutal military dictatorship from 1973 through 1990 was, in part, precipitated by the acute polarization that arose when President Eduardo Frei pushed through a constitutional amendment designed to expedite land reform by permitting the expropriation of property in general even if compensation had to be delayed (Kaufman 1972; Loveman 1976).

Yet, as mentioned earlier, initiatives can have salutary deterrence effects. These fall into three categories. Those intended to reduce the overall levels of hostility can be effective insofar as they raise the threshold at which provocations will result in violence. Other provisions within a specific initiative may be designed to reduce its particular conflict-risking impact. Yet other provisions are designed to strengthen the presence and capability of the government to preempt potentially violent confrontations or outright attacks.

Within the category of measures intended to reduce overall levels of hostility, a common thrust is the broad set of "community development" initiatives. It is thought that by supporting cooperative activities and promoting common identification would reduce the potential for conflict among groups. While "community development" can be inclusive enough to strengthen common identification, the ambiguity of the concept of "community" and its geographic scope frequently raises difficult issues. The "community" may be defined as all residents within a geographic area, but often it is defined as the set of people with common characteristics, typically defined along ethnic or religious lines. Even if the initiative is intended to serve all, its control by whoever has authority within the area may tilt toward benefiting those with whom these authorities have the closest identifications. In short, the intention to build "community" through additional funding may result in exacerbating conflicts within the broader community. Development practitioners, particularly outsiders, need to track indicators of benefit distribution, while also monitoring whether identifications within the jurisdiction are converging or diverging.

In addition, the government may be able to bring greater general prosperity to the areas with very high potential for violence. An example is the greater emphasis on conditional cash transfers in regions of Colombia that had high levels of guerilla activity. The Colombian government, with the support of the World Bank, added to the standard considerations of "economic growth, building quality government, and sharing the fruits of growth" "a fourth pillar ... building the foundations of peace ... The Project also contributed to this pillar since it supported the expansion of [the conditional cash transfer program] *Familias* to areas previously affected by violence" (World Bank 2009, 2).

In Burundi, following several horrendous genocidal episodes, the government and civil society groups have been trying to restore the precolonial, balanced Hutu-Tutsi council of elders, with broad local authority. Kamungi, Oketch, and Huggins (2005, 233–234) report that:

Land tenure conflicts were mediated by the local council of elders, the Bashingantahe. The Bashingantahe council was made up of Hutu and Tutsi men of integrity ... They were an organized corporate group in whom was vested the social, political and judicial power of their society. The council settled disputes by conciliation or judgment, authenticated contracts such as marriage, sale or land inheritance, oversaw the maintenance of justice, and provided guidance and balance to politicians ... They were accountable to the people. Most of the disputes in which they were expected to intervene pertained to property, but they engaged in other types of conciliation on family or other matters.

... Current efforts to revive the institution of Ubushingantahe [sic] are premised on the conviction that a return to traditional cultural values and to traditional methods of conflict resolution after years of conflict stands a chance of contributing to the restoration of peace and stability in Burundi.

The propensity of younger adults, particularly young men, to engage in aggressive behavior is the basis for targeting this demographic with income-earning opportunities or other opportunities to keep them occupied in ways other than joining gangs, insurrections, violent demonstrations, and so on. This has been particularly important in coping with the demobilization of civil war combatants (Knight 2004), but it has also been relevant for preempting violence by underemployed youth.

Eliminating some sources of conflict can reduce the willingness to engage in potentially violent confrontations that otherwise could be triggered by specific initiatives. Thus, some policies may induce cooperation, thereby reducing the incentives for conflict. For example, Tobias and Boudreaux (2011. 235) point to Rwanda's recent opening up of the coffee industry, which placed Tutsis and Hutus in economically inter-dependent roles. This policy

prompted the creation of new entrepreneurial ventures and associations such as coffee cooperatives and privately owned CWSs [coffee washing stations]. This new infrastructure in Rwanda's coffee sector has provided opportunities for quality improvement in coffee trade, as well as inter-group contact between Hutu and Tutsi coffee farmers at newly created coffee mills that did not exist before coffee industry liberalisation. It specifically targeted a group benefiting from institutional change in a particular industry in a society that has experienced extreme violence and trauma in the recent past.

Another approach is to fortify one or more groups that otherwise would be vulnerable to attack by another group. This approach can range from providing arms to weaker groups or providing greater economic assets so that they could purchase defensive resources, to increasing the harshness of penalties for attacking these groups.

These "background" hostility-reducing approaches may be somewhat more closely connected to the primary initiative. Johnson (2014, 7) notes the preemptive impact that land tenuring in Ecuador can reduce the hostility surrounding the contested expansion of palm oil plantations:

In order to address and further prevent social and environmental conflicts from emerging due to palm oil expansion, land registration is made mandatory. At the most recent Latin American RSPO [Roundtable on Sustainable Palm Oil] meeting in Ecuador, this process was strongly promoted to companies as a way to address current conflicts with communities surrounding palm oil plantations as well as a method to prevent future conflicts. To independent farmers attending the RSPO meeting and even during follow-up regional workshops on the RSPO process in Ecuador, representatives from ANCUPA [the Asociación Nacional de Cultivadores de Palma Aceitera] – the palm oil producers Association] praised land registration as a 'progressive measure' that is 'a-must' due to its likelihood of preempting conflict even before it starts. With land registration and proof of land ownership, it is believed that no other third-party – company or community – can contest one's claims to land.

Within the category of conflict-deterring measures closely associated with the primary initiative, one approach is to include provisions that provide incentives for multiple groups to cooperate with one another in carrying out the initiative (Brouwer 2015). Kehl (2012) documents experiences in India, Mexico, and South Africa in which water policy reforms were subjected to lower conflict in the locales where the governments had facilitated multi-group water-user associations.

INVOCATION AND APPLICATION

As mentioned in Chapters 6 and 7, the invocation and application of policies can depart from the intentions of higher-level government policymakers, and, in so doing, can lead to harsh deprivations for particular groups. Insofar as these deprivations generate greater hostility, favoritism in implementation can exacerbate conflict. Therefore, in contexts of high levels of inter-group competition for resources, in which implementers belong to the groups involved in this competition, it may well be important to limit the scope of discretion of enactment in order to reduce the potential for favoritism.

Another potential deterrence rationale of the Burundian effort to resurrect the Ubushingantahe (Kamungi, Oketch, and Huggins 2005, 171) is that it would place the decisions on implementing provisions of the land law in the hands of a combined set of Hutus and Tutsis. In other contexts, the effectiveness of this multi-ethnic implementation approach depends on whether the leaders themselves can avoid impasse and whether people otherwise prone to violence will accept the leaders' collaboration as sufficient reason to forgo potentially violent confrontations.

Yet for policies, programs, or projects in ethnically divided jurisdictions that cannot be enacted with sufficient fairness by local leaders, the enactment strategy may call for the deconcentration form of decentralization, through which government personnel from outside of the area are brought in as more neutral arbiters. The viability of this approach depends on whether these officials are sufficiently compensated and provisioned so as to avoid having to rely more heavily on some local groups than others. For instance, Chandavarkar (2007, 466), after noting that Indian Administrative Service officers arbitrate disputes, also points out that "[r]ecruited into a national cadre, IAS officers are assigned to a specific state and spend a significant part of their careers in them ... As a result, they, and even more fully, the subordinate bureaucracy, have been vulnerable to the pressure and influence exerted by rural elites, often a prosperous peasant strata [*sic*] which has done well out of the Green Revolution ..."

In the vein of deterrence, the formulation of every resettlement program ought to consider the need for assigning more personnel capable of serving the roles of mediation, adjudication, or peacekeeping. Whether or not the personnel ought to be of the national or subnational government levels depends not only on the level of animosity at the resettlement sites, but also on how thin the administrative capacity is in resettlement areas, which often are "frontiers" with relatively low levels of subnational administrative capacity.

TERMINATION

As a potential tipping point in pushing groups into violent responses, the termination of benefits has to be planned in light of minimizing the risk. Riots and insurrections are often triggered by the termination of subsidies or property-rights guarantees. If different ethnicities are involved, it is compelling to balance the deprivations across groups, which requires diagnosing how people define their ingroup and the outgroups. As mentioned in Chapters 6 and 7, providing some compensation, whether through cash transfers or other means, can at least signal that the government has not ignored those deprived by the primary termination.

However, government leaders may be intentionally reducing the benefits to particular groups in order to reduce their power, another point mentioned in Chapter 7. This may be to reduce the capacity of those groups to rise up against the government, or to attack yet other groups, but it may backfire by increasing the animosity and defensiveness of the newly deprived groups, who then might be more predisposed to violence. Therefore, understanding the government leaders' intentions, and gauging the kind of reaction deliberate asset deprivation would provoke, are very important analytic challenges.

Decentralization that alters the relative power of a group with more influence with the national government vs. a group with more influence with the newly-empowered subnational government will increase the likelihood that the now less powerful group will expect the deterioration of its privileges, and may embolden the newly powerful group to terminate these privileges. Once property rights and civic rights are under threat of termination, the likelihood of violent confrontations may well rights.

APPRAISAL

As the consequences of a policy initiative unfold, the likelihood of violent conflict will increase or decrease, depending on both the objective and subjective impacts attributed to the initiative. The breakdown of the appraisal process needed to assess whether modifications are required to reduce the likelihood of violence begins with the suppression of information about predispositions to violence. As mentioned earlier, in some circumstances disaffected or threatened groups may not openly express their attitudes, for fear of reprisals. Officials in the areas where the likelihood of violence is mounting, or has already begun, may be reluctant to report about this to higher-level policymakers, for fear of seeming ineffective. A special case of this risk holds when leaders in decentralized jurisdictions fear that the central government might rescind the subnational autonomy because of the violence. Even when information about violent clashes or heightened dissatisfaction does reach government leaders, denials stemming from overconfidence may blunt the impact of the appraisal.

For the development practitioner who understands all of these considerations but cannot create the policies and institutions to reduce the threat of violence, it is still important to diagnose the likelihood that government leaders will know how to take these actions and whether they are willing to do so. Such diagnostics require the development practitioner to have deep knowledge of the risks of destructive conflict. Therefore, resorting to the expertise of reliable country experts may be a crucial resource.

SUMMARY

This chapter demonstrates that dangers of provoking destructive conflict may lie in any of the decision functions. To reiterate some of them: Unless the intelligence and appraisal functions are sufficiently strong, it is difficult for analysts who are not embedded in inter-group contention to understand how deep the animosities may run and how vulnerable inter-group coexistence is to initiatives believed to favor or threaten particular groups. In promoting an initiative, unless policymakers desist from denying the potential harm to a particular group, they may exacerbate the threat that this group may feel when the deprivations are greater than expected. In promoting an initiative by disparaging a group that would be negatively targeted by the initiative, the government may increase both the defensiveness of that group and the willingness of other groups to aggress against that group. The exclusion of groups from participating in the prescription function similarly can lead to hostility toward the government and groups believed to be in league with it. Initiatives of under-financed decentralization also can provoke animosity among the newly deprived. The content of many initiatives, most strikingly the record of resettlement programs, creates the opportunities for confrontations that often lead to violence. The risk that faces top-level policymakers who themselves are conflict-sensitive is that implementers involved in the invocation and application functions, whether on the national or subnational levels, will reflect their own biases. Finally, the termination of benefits is often ammunition for provocateurs. Yet we have also seen that performing these functions more effectively can contribute to deterrence of destructive conflict. This requires more careful planning, stronger and more responsible state presence, and institutions that bring members of potentially antagonistic groups into mutually rewarding interaction.

TABLE 8.1 *Core Problems, Causes, and Potential Indicators of Failing to Reduce Avoidable Conflict*

Root problem	Causes	Potential indicators
Inter-group polarization	Strong ideological differences	Communications conveying polarized ideologies and critiques of other groups' positions
	Ethnic/religious differences	Degree of disparaging communications about other groups
	Perception that other groups are overly advantaged by policies	Stakeholder communications denouncing government favoritism toward other groups
	Stereotyping	Extent of communications negatively over-simplifying outgroup characteristics, including exploitative roles
	Endorsement of collective culpability	
	Highly-resourced provocateurs	Extent of provocateurs' mobilization success
	Perceptions of unfair exploitation by another group	Communications complaining of unfair exploitation; stereotyping another group as dominated by exploitative roles
	Cultural clashes	Degree of close inter-group proximity
Threats seen as requiring aggressive actions	Unequal deprivation of particular groups (see also Chapter 7 for elaboration)	Multiple indicators (see Chapter 7)
	Severe economic or political competition	Extent of economic or political role overlap; degree of close inter-group proximity

9

Minimizing Shortsighted Policies

The tasks of identifying shortsighted initiatives and promoting farsighted ones require identifying the causal factors that predispose people to shortsighted actions, and where in the decision process these predispositions can be reversed. This chapter illustrates how the conditioning factors that account for shortsightedness can be addressed through tactics altering the operation of the decision functions. The insights about averting shortsightedness reinforce the importance of understanding how planners, policymakers, implementers, and the public interact. It is all too commonplace for critics to engage in overly narrow blame. For instance, the weakness of sub-Saharan governments' policies regarding commercial agricultural promotion have been attributed to myopic planning; Tyler et al. (2008, 52–53) conclude:

> In theory, many of the major impacts of commercial agriculture can be foreseen, such that a sound planning process could specify the design features and management actions necessary to mitigate them. The problem is that, for a whole range of reasons, well-informed, far-sighted and impartial planning processes rarely exist in Africa ... Thus, negative impacts from commercial agriculture continue to be observed, the extent of such impacts in Africa perhaps limited as much by the limited scale of commercial agricultural development to date as by anything else.

Alternatively, top policymakers are frequently cast as shortsighted and selfish – reflecting a failure of character. The Argentine economist Mariano Tommasi (2011, 4) expresses the bluntest denunciation of the leadership of his own country:

> Two centuries after independence we encounter Argentina and Chile immersed in quite different trajectories. Argentina's trajectory is defined by dramatic policy

swings and by great uncertainty about the future, brought about by weak institutions and shortsighted leaders. Chile, by contrast, is on a positive trajectory of growth and development, facilitated by strong policy institutions that keep political leaders focused on long-term objectives.

In other instances, the proposed diagnosis is bureaucratic obstruction; the implementers resist change in general, but especially initiatives with long-term impacts that threaten their standing. Kabiri (2007, 27–29, 60–63) attributes the stalling of Tanzanian wildlife management to bureaucratic obstruction. He notes the institutional interests of the wildlife bureaucracy: "There is then no doubt that the wildlife bureaucrats understand the financial dispossession inherent in implementing WMA [Wildlife Management Areas]. If the wildlife division was deprived of control over tourist hunting ventures, it would have to queue with other government departments in applying for appropriations from the treasury" (Kabiri 2007, 60).

THE BREADTH OF SHORTSIGHTEDNESS PROBLEMS

Across the full range of sectors, four limitations are prevalent. First, policy initiatives may be shortsighted because they are not recognized as having longer-term negative consequences. Second, such initiatives may be adopted because of the inability to visualize farsighted initiatives that promise sufficiently positive gains. Third, even when positive long-term scenarios are on the table, they may be passed over if they are not viewed as compelling enough to be worth the short-term sacrifices. Fourth, even though farsighted behaviors on the part of citizens are no less crucial for long-term progress, policymakers may not be able to inspire stakeholders to engage in farsighted actions such as community upgrading, keeping children in school, conserving natural resources, and responsible savings. Stakeholders outside of government are important not only for their own behavior, but also in whether they support the government's initiatives.

BASIC CAUSES OF SHORTSIGHTEDNESS

To address all four of these scenarios requires understanding the consequences of analytic limitations, impatience, selfishness, and vulnerability.

Analytic Limitations

The fundamental problems of shortsightedness begin with the analytic limitations that restrict the capacity to envision future costs of shortsighted initiatives, and the benefits worth the short-term sacrifices required for farsighted initiatives. The *expected* benefits must reflect the level of confidence these benefits will occur; therefore, assessments of the policymakers' credibility, effectiveness, and longevity in office are relevant. These intelligence burdens pertain not just to the planners and policymakers, but also to any stakeholders whose support or compliance is required for the success of the initiative. The credibility requirements for policymakers entail not only their personal commitment and effectiveness, but also their ability to convince these stakeholders that the projections of success are believable. This, in turn, depends on stakeholders' perceptions of the strength of policymakers' commitments to the initiative; whether the policymakers will either remain in office long enough to follow through on serious commitments, or their successors will do so; and whether serious commitment can result in the desired objectives.

Impatience

Even if the magnitude of a later benefit is equal to that of an earlier one, in many (but not all) circumstances the earlier benefit is valued more highly. By the same token, an earlier cost is regarded as more severe than a later one. This pervasive tendency of "pure" impatience, typically reflected by discounting the present value with which people regard benefits or costs further and further into the future, can be conceived without any consideration of the likelihood of the outcomes. Obviously, the unwillingness to delay gratification is a fundamental factor in determining the reluctance to support farsighted initiatives requiring short-term sacrifice.

One of the most telling signs of impatience is goal displacement that elevates the standing of intermediate goals in place of more fundamental, long-term goals. This has two adverse implications. First, the pursuit of the newly emphasized intermediate goals may come at the cost of the longer-term goals. For example, as outlined in Chapter 3, the goal of maximizing the number of families registered for cash transfer programs might draw funds away from the neediest families and thin the staff to the point of poor assistance and oversight. Second, and more generally, the goal displacement may distract attention away from the key focus on the needs of stakeholders. The discourse must keep the stakeholders' interests at the center of attention. The prevalence of communications that appear to over-emphasize intermediate goals may be an indicator of impatience.

It is important to note that pure impatience for consumption is neither rational nor irrational, no matter the degree of impatience; it is a matter of personal preference.[1] Therefore the support for such initiatives is sensitive to cultural factors, pervasive moods, time horizons, and other considerations requiring nuanced understanding.

Of equal importance to pure impatience is the preference for delaying deprivations, whether economic, political, psychological, or otherwise costly. For example, spending on slum upgrading is often very costly; yet leaving ugly, environmentally damaging slums intact can have severe political and social costs. The shortsighted strategy is to bulldoze the slums, even when it is recognized that the slum dwellers simply will rebuild. For Indonesia, Sugiri (2009, 20–21) emphasizes:

> that slum bulldozing is most certainly not the best option for local governments ... [yet] [f]rom 2000–05, the Local Government of Jakarta has forced more than 90,000 slum dwellers to move out from their homes, and threatened another 1.5 million of the urban poor ... [S]lum bulldozing would decrease the housing supply and make the dwellers unsheltered. Rather than going back to their origin in rural areas, these unsheltered urban poor would most probably find other places to quickly build their new slums. Slum bulldozing has been proven by experience as unable to eliminate slums.

However, sometimes the preference to delay costs does not hold. The "get it over with" impulse, perhaps heightened by communications instilling dread (Loewenstein and Prelec 1993), can prompt a reversal of the time preference.

Another form of impatience is "strategic," in taking into account the prospects for achieving long-term goals. Thus, strategic impatience reflects the preference for earlier benefits over otherwise equally-valued later benefits, due to the concern that the later benefits will not be realized. Either implicitly or explicitly, people gauge the probabilities of success, and may opt for the "bird in the hand." Uncertainty clearly contributes to this form of impatience, just as it makes it more difficult to envision desirable long-term consequences.

Unjustified Selfishness

The third fundamental problem is that people are often selfish in pursuing their own interests, even when they have a responsibility to their

---

[1] This contrasts with the logic of discounting applied to investment, for which there is a technically optimal rate in light of alternative investment opportunities.

constituents or employers. This "principal-agent problem" does not deny that people have a right to seek benefits for themselves, only that it is problematic when they do so in violation of their responsibilities. Leaders may curry support through reckless spending, radical tax reductions, invasion of other countries, and so on, for which adverse consequences are likely to emerge after the leaders are no longer in office,

The relationship between selfishness and shortsightedness is based on the fact that people often can get away with shortsighted actions that improve their situation with little accountability for the long-term problems that may emerge. As multiple events and trends accumulate from the time that a selfish action is taken to more distant future consequences, the responsibility for adverse outcomes is typically more difficult to establish. For example, program administrators may be rewarded for enrolling very large numbers of program participants, even if in the long run the program services deteriorate because the personnel are overburdened; by then the administrator may have shifted to an entirely different position.

A broader form of *organizational* selfishness may lead a government agency to take actions that strengthen its position vis-à-vis competing agencies even if those actions sacrifice sound farsighted goals. This would be reflected, for example, by a population resettlement agency that rushes in to establish jurisdiction over areas otherwise claimed by the agriculture or forestry ministries, even if soil fertility or access to inputs and markets have not been determined. Thus, the agency rivalries sometimes responsible for intelligence failures and implementation problems (reviewed in Chapters 2 through 5) are also implicated in shortsightedness.

Vulnerability

In many cases, policymakers and others would wish to engage in farsighted behavior, but are too vulnerable to do so. They may fear that their pursuit of farsighted initiatives would lead to the loss of their position or an intolerable portion of their assets; even the policymakers wishing to pursue farsighted initiatives may conclude that they are too politically vulnerable for the initiative to succeed. For some cases, one might consider the unwillingness to pursue farsighted initiatives as simply a form of selfishness, if decision-makers reduce their vulnerability at the expense of deprivations of others. Yet it is not the common selfishness of seeking gain, but rather of avoiding loss. In addition, overcoming vulnerability calls for approaches distinct from – and perhaps opposite to –

those to reduce selfishness, such as insulating positions from removal or retaliation, providing a cushion against losses, and so on.

Policymakers in precarious political situations may feel compelled to overspend in order to placate shortsighted stakeholders demanding immediate benefits. Samuels and Mainwaring (2004, 107) attribute a significant part of the Brazilian fiscal problems of the 1990s to the political vulnerability of both the state governors and the state bank directors:

> Brazil's state banks gained a reputation for profligate spending to bolster the political careers of the politicians who oversee them . . . The banks made billions of dollars in unsound loans to state governments. State bank debt totaled U.S.$96 billion as of 1998 . . . As political appointees who would be likely to remain in their positions only as long as the governors did, the directors of state banks functioned with a short-term logic that often violated elementary principles of private banks . . .

OVERCOMING DECISION MALFUNCTIONS RELATED TO SHORTSIGHTEDNESS

Many of the causes, indicators, and potential correctives of shortsightedness can be identified by examining each of the decision functions.

Intelligence

To help mobilize support for farsighted actions, and to offset the uncertainty about future possibilities, fuller information could promote greater attention to the longer-term future, aid in assessing strategies for pursuing longer-term gains, and increase confidence that the proposed policies can be successful. Deeper problem definitions will focus attention on longer past and future time frames; greater awareness of impacts on future generations may do so as well.

Fleshed-out scenarios on how to achieve long-term objectives obviously can be helpful, if they are realistic. The time horizon of the intelligence presented to stakeholders must have at least rough correspondence with their time horizons (although time horizons can be stretched to a certain degree, as discussed below under promotional tactics). Very long time horizons will provoke superficial analysis, raise doubts about the commitment of the policymakers, and stoke uncertainty. For example, South Africa's National Development Plan 2030 (South African National Planning Commission), published in 2012, strains credibility. Rennkamp (2012, 8) assessed that:

development targets are clearly quantified, but unclear how they will be achieved yet. The National Planning Commission prioritized to reduce poverty and inequalities as the main development objective in its national development plan. By 2030, the number of 39% of the population living below the national poverty line ... should be reduced to 0%. Income inequality (as measured in GINI) should decrease from 0.7 to 0.6 by 2030 ... Yet, it is not clear how these targets will be achieved. The targets for poverty and inequality reduction in the national development plan are not national policy (yet).

Henley (2010, 11) is even more dismissive of Kenya's 2007 plan:

Kenya Vision 2030 ... is a striking example of a fantasy of modernity masquerading as a development plan. Its economic platform begins not with agriculture, the sector in which three quarters of the nation's workforce is employed, but with tourism – in which sector the plan, reading more like a travel brochure, promises that Kenya will provide 'a high-end, diverse, and distinctive visitor experience which few of her competitors can offer.' After a brief look at agriculture, with an emphasis on 'improving the value gained in the production and supply chain,' Kenya Vision 2030 then moves on to the third sectoral priority, wholesale and retail trading. Here the main aim, astonishingly, is to 'raise the market share of products sold through formal channels (e.g. supermarkets) from the current 5% to 30% by 2012,' a change which will make for 'greater efficiency in the country's marketing system.'

Less obviously than having a plan with a plausible time horizon, clarifying how the pursuit of farsighted policies is in the interest of the policymaker may be able to dispel the concern that the initiative does not reflect a serious commitment. Therefore, the development practitioner ought to pay attention to whether the policymakers are transparent about how they would benefit from their own policies. Ironically, if policymakers employ the tactic of claiming that they are making self-sacrifices for the benefit of the society, stakeholders may become even more skeptical about the willingness of policymakers to follow through.

Promotion

While clarifying the bases for regarding farsighted plans as credible is as much a focus of the promotion function as the intelligence function, other promotion strategies are more distinctive to the promotion function per se. The management of perceptions of crisis can be key: insofar as crises arouse strong emotions, people may be less likely to engage in farsighted thinking and action; as mentioned in Chapter 4, crises often lead to the contraction of attention in terms of both the range of issues and the time horizon. However, evoking a longer-term crisis scenario may stimulate sufficient dread to provoke the "get it over with" reaction to make the short-term sacrifices rather than postponing actions necessary for the long run.

Prescription

The prescription process and the content of initiatives that emerge from this process also hold techniques for averting shortsightedness. Although the processes and content are intimately connected, many of the problems and strategies can be separated analytically.

Process. Regarding the process, participation in formulating and enacting policies will increase participants' assessment that the policy will be enacted. More specifically, shared decision-making authority ("checks and balances") may reduce the possibility that impetuous, shortsighted actions will be taken, including terminating sound farsighted initiatives at the first sign of sacrifices. In this regard, Knott and Miller (2006, 240–246) argue that multiple groups with veto power with respect to policy changes can stabilize the government's policy commitments; this could encourage the business sector's pursuit of long-term economic investments rather than the pursuit of immediate profit. In addition, a broader range of perspectives brought to bear in addressing problems may deepen the problem definition.

The formal analytical processes by which government policies are formulated can be structured to require attention to longer-term consequences. Multi-year budgeting (discussed at length in Chapter 10) is an obvious approach, though it rarely extends beyond a few years.

Part of the machinery of the prescription function are the provisions that insulate decision-makers from various threats, in order to reduce the vulnerability that would dissuade them from pursuing farsighted initiatives. The most direct form of insulation is the guarantee that an official can serve his or her term without fear of dismissal. This is characteristic of some central bank heads, regulatory commissioners, attorneys general, inspectors general, and so on. For example, Padmanabhan (2002, 1165–1166) notes that South Africa's Independent Electoral Commission Act 150 of 1993 "limited removal of commissioners to situations of misconduct or incapacity ... Commissioners could only be removed by the Special Electoral Court acting on the basis of an application lodged by the President, the Transitional Executive Council, Parliament, or a political party ... This provision insulated commissioners from politically motivated removals." The same protection from dismissal has been the case for attorneys general in South Africa and Zimbabwe (Goredema 1997).

However, loopholes in these cases do exist. For Zimbabwe, dismissal can be effected because of "misconduct, incompetence or incapacity"; in South Africa because of "misconduct, incapacity or inefficiency" (Goredema 1997, 50–51). Thus, the degree of insulation can vary; this is true not only in terms of the grounds for dismissal, but also by which organs must agree to dismiss the official. For example, prior to 1988 the Brazilian attorney general could have been dismissed simply by the president; the 1988 Constitution strengthened the protection by requiring a majority of the Senate to propose dismissal, while still requiring the decision of the president (Carvalho and Leitão de Melo 2012, 19).

In terms of insulating top officials involved with economic policy, for which short-term profligate spending is a common danger, the installation of the head of the central bank is of particular importance. Herbert (2002, 126), referring to the ambitious New Partnership for Africa's Development (NEPAD) liberalization programs, argues:

The standards for proper operation and independence of central banks are now globally accepted. NEPAD participants should be expected to put in place within 18 months clear standards equal to developed world standards over the independence of bank operations, *insulation of officials from political removal from office* and clear standards for maintenance of fiscal stability, low inflation, positive real interest rates, and enforcement of proper capital adequacy ratios on commercial banks. (emphasis added).

Note that Herbert asserts that central bank independence is "globally accepted" as a standard, and yet the quote makes it clear that this standard had not been upheld in some sub-Saharan African countries.

To fend off vulnerability to the withdrawal of financial resources required to perform their duties, officials could benefit from budget guarantees. Hammergren (2006, 67) cites the post-1980 innovation of budgetary earmarks for courts in Latin America, to reduce their dependence on the executive and legislative authorities.

Other forms of insulation include straightforward political strength and the prospect of dire consequences should a policymaker, or other actor, be blocked from pursuing a farsighted initiative. Biglaiser and Brown (2005, 672–673) summarize the circumstances in which policymakers often can ride out the opposition to farsighted initiatives: centralized executive authority, especially if special provisions and emergency powers exist to bypass pressures; presidents enjoying a legislative majority for his or her party; fewer or weaker actors who could veto the initiative; and fewer or weaker actors with ideological differences from the policymakers. While development practitioners may not be able to change these conditions, they can pay attention to the degree in which each holds as an indicator of the government's capacity to carry out the initiative.

Content of Prescriptions. The most straightforward approach to promote farsighted over shortsighted actions is to change the relative benefits and costs of each. Even if long-term consequences of farsighted initiatives are less valued than more immediate consequences, approaches do exist to induce people to internalize future consequences through creating or publicizing near-term conditions or events. One obvious strategy is to create rewards for behavior consistent with the pursuit of farsighted objectives. If higher-level government officials can identify actions of subordinates clearly associated with the pursuit of farsighted goals, the performance evaluation process would bring rewards closer to the present. In general, intensive monitoring will discourage shortsighted selfish actions. Such monitoring can be expanded to include a broad range of stakeholders.

For initiatives to promote farsighted actions by stakeholder groups, co-financing of self-help efforts can reduce stakeholders' short-term costs. For example, in the Philippine city of Naga, the Kaantabay sa Kauswagan (Partners in Development) program, funded by the local government and NGOs, reduced the costs for the urban poor without land titles to purchase their land, improve their housing, and work collectively to improve roads and sanitation (Prilles 2005). Similarly, Obeed, Ali, and Ward (2017, 642–643) note the potential for the government to co-finance the conversion of flood irrigation to drip irrigation in Iraq. Assessing policymakers' willingness to engage with communities, rather than monopolize the actions involved in community initiatives, may help the development practitioner gauge the prospects for co-financing or other means to improve the balance of short- and long-term benefits.

The credibility of top leaders' capacity to follow through may be enhanced by tightly linking to other important, widely supported initiatives. For example, the multi-year process necessary for the reform of the Mexican oil sector, reviewed in Chapter 5, is insulated by its connections with reforms targeting labor markets, education, and telecommunications, all of which were priorities to the opposition parties and many other stakeholders.

The content of initiatives can also reduce uncertainty – even though uncertainty is typically regarded as an intelligence problem. As to whether the policymakers are sufficiently committed to the initiative, policymakers can go beyond communicating how they would benefit if the initiative is successful, they can build in "hands-tying" provisions that would result in costs for the policymakers if the initiative is unsuccessful or is not pursued. For the sake of the programs and projects that are most crucial to sustain at pre-determined levels in the long run, locking in the commitment can be accomplished through a host of instruments, with varying degrees of difficulty to reverse. Constitutional provisions, such as the Brazilian constitution's budgetary commitment to education, are in principle the least reversible, though, of course, constitutions can be abrogated or amended. Trust funds with designated income streams are another alternative. For example, the Ghana Education Trust Fund, enacted in 2000 to earmark 2.5 percent of the value-added tax, is still in effect. Yet in the past several years, the Finance Ministry has been withholding substantial portions of the funds (Government of Ghana 2015).

Even initiatives backed by the fullest commitment need not lead to adverse outcomes if indications emerge that the initiative would be ill-fated. Credible *conditional* commitments will enhance the willingness of people to accept short-term sacrifices for long-term gains but also allow initiators or their successors to change the policies if pre-specified conditions arise, thereby safeguarding the quality of policy and providing greater certainty regarding future contingencies.

Another approach (also introduced in Chapter 3) is to enter into agreements with external bodies, such as multilateral or bilateral foreign assistance agencies. These agencies not only cover some of the costs, but they also bind the current and successor governments to the initiative through the period specified by the agreement. Finally, the movement toward more comprehensive international trade agreements provides an opportunity to gain support for policy reforms required to bring the policies of trading partners into enough conformity ("harmonization") for trade agreements to be strengthened.

In short, prescriptions that subject the initiators to heavy costs if they renege can also enhance the perceptions of seriousness of the commitment. Often a loan agreement with a bilateral or multilateral foreign assistance agency would have adverse economic and political consequences if the government reneges on its commitments entailed in the agreement. Enhancing credibility may be one of the motives of the foreign assistance agencies as well. For example, the World Bank's contribution to sub-Saharan Africa's NEPAD programs undertaken included "strengthening credibility" (Nankani 2004, 1).

Another application of the hands-tying logic is to counter shortsighted favoritism that might undermine broad support for farsighted initiatives through fixed, explicit formulas for allocating benefits, rather than the discretion of government decision-makers. This form of "stimulus avoidance," a form of hands-tying by eliminating discretion, exists in nations as diverse as Costa Rica and Kenya, which have formulas that allocate certain funds across different areas according to income levels, population, and so on. In Kenya, the Constituency Development Fund (CDF), established in 2003, earmarked 2.5 percent of national revenues. "with the aim of ironing out regional imbalances brought about by patronage politics." (Bagaka 2008, 2) The approach, therefore, was to mandate a fixed distributive formula. As Bagaka (2008, 3) reports: "Allocations to the 210 parliamentary jurisdictions are clearly spelled out in the CDF Act, where 75% of the fund is allocated equally among all 210 constituencies. The remaining 25% is allocated based on constituency poverty levels, population size and the size of the constituency." The formula itself initially could be manipulated to favor particular areas, but as long as the formula remains intact, the opportunities for further favoritism are limited.

Implementation

Obstacles to implementing farsighted initiatives rest on the contrasting risks posed by implementing agencies: inaction or shortsighted action. The analysis of incentives must be extended to both agency interests and individual interests. Responsibly farsighted implementation calls for moderate ambition – avoiding self-protective inaction that would expose individuals or agencies to risks, but also avoiding aggressively self-serving actions to put the individual or the agency above the others. Individual ambition is sensitive to performance appraisal, best examined in the section on appraisal.

The ambition of agency leaders to gain greater standing, insofar as it arises because of jurisdictional overlaps can be addressed by restructuring of roles. Streamlining agency mandates to reduce overlapping jurisdictions can reduce the incentives for agencies to take hasty actions in the competition for laying claim to jurisdiction. The creation or strengthening of watchdog agencies may be able to restrain what are identifiably shortsighted obstructions. A more thorough though more challenging watchdog function is for top officials to direct highly qualified specialists to assess whether the actions proposed by administrators are likely to serve the long-term goals they claim: do the highway projects really have acceptable rates of return; are the proposed shifts in school personnel likely to have the claimed improvements in student achievement? Such parallel analytical efforts, which in essence bring the costs or benefits for agency personnel closer to the present, can serve the dual functions of deterring efforts to improve the standing of the agency through shortsighted approaches and assessing the integrity and technical caliber of agency personnel.[2]

Insofar as government institutions have their own inertia, establishing agencies dedicated to broad sets of long-term initiatives can insulate these initiatives. The key is that some mandates and agencies established to pursue these mandates will attract and reward people with farsighted perspectives. In addition to the environmental agencies mentioned in Chapters 3 and 5, regional development authorities such as Brazil's Superintendency for the Development of the Northeast (founded in 1959) and its Superintendency for the Development of the Amazon (founded in 1966) had been given development authority beyond the individual sectoral ministries and beyond the individual states within the respective regions. There would seem to be good reasons to expect that these agencies would not survive – the jurisdictional threats they pose to the prerogatives of federal ministries and the state governments, and the corruption scandals that occasioned their temporary dismantling – thus their longevity is testament to the potential for insulating institutions created to pursue long-term objectives.

---

[2] A useful model was the World Bank's Quality Assurance Group (QAG), which selectively assessed, among other analytical work, the rate-of-return estimates of projects evaluated by country-specific World Bank units. Because sufficiently high rate-of-return estimates were necessary for the unit to have projects in the pipeline, personnel had an incentive to exaggerate these estimates. The risk of a poor QAG assessment became a deterrent to such exaggeration. Although the QAG was eliminated, the World Bank Group retains the Independent Evaluation Group (IEG) to evaluate projects and programs. Yet, despite the IEG's deservedly strong reputation, its evaluations come largely after implementation has occurred. Therefore, some of the staff involved in developing and approving the initiatives are no longer subject to accountability. See Ascher 2009, 109–11.

Appraisal

In the context of concern about farsightedness, the appraisal function has two distinctive purposes: to assess how well initiatives are doing, and, when conditions are appropriate, to provide incentives for planners, policymakers, and implementers to act in farsighted ways. The criteria of evaluation determine both whether ongoing farsighted initiatives are deemed sound enough to continue, and whether the combination of criteria and rewards will motivate farsightedness. These points hold for performance appraisal of programs and projects, and the agencies associated with them, as well as for the personnel appraisal that may reward or deprive individuals.

Program and Project Appraisal. How would policymakers, as well as development practitioners, know whether a farsighted initiative is panning out? Ironically, the sustainability of farsighted initiatives may call for paying less critical attention to ongoing appraisal, simply by the very nature of long-term goals and because the sacrifices appear early on. For instance, improved curricula may require considerable adjustment time before materials are perfected, teachers are trained, and testing routines are perfected. New towns may take many years until the full range of services are developed. Constructive appraisal would have to clarify reasonable expectations at each point in time, even if it is tempting for policymakers to exaggerate progress and expectations. Therefore, for appraisal to be sensitive to long-term goals, it cannot rely simply on indicators, but rather must engage in the analysis of projecting consequences for which indicators are not yet available. Such an analysis, insofar as it demonstrates that the agency is on the sound track to pursue long-term objectives, would reduce the perceived vulnerability of agency leaders, and thereby reduce the temptation to engage in goal displacement.

Personnel Evaluation. Although the appraisal of ongoing initiatives is – and often ought to be – separate from the appraisal of personnel involved in formulating and implementing initiatives, personnel appraisal has the potential to play an important role in whether administrators will support or undermine farsighted initiatives. The logic is that administrators will pursue the objectives corresponding to the most important among the criteria of evaluation.

Three quite distinct contexts can be found. In many developing countries, the personnel evaluations for retention, compensation, and promotion are virtually irrelevant; as long as officials are not egregiously incompetent or corrupt, the periodic evaluations are pro forma. In these cases, no performance criteria can orient bureaucrats toward either short-term or long-term pursuits. Typical of this scenario is Pakistan, for which Tanwir and Chaudry (2015, 98) note the "significant disconnect between the present performance evaluation system and the actual performance of civil servants." This is especially true in countries where compensation and promotion are based on years in service.

A second scenario, epitomized by Malaysia, involves politicized appointments, promotions, and other rewards. Chin (2011, 152–153) highlights Prime Minister Mahathir's success in creating a loyal, Islamic bureaucracy: "The end result was a highly politicized civil service where high-level corruption was left unchecked for political reasons. The Islamization of the civil service also meant that the civil service took on a more religious character."

The third scenario involves both agency and individual rewards for assessments of good performance. For example, in China, where officials begin with local assignments, Wang (2007, 226) notes that "[o]ne of the most important criteria for promotion is economic performance." While this may seem to tie promotions mechanically to rates of growth, higher officials can assess for the difficulty of overseeing growth in particular jurisdictions. A key point, however, is that the assessment of good performance may be deceptive. This performance may not be truly farsighted, if it pursues impressive short-term but unsustainable gains, as in the example of seeming success in signing up a huge number of cash transfer recipients. In short, rewards can motivate farsighted or shortsighted behavior, depending on the accuracy of the performance appraisal.

Termination

The challenges of terminating shortsighted initiatives selected for their short-term rewards are obviously more complicated than terminating initiatives that have already proven their short-term weaknesses. The intelligence and promotion functions have the burden of demonstrating and conveying both the longer-term difficulties of the shortsighted initiative and the credible long-term gains of farsighted alternatives.

To address the opposition to terminating shortsighted initiatives effectively, it is useful to assess which of the four causes of shortsightedness may be in play.

Insofar as the cause is straightforward impatience, proposing alternatives that promise sufficient short-term rewards but impressive enough long-term benefits to outweigh the discounting. In some circumstances, such alternatives may not exist. In that case, the development practitioner ought to be sensitive to the likelihood that the initiative will be ill-fated.

Insofar as the cause is inappropriate selfishness, clarifying that those responsible for the initiative will not be held sufficiently accountable should the initiative have adverse longer-term outcomes could be combined with reforms in program and personnel evaluation to reduce the incentives for selfish actions to be rewarded.

Insofar as the cause is uncertainty leading to strategic impatience, the credibility-enhancing measures outlined earlier in this chapter are clearly important. For example, the assurance that benefits will materialize can be cemented by hands-tying commitments such as the trade pacts or agreements with international organizations or bilateral development agencies, as outlined above.

Insofar as the cause is vulnerability, the approach ought to be to reduce the reality and perceptions of the magnitude of costs that some would incur if farsighted initiatives are successful, and the costs if they are not. For the poor, alternatives range across the very broad set of social safety nets (Grosh et al. 2008); for the non-poor, instruments such as decent unemployment and retirement guarantees, tax provisions permitting loss carryovers, and so on.

SUMMARY

This chapter has demonstrated that combining the analysis of rather simple conditioning factors (impatience, selfishness, analytic limitations, and vulnerability) with the distinctions emerging from parsing the decision process provides a fertile basis for identifying the obstacles, indicators, and potential remedies regarding shortsightedness. The range of promising mechanisms – for recognizing and discouraging shortsighted initiatives through intelligence and appraisal, and for promoting farsighted initiatives through credibility enhancement and insulating otherwise vulnerable decision-makers – is truly encouraging.

TABLE 9.1 *Core Problems, Causes, and Potential Indicators of Shortsighted Policies*

Root problem	Causes	Potential indicators
Pure impatience	Limited interest in envisioning future circumstances	Thinness of discourse about future circumstances
	Superficial problem definitions	Truncated causal analysis of problems
	Personal preferences; culturally-influenced time horizons	Among policymakers: short-term targets of initiatives, emphasis on intermediate objectives and goal displacement; among stakeholders: extent of opposition to appeals for sacrifice, &/or goal substitution
Strategic impatience	General dismissal of feasibility of long-term goals	"
	Limited capacity to envision future circumstances	Thinness of discourse about future circumstances
	Lack of leadership credibility	Extent of concerns voiced about top leaders' commitment, capacity, &/or continuity
	Political vulnerability	Degree of irregular turnover of government leadership
	Socioeconomic vulnerability	Degree of stakeholders' socioeconomic marginality
	Superficial problem definitions	Truncated causal analysis of problems
Selfishness in agents' neglect of responsibility	Low current compensation	Low levels of bureaucratic salaries compared to benchmarks
	Weak monitoring and sanctions against selfish shortsighted actions	Extent of prosecutions for corruption; relatively weak punishments for shortsighted decisions
Threats to farsighted initiatives from opposition	See table 3.1 for elaborations	See table 3.1 for elaborations

10

Adapting Policy Initiatives and Institutions

The premise that distinctive policy challenges arise from the underdevelopment syndrome can be extended more broadly to consider how initiatives and institutions can be designed or reformed to enable development practitioners to be more effective. If, as Chapter 2 argues, certain distinctive characteristics of developing countries present greater obstacles to effectiveness, addressing these characteristics is a key to discovering more appropriate policies and institutions.

ADAPTING POLICY CONTENT

It is easy simply to advocate stronger institutions – surely a worthwhile long-term goal – but even if leaders follow sound advice of governance experts, and prioritize institutional changes in terms of contributions to economic and sociopolitical development, institutional change is often a slow, inconsistent, and politically costly process. In the meantime, initiatives have to accommodate existing limitations, which is what robustness is all about.

Therefore, the need to adapt policies embraced in developed countries raises the question of what characteristics of prescriptions are more resilient under low institutional strength. How should policy initiatives per se be formulated and enacted in light of the typical problems facing developing countries? Because highly complicated policies may outstrip the capacity of the existing process to merge adequate information, expertise, and administrative capacity, simpler policies may have greater success. An initiative must yield a prescription that can be invoked and applied effectively, and terminated, if necessary, in a timely, humane, and conflict-sensitive fashion. It has to be based on intelligence on what is institutionally feasible, typically drawing on appraisals of past initiatives that underestimated institutional weaknesses. This intelligence consists, in large part, of experience with the malfunctions of each decision function.

Robust Policies in the Face of Imperfect Information

In the face of weak intelligence, it is often sensible to rely on policy instruments that are less sensitive to mis-estimates of costs, intended impacts, and secondary consequences. Consider the difference between committing to a very large-scale program and phasing in a program without a commitment to continue beyond the current phase. For example, phasing in highway initiatives may be able to avoid the problems of massive highway network initiatives that could fail if the expected toll revenues do not materialize. However, this requires continual, realistic appraisal of whether the results are sufficiently successful to be extended, possibly facing opposition from the champions of expanding an initiative if the appraisal deems the initiative as less successful than planned. Champions often argue that appraisal is premature – claiming that more time is needed to see the fruits of the initiative. Thus, many policy prescriptions can be more robust if planners and policymakers recognize the need to adapt to limited intelligence. For example, Orphanides and Williams (2007, 1432) suggest adjustments in monetary policy approaches (too technical to report here) to adjust for imperfect knowledge, concluding:

Policies that appear to be optimal under perfect knowledge can perform very poorly if they are implemented in such an environment. In our model economy, the presence of imperfect knowledge tends to raise the persistence of inflation, partly as a result of the persistent policy errors due to misperceptions of the natural rates and partly as a result of the learning process agents may rely upon to form expectations. This leads to a deterioration in economic performance, especially with regard to a policymaker's price stability objective. Policymakers who recognize the presence of these imperfections in the economy can adjust their policies and protect against this deterioration in economic outcomes.

Principles of Adaptability in the Face of Uncertainty. Swanson et al. (2010) distinguish between two circumstances of uncertainty. First, the nature of the conditions within which the policy may operate is known, but planners and policymakers are uncertain as to the relative strength of these conditions. Swanson et al. (2010, 927) note that:

This capacity to adapt to anticipated conditions is the more traditional of the two capacities, but is by no means a well-formed ability in most policymaking processes. A policy with this capacity can be crafted to:

- perform well under a range of anticipated conditions with little or no alteration;
- monitor changes in context and identify when these are significant enough to affect performance; and
- trigger built-in policy adjustments or deliberations necessary to determine policy adjustments to maintain performance or terminate the policy when it is no longer relevant.

In contrast, the possibility of unanticipated conditions may exist: the so-called "unknown unknowns" – uncertainty of the deepest level. Swanson et al. (2010, 928) note that a policy under such conditions can still be "crafted" so as to:

- accommodate unforeseen issues and changes in context for which the policy was not originally designed, but in ways that support the policy's goals;
- recognize emerging issues that will need to be addressed; and
- trigger further analysis and deliberation necessary to make policy adjustments to address emerging issues, maintain performance, or terminate the policy if it is no longer relevant.

In addition, some policies have adaptability built-in, particularly in adjusting coverage and magnitudes according to pre-set formulas. For example, Swanson et al. (2010, 930) cite the example of crop insurance payouts in India:

Weather-indexed insurance in India is a particularly good example [of fully-automatic policy adjustment]. It has emerged as an alternative to traditional crop insurance in India where settling a claim was a time-consuming process. Weather-indexed crop insurance is linked to the underlying weather risk measured by an index based on historical climate data, rather than the extent of crop yield loss. These weather insurance contracts have been found to offer quick payouts triggered by independently monitored weather indices and result in improved recovery times from weather-related stress. The built-in adjustment feature provides a simple mechanism for managing insurer risk and determining farmer eligibility for benefit payments.

The additional virtues of this approach are that it reduces the scope for favoritism and corruption, and, because of the involvement of stakeholders, they were able to "self-organize" to minimize potential adverse effects of the initiative (Swanson et al. 2010, 932–933). This implies leaving some flexibility in the regulations of stakeholder activities, facilitating stakeholders to organize in constructive ways, and providing sufficient certainty so as to motivate the efforts to engage in organizing.

Robust Policies in the Face of Administrative and Compliance Challenges

Where administrative weaknesses pose serious problems, the possibilities of initiatives with lesser administrative burdens obviously ought to be considered. For some aspects of policy – especially tax policy and stream-lining regulation – significant progress has been made, though many countries have not embraced the opportunities.

Taxation. One of the most impressive examples of adapting prescriptions to weak institutions has been in the sphere of taxation. International tax experts focusing on developing countries advocate elim-inating exemptions, reducing the marginal rates, broadening the base, and giving greater weight to value-added taxes (VAT) as opposed to income or profit taxes. These recommendations are based on the skepticism regarding ambitious efforts to use the tax code to promote investment in subsectors that government planners deem as highly promising. This ambition is appropriately challenged by recognizing that the intelligence function may be limited in terms of identifying the most productive investments, that an imbalanced promotion process often pressures gov-ernment leaders to invest in suboptimal pursuits, and that implementation is often too weak to prevent the evasion of income and profit taxes (Gillis 1989; Bird, Martínez-Vázquez, and Torgler 2008). By reducing or com-pletely supplanting income taxation with its multiple rates, exemptions, and ease of evasion, value-added taxation reduces the erosion of tax effort that plagues tax collection where governments are too weak to resist unsound exemptions or to discipline evaders.

Streamlining Programs. Programs can also be less complex by having fewer, broader categories and simpler decision criteria. Successful social safety net programs are typically broad, simple, and uniform. Support based on their breadth is likely to make them resilient in resisting efforts to terminate or weaken the program. Simplicity and uniformity reduce the administrative challenges and costs; and uniformity also reduces the likelihood of conflicts among potential recipients competing for higher benefits. In addition, initiatives can often reduce uncertainty of responsi-bility and bureaucratic conflicts if they are managed by the minimum number of agencies.

Streamlining Regulation. Although it is easy to lament the weak capacity to enforce regulations, the scope of regulation and the magnitude of resources devoted to regulatory enforcement have to be questioned. One approach to make regulation more effective with a given level of enforcement resources is to reduce the scope of regulation. Some regulations are, of course, truly constructive; they protect against damaging behavior and inappropriate restrictions of competition. However, many regulations in developing countries, ranging from licensing requirements to onerous burdens that only well-established firms can bear, may restrict competition in order to favor privileged firms or individuals.[1] The institutional weakness in reducing predominantly competition-restricting regulations is often the inability or unwillingness of leaders to fend off rent-seeking efforts. Avoiding overly stringent regulations that would require greater enforcement effort would address the limitations of administrative capacity. Streamlined regulations, consistent with the monitoring limitations of many developing countries, can also contribute to the capacity of enforcement. For constructive regulations, the interplay between governance and economic policy points to strengthening governance by devoting both budgetary and political resources to enforcement, but an alternative tack is to streamline regulations such that they are more easily monitored and enforced. Where institutional capacity, including voluntary compliance and credible sanctions, are weak, more resources ought to be devoted to enforcing important regulations, and to enhancing regulatory control by maintaining centralized enforcement (Araral 2014, 295).

Policy Arenas. Simplicity can also be achieved by relying on initiatives that involve fewer procedures to formulate a prescription. For example, monetary policies involving fairly insulated decisions by a central bank typically involve fewer steps, agencies, and actors outside of government. This does not mean that a chosen monetary policy is optimal, but rather that an initiative to establish sound macroeconomic levels (money supply, inflation rate, interest rates) faces fewer pitfalls through such decisions than pursuing the same targets through the fiscal policy route of government spending.

Prototyping

Pilot efforts that restrict either the geographic area or the budgetary magnitude of an initiative may be able to reveal whether the underlying

---

[1] Much of "rent-seeking" involves benefiting government officials in order for private actors to gain protection from competition, thereby resulting in excess profits ("rents").

assumptions have been borne out before large-scale or irreversible missteps have been undertaken. Special enterprise zones, such as export-processing zones, free-trade zones, industrial parks, free ports, and technology development zones, have been established in a number of countries to "test out" development approaches, particularly to see whether market-opening strategies, technology-promotion measures, or foreign investment-attracting approaches will pay off. China has had the most ambitious initiatives, especially with export-processing zones. Zeng (2015, 4) notes not only the initial limited scope, but also how the establishment of the diverse forms of special enterprise zones contributed to policy learning; it has been an example of "gradualism with a pragmatic and experimental approach; reform-oriented mindset." After some initial successes, many more special enterprise zones were established. Some failed, and were terminated; yet China's growth has certainly been strengthened by this adaptive approach.

Similarly, India's weather-indexed insurance program mentioned above was also implemented as a series of pilots, varying the target crops and locations with a range of delivery models. Swanson et al. (2010, 931) note that:

> The implementing agencies ... have reported that this pilot experience was valuable to better understand risk parameters and the potential for commercial expansion. It was also an opportunity to create awareness among farmers, build trust through timely payouts and improve the design in response to customer feedback. Moreover, the early pilot schemes offered by the private sector were followed by the entry of the public sector.

Like any "experiment" outside of carefully controlled laboratory conditions, the lessons derived from pilot programs have to be interpreted in the context of other trends and conditions that may account for success or failure beyond the nature of the initiative. For example, Farole (2011) notes that some special enterprise zones in sub-Saharan Africa may have failed because of the overall weakness of the economies.

For any pilot or prototype initiative, the remaining challenge is that scaling up the initiative may introduce different dynamics, or may not be as appropriate in different areas. Therefore, scaling up ought to be complemented by adaptability, as the Chinese experience indicates.

ADAPTING THE POLICY PROCESS

Insofar as the development practitioner can influence the policy process, a broad range of alterations in that process may be able to reduce decision malfunctions, stabilize the economy and the budget.

Stabilizing the Budget

A stable budget averts some of the problems that sap the enthusiasm of policymakers to fulfill the commitments of their initiatives, reduce the capacity to compensate groups deprived by an initiative, hobble the planning effort, and weaken administrative capacity. Therefore, any arrangements that reduce budget volatility from year to year can help to counter the overall economic volatility that plagues many developing countries. Huidrom, Kose, and Ohnsorge. (2016, 10–12) note that three arrangements have been prominent: fiscal rules that "impose lasting numerical constraints on budgetary aggregates–debt, overall balance, expenditures, or revenues"; stabilization funds that "set aside receipts from significant natural resource revenues such as oil and natural gas"; and the Medium-Term Expenditure Framework (MTEF) that most commonly "translates macroeconomic objectives into budget aggregates and detailed spending plans."

Fiscal Rules. Budget expenditure rules, in particular, are designed to check the impulse of excessive spending, frequently arising either when government revenues are high, or when government leaders feel particularly vulnerable unless they engage in such spending. Cordes et al. (2015, 3) explain the rationales of these rules:

Expenditure rules, in particular, have received increasing attention as they exhibit a number of features ... In particular, they are directly aimed at addressing the expenditure pressures often at the origin of excessive deficits, they are transparent and generally easy to monitor, they fully accommodate revenue shortfalls resulting from adverse economic shocks (allowing for a stabilizing role of fiscal policy), and they are most directly related to the formulation of the annual budget, which sets legally binding appropriations, thus contributing to the rules' enforceability. Importantly, and unlike deficit caps, expenditure rules also help creating buffers in good times, when revenue windfalls can make spending pressures difficult to resist.

Céspedes, Parrado, and Velasco (2014, 119) point out that having a firm fiscal rule limiting overall government spending for the coming budget period disciplines the budget process that is such a crucial arena of bureaucratic rivalry:

[I]n the early phase of budget preparation, the rules for the negotiation among ministers are key. One alternative is to channel individual spending requests first and then let the spending limit emerge from the simple aggregation of those petitions. Another alternative is for a ceiling to be preset and then within that ceiling allow spending ministers to bargain over their spending shares. The latter system is clearly superior because it encourages individual players to internalize the aggregate budget constraint. But how is the spending ceiling to be determined? The fiscal rule provides the answer.

Some expenditure rules are designed to cover multi-year commitments. The International Monetary Fund (Cordes et al. 2015) has examined the expenditure rules in Argentina, Botswana, Brazil, Ecuador, Mongolia, Namibia, and Peru, that limit government expenditures over at least a three-year time horizon. They find that having formal expenditure rules does seem to correspond with lower budget volatility, although the discipline reflected by the very fact of having expenditure rules may account for the lower volatility. Sarr (2015, 25–26) notes that the multi-year budget process brings longer-term forecasting formally within the budget process:

The most visible element in a sustainable budgetary framework is the MTEF (Medium-Term Expenditure Framework). MTEFs translate macro-fiscal objectives and constraints into broad budget aggregates as well as detailed expenditure plans by sector. The rationale of this budgeting tool is to enable the central government to more adequately incorporate future fiscal challenges into the annual budgets, thereby reducing an undue emphasis on short-term goals. The key public finance problems that MTEFs are intended to overcome are dynamic common pool and time-inconsistent voters, which can lead to higher government spending and borrowing, resulting in sub-optimally high deficits and debt.

Multi-year budgeting can also impart discipline in fiscal decentralization. Just as the annual expenditure rules can take pressure off top government leaders, so too can multi-year budgeting, insofar as it focuses attention on the possibility of future revenue shortfalls and the need to be cautious about current spending.

With respect to fiscal decentralization, Kamugisha (2014, 9) argues that for Tanzania, the three-year budget exercise is designed to impart discipline on both the national and decentralized levels:

financial interdependence between different tiers of governments enhances effective budgeting and evaluation of transfers to be carried out to ensure efficient service delivery and getting value for money. A three year medium term framework (MTEF) is used to make local government participate in a multi- year budgeting system. In order for it to be effective, predictability [of] fiscal transfer system is undisputable.

Stabilization Funds. While fiscal rules discussed above are designed to constrain spending in the face of pressures to overspend, it is also important to strengthen the capacity to ride out years of budget shortfalls by creating politically-protected savings instruments to shield revenues that come in during boom times. This aspect of budget discipline can also be accomplished through stabilization funds, particularly for commodity-export-dependent countries. The central budget receives revenues from specific exports (typically hydrocarbons or hard minerals such as copper) up to a predetermined volume; the rest goes into the fund. When revenues fall short of the predetermined volume, money from the stabilization fund flows into the budget. The most prominent stabilization fund success has been Chile's Economic and Social Stabilization Fund (ESSF), often called the Copper Stabilization Fund. In light of the unusually high volatility of world copper prices, it is remarkable that "Chile has become somewhat of a poster child for prudent macroeconomic management" (Céspedes, Parrado, and Velasco (2014, 106). Due to the copper-revenue savings deposited in the ESSF during the remarkably high copper prices in 2006–2007 (nearly three-and-a-half times greater than in the 2000–2003 period), in 2009 the Chilean budget was able to withdraw US$8 billion from the ESSF, averting the economic disaster that struck so many countries during the Great Recession. Céspedes, Parrado, and Velasco (2014, 128) point out that during the crisis, Chile "stood out as the country with the most aggressive countercyclical policies, with substantially eased credit conditions and a large fiscal stimulus."

However, stabilization funds require discipline on the part of the government to desist from raiding the fund when the formula does not warrant withdrawals. Huidrom, Kose, and Ohnsorge (2016, 11) conclude that:

While a stabilization fund can be a powerful fiscal tool to manage fiscal resources and create fiscal space, the establishment itself does not guarantee its success. Cross-country evidence even suggests that the effectiveness of a particular stabilization fund in shielding the domestic economy from commodity price volatility depends largely on government commitment to fiscal discipline and macroeconomic management, rather than on just the existence of the instrument itself.

Stabilizing Specific Project or Program Budgets. As outlined in Chapter 9, safeguarding the commitments to farsighted projects or programs can be accomplished by such measures as constitutional provisions, funds with continual income streams, and new government agencies dedicated to the commitment. For the sake of the programs and projects that are most crucial to sustain at predetermined levels, locking in the commitment can be accomplished through a host of instruments: constitutional provisions, dedicated bonds, trust funds, and establishing agencies to carry out a set of projects or programs (such as the environmental agencies mentioned in Chapters 3 and 5). Another approach (also introduced in Chapter 3) is to enter into agreements with external bodies, such as the multilateral or bilateral foreign assistance agencies, which not only cover some of the costs, but also bind the current and successor governments to continue the initiative through the period specified by the agreement. Finally, the movement toward more comprehensive international trade agreements provides an opportunity to gain support for policy reforms required to bring the policies of trading partners into enough conformity ("harmonization") for trade agreements to be strengthened.

Gaining Administrative Compliance

The most promising way to address the classic "principal-agent" challenge of conflicts between the incentives of top-level policymakers and administrators involved in enactment is to design policies that reward the implementers if the initiatives are enacted successfully and in conformity with the goals that underlie the initiatives. This requires either building the rewards (bonuses, promotions, or other recognition) into the initiative itself, or providing more general incentives for administrative competence beyond any particular program or project initiative.

Roberts (2003) summarizes an Overseas Development Institute assessment of the experiences of seven low-income countries[2] with "performance budgeting" (basing government expenditures on policy objectives rather than incremental changes from existing budget allocations) and the reinforcing movement to "results-based management" (rewarding administrators for "effective contributions to their organisations' declared objectives") (Roberts 2003, 47). A major conclusion is that these complementary approaches create the conditions needed for administrators to share the objectives of the top-level policymakers. Roberts (2003, 47–48) reports:

Tanzania and Uganda quite appropriately embarked on programmes of results-based management reform at approximately the same time as they formalised results-based budget practice . . . Both are techniques for overcoming divergence of objectives and motives between principal and agent. The logic of the two reforms is that responsibility for financial and resource management decisions should be devolved to front-line managers, subject only to prior agreement on the results to be achieved, the resource envelope available for achieving them, and the rules governing the processes used.

---

[2] These countries were Bolivia, Burkina Faso, Cambodia, Ghana, Mali, Tanzania, and Uganda.

In addition, however, the initiative must be accompanied by sufficient monitoring and evaluation to assess success, and administrative capacity must be high enough to reduce the likelihood that administrators would feel compelled or justified to engage in corruption.

Streamlining Agency Mandates

In light of the risks arising from bureaucratic rivalries and general coordination challenges, it is often advisable to streamline the policy process. One approach is to simplify the mandates of a given agency to minimize conflicting objectives. Potential conflicts range from asking an agricultural ministry to promote agriculture production while also leading the initiative for stronger environmental regulation of agroindustry, to requiring a state mining company to maximize profits on behalf of the government, but also investing heavily in housing and other physical infrastructure for communities in the area. This is not to say that agricultural ministries or state mining enterprises should neglect environmental protection, nor that mining enterprises lack obligations to treat local communities respectfully and constructively. However, the norms to which such governmental and state entities must adhere ought to be established, monitored, and enforced by other government units specifically mandated to do so. The agricultural ministry and the state mining enterprise should have units (often labeled "inspectors general" offices) mandated to monitor compliance with all regulations, so that the ministry or enterprise can avoid sanctions by the regulatory agency.

Other simplifications could involve minimizing the number of agencies involved in delivering services or to give one entity – whether an agency, community, council, etc. – unambiguous authority to manage the program or project. It may also involve simpler contracting. Araral (2014, 295) calls for simple contracts and price caps for government contracts rather than more complex and uncertain rate-of-return provisions.

However, simplicity is not equivalent to directness. A common conditioning factor in developing countries is the shift to more direct interventions in reaction to the frustration of ineffective policies and programs, reinforced by the uncertainties of whether indirect approaches will be effective. Influencing behavior by changing incentives often requires careful calibration of pricing, interest rates, program timing, etc.; these, in turn, require analytic subtlety, enough control over the prescription functions, administrative capacity, and substantial patience. The direct measures are often too heavy-handed to be effective. Instead of adjusting money supply or government spending to reduce inflation, the government may impose price controls, at the risk of rigidity and black markets. Rather than providing physical and social infrastructure in the hope that people would relocate, governments may coerce them into doing so. Instead of creating enabling conditions to spur investment, the government may grant monopolies, ban imports, or take other direct actions counter to market efficiency.

Selective Decentralization

Despite the numerous pitfalls of decentralization mentioned previously in this book, ranging from distortions of sound initiatives to the greater conflict over local control, selective decentralization can overcome some institutional weaknesses. The crucial point to keep in mind is that neither centralization or decentralization is *the* answer overall. Whether decentralized policymaking makes sense depends on the specific service at issue, and whether centralized or decentralized provision of that service better meets the criteria of responsiveness, efficiency, fairness, minimization of harmful spillover effects, and conflict sensitivity.

Placing initiatives in the control of subnational governments does not preclude the possibility of participation by national-level agencies. Subnational governments can contract with either national-level agencies to provide goods and services, or to look to the private sector. As long as the subnational agencies have the fiscal resources, the competence to decide on the right mix of goods and services, and the capacity to keep corruption at a reasonably low level, this instrument of decentralization can be effective. Clearly, however, the efficiency, fairness, and conflict sensitivity criteria must be observed, and fiscal decentralization is essential (European Commission 2007).

Decentralized governance can also be helpful for prototyping. Decentralized decisions by early adopters as to whether to adopt (and adapt) a particular type of policy, program, or project will limit the initial scope, as well as allow for variations. Many of the pilot initiatives in China were launched by provincial or even lower-level governments (Zeng 2015); some failed and were discontinued, yet others have been a major basis of China's economic boom. This approach, of course, has to be tempered by recognition of the potential pitfalls of decentralization, outlined at several points earlier in this book.

Relying on Internationally Provided Services

When confronted with corruption that has been resistant to domestic reform efforts, the government may have to consider farming out key services to international providers. To minimize nationalistic or anti-colonial backlash, it may be advisable to contract with private international firms rather than with foreign governments. Thus, customs management in Indonesia was contracted out to the Swiss firm SGS from 1985 to 1997 (Krasner 2010, 106)

Investing in Intelligence through More Open, More Deliberative Processes

So many of the shortcomings that have been cited throughout this book stem from intelligence failures. The deficit in investments in intelligence often stems from the fact that expenditures on the government's intelligence infrastructure is interpreted as adding to a bloated bureaucracy. Because of the historical association between national planning agencies and statist policies, some of these agencies have been under siege. For example, as part of India's liberalization, the Narasimha Rao administration reduced the power of the Planning Commission (Jaffrelot 2011, xxv). New administrations sometimes dismantle the policy planning units in a wholesale dismantling of the government apparatus, as occurred in Nepal in the "Panchayat" period beginning in the 1960s and extending through the 1980s (Panday 1989).

The importance of investing in intelligence also is reinforced by the centrality of monitoring and diagnosis for adaptation. Angel (2000, 45) notes:

In the absence of a final plan, the dynamism of self-organizing cities requires the implementation of self-correcting policies that are regularly updated and refined to respond, guide, regulate, and motivate evolving housing markets. To be self-correcting, such policies need accepted norms on the one hand, regular feedback to monitor deviations from these norms on the others, and better explanations on how and why these variations occur.

Undoubtedly, government funding for intelligence has its limits. Yet not all of the "investments" in intelligence require governmental expenditure are financial. An open prescription process that encourages both non-governmental technical input and stakeholder participation can increase the stock of data and knowledge, as well as reduce the discrepancies between government intelligence and other intelligence sources that are less prone to the narrowness and wishful thinking that otherwise might distort government intelligence.

In addition, the pace of the prescription process ought to be timed so as to permit both sufficient technical intelligence and the current political intelligence of the early feedback as to whether the policy is likely to trigger unwanted consequences, more opportunity for the interests of relevant stakeholders, and the consideration of longer-term consequences, to be taken into account. Avoiding hasty enactment, despite the popularity of bold action, may have the additional virtue of preparing stakeholders to adapt their expectations and actions to the new policy context.

II

Conclusions

One of the most disconcerting insights gained in examining the challenges to formulate and enact sound development policies is that often being an expert in the policy process simply is not enough. Lack of expertise *of* the policy process has led experts to endorse an initiative that appears to be well formulated but is distorted in enactment, or to waste their efforts when policymakers are not really interested in listening. Without understanding the importance of linking different policies, experts may ignore the opportunities to avert impasses; without understanding how overly vague or overly rigid laws can distort sound enactment, experts may blame the implementers rather than revising the laws. Without recognizing how implementation may diverge from the intentions of top-level policymakers to minimize avoidable deprivation or destructive conflict, experts may fail to press for modifications in the prescriptions to channel implementation in more humane and conflict-sensitive directions.

SUMMARIZING THE DIAGNOSTIC INDICATORS

As aspiring experts *of* the policy process, development practitioners' most useful asset is the set of indicators that both alert them to potential decision-process malfunctions and their causes, and point to ways to shape policies and institutions. Chapters 3 through 9 identify the dynamics that commonly produce process problems, explaining how particular indicators are useful in diagnosis. A more comprehensive way to alert the development practitioner to risks and opportunities is to aggregate the indicators cited throughout this book, and to remind the reader of the links to relevant dynamics and consequences.

Indicators and Possible Implications

The following is a condensed summary that could be useful if the development practitioner detects a condition or trend that may serve as an indicator of potential problems:

Indicators focusing on the processes of formulating and launching initiatives by top-level policymakers:

1. The **thoroughness of the analysis going into the initiative** may indicate how coherently planners and policymakers have identified goals and/or avoidance of avoidable deprivation.

2. The **thoroughness of analysis conveyed to stakeholders about how farsighted policies can succeed** may indicate the seriousness of policymakers' commitment, the confidence of stakeholders that the initiative will succeed, and/or the degree of support for the initiative.

3. The **degree to which policymakers can convincingly convey their own interest in pursuing farsighted policies** may indicate the seriousness of policymakers' commitment, the confidence of stakeholders that the initiative will succeed, and/or the degree of support for the initiative.

4. The **speed of policy decisions** may indicate overconfidence of policymakers, groupthink, and/or their reactions to political pressures, increasing the risk of problematic initiative design, possibly leading to avoidable deprivations.

5. The **degree of discrepancies between information available to top-level policymakers and lower-level officials** may indicate the tactic of gaining information asymmetry advantage, increasing the risk of poorly designed initiatives.

6. The **discrepancies between government analysis and other analyses,** possibly because government analysts reflect pressures to seem supportive, or because of the assumption that stakeholders will regard the reform as intended, may indicate poorly designed initiatives and/or policymakers' overconfidence insofar as the analysts' assessments underemphasize risks.

7. The **prevalence of rejecting challenging information,** possibly due to confirmation disconfirmation biases, and conflicting external input, may indicate planners' and/or policymakers' overconfidence.

8. The **extent of discrepancies among goal articulations** may reflect mandate differences among implementers and/or external development practitioners.

9. The **shortness of planning horizons** may indicate short-term pressures on policymakers, their pure or strategic impatience, and/or their vulnerability.

10. The **prevalence of short-term targets of initiatives** may indicate pure impatience, short time horizons, and/or political vulnerability, increasing the likelihood of shortsighted initiatives.

11. The **extent of emphasis on intermediate objectives and goal displacement** may indicate pure and/or strategic impatience.

12. The **thinness of discourse about future circumstances** may indicate limited interest in envisioning future conditions and/or addressing problems with short-term sacrifice.

13. The **narrowness of information cited by government planners and policymakers** may indicate disregard for potentially relevant intelligence and higher risk of problematic design of initiatives.

14. The **scarcity of information about the informal sector** may indicate the likelihood of poorly designed initiatives, which may cause avoidable deprivation.

15. The **prevalence of truncated causal analyses of problems** may indicate superficial problem definitions and greater likelihood of pure or strategic impatience.

16. The **extent of concerns voiced about top leaders' commitment, capacity, and/or continuity** may indicate lack of leadership credibility and greater likelihood of strategic impatience.

17. The **extent of discrepancies among levels/causes of problem definitions** may indicate different ideological or disciplinary backgrounds, impeding effective communication and cooperation.

18. The **scarcity of comprehensive appraisal** (qualitative and quantitative as appropriate; covering input, output, and outcome dimensions relevant to the full range of valued outcomes) may indicate limitations in effectively adapting initiatives when necessary.

19. The **prevalence of communications overemphasizing intermediate goals** may indicate excessive impatience.

20. The **prevalence of communications questioning development agencies' motives** may indicate a presumption of ulterior motives and hence distrust of these agencies.

21. The **extent of discrepancies among advice from different external sources** may indicate greater uncertainty and disagreement concerning development doctrines and their use in generating initiatives.

22. The **prevalence of veto actions by other top-level government policymakers** (e.g., the legislature, the courts, autonomous bodies) may reflect "divided government," making impasses more likely.

23. The **degree of non-participation or perception of superficiality of stakeholder participation** may indicate poorly designed initiatives, avoidable deprivations to particular groups, and greater likelihood of destructive conflict.

24. The **degree of failure to transmit stakeholder input to higher policy-making levels** may indicate unresponsiveness to stakeholder needs and wants, greater risk of avoidable deprivations, and/or greater risk of destructive conflict.

25. The **extent of hostile government rhetoric against stakeholder groups** may indicate polarization between government leaders and stakeholder groups, possibly to mobilize efforts to justify harsh treatment of targeted stakeholders.

26. The **general prevalence of budgetary incrementalism** may indicate an unwillingness to finance major new initiatives adequately.

27. The **degree of restructuring of top-level policymaking units (e.g., ministries)** may indicate greater risk of premature program or project termination and/or emasculation.

28. The **prevalence of policymakers' efforts to alter processes or to shift arenas** may indicate the capacity to overcome impasses through venue shifting.

29. The **degree of narrowness of targets and considerations specified in the initiative** may indicate incoherence of goal identification by planners and/or policymakers, and/or the policymakers' tactic of restriction by partial incorporation.

30. The **extent of isolation of policymaking on linkable issues** may indicate non-integrated policy venues, possibly increasing the likelihood of impasses and/or the inability to minimize avoidable deprivation.

31. The **prevalence of leaders' communications emphasizing their toughmindedness** may indicate leaders' unwillingness to compromise; hence greater likelihood of impasses.

32. The **extent of irregular turnover of government leadership** may indicate high levels of inter-group conflict, incomplete or distorted implementation, and/or political vulnerability leading to short-sighted initiatives.

33. The **prevalence of sharp ideological differences among government entities** may indicate higher levels of intragovernmental opposition and incomplete or distorted implementation.

34. The **chief executive's lack of a legislative majority** may indicate intragovernmental opposition.

Indicators focusing on the content of initiatives launched by top-level policymakers:

1. The **discrepancies between the ambition of initiative goals and external assessments** may indicate problematic initiative design, due to overconfidence of policymakers, and/or resistance to external advice.

2. The **narrowness of policy provisions of potentially multi-issue initiatives** may indicate non-integrated policy venues, lack of side-payment mechanisms; hence lower likelihood to mitigate or compensate to reduce deprivations and/or impasses.

3. The **discrepancies between budgeted and actual outlays for programs and projects** may indicate the differences between formal and effective prescriptions and/or administrative weaknesses.

4. The **degree of restructuring of administrative units** may indicate a greater risk of premature program or project termination and/or emasculation.

5. The **complexity of an initiative's provisions** may indicate greater difficulties in the coherence of the measures and/or the coordination of implementation.

6. The **indirectness of metrics embedded in the initiative and pronouncements about it** may reflect lack of commitment.

7. The **degree of regulatory proliferation** may indicate greater likelihood of rent-seeking, the political tactic of undermining certain stakeholders through onerous regulations, and/or incomplete or distorted implementation by overtaxed regulatory agencies.

8. The **extent of unrealistically stringent regulations** may reflect lack of commitment and/or higher likelihood of incomplete or distorted implementation.

9. The **degree of the initiative's inconsistency with policymakers' and core supporters' ideology** may reflect lack of commitment and/or higher likelihood of incomplete or distorted implementation.

10. The **extent of unwillingness to punish lower-level officials for not enacting initiatives** may indicate lack of commitment, and/or higher likelihood of incomplete or distorted implementation.

11. The **discrepancies between the required and actual budget for full enactment of the program or project** may indicate incomplete enactment; possibly reflecting the policymakers' tactic of restriction by partial incorporation; possibly reflecting budgetary incrementalism that may reduce inter-agency conflict but limits the capacity to finance new initiatives.

12. The **degree of vagueness of policymakers' formal initiatives (breadth and multiplicity of interpretation of prescriptions)** may

indicate intelligence too weak to develop specific measures, opportunities for favoritism, reducing accountability due to vague goals and targets, and/or the tactic of restriction by partial incorporation through nonspecific provisions that limit their application; all risking distorted enactment.

13. The **definitiveness of language promoting the initiative** may indicate policymakers' overconfidence.

14. The **extent of unwillingness to embed the initiative within broader programs or agreements** may indicate lack of commitment.

15. The **extent of unwillingness to enter into external commitments** may indicate lack of commitment, and/or greater need to renege on the commitment.

Indicators focusing on implementation issues:

1. The **degree of excessive rigidity of policymakers' formal initiatives** may indicate concern over implementers' discretion and/or resistance, increasing the risk of distorted enactment.

2. The **volume and seriousness of unprosecuted regulatory violations** may indicate the discrepancy between formal and effective regulation.

3. The **degree of discrepancies among problem definitions expressed by different agencies** may indicate lack of coordination among implementers.

4. The **prevalence of communications of contrasting ideological positions by different agencies** may indicate ideological differences among implementers, increasing the likelihood of incomplete or distorted implementation.

5. The **history of inter-agency conflict (e.g., reports of inter-agency non-cooperation)** may indicate inter-agency rivalry for resources, jurisdiction, and/or standing, increasing the risk of impasses or incomplete and/or distorted enactment of initiatives.

6. The **extent to which agencies were established and staffed by different administrations** may indicate higher likelihood of inter-agency conflict.

7. The **paucity of communication among agencies with connected responsibilities** may indicate inter-agency rivalry, dysfunctional agency isolation, and/or incomplete or distorted implementation.

8. The **degree of willingness of agencies to withhold information from other agencies** may indicate inter-agency rivalry; all increasing the risk of impasses or distorted implementation.

9. The **extent of complexity of agency mandates** may indicate conflicting goals, lower accountability, and/or jurisdictional conflicts with other agencies.

10. The **prevalence of veto actions by implementing agencies** may indicate jurisdictional conflicts, and/or implementers hired by previous administrations, and/or disagreements between national and subnational policymakers.

11. The **discrepancies between overall administrative budgets and benchmarked administrative budgetary needs** may indicate incomplete and/or distorted enactment.

12. The **degree of top leaders' past incursions against the prerogatives of formally autonomous agencies** may indicate the lack of definitiveness of formally autonomous agencies.

13. The **extent of failures to enact feasible provisions of initiatives** may indicate administrators' disagreement with initiatives' goals and/or consequences.

14. The **prevalence of communications disparaging other agencies** may indicate inter-agency rivalries and/or status resentment of staff of one agency vis-à-vis others; both increasing the risk of impasses or distorted implementation.

15. The **volatility of budget allocations among agencies** may indicate high levels of budgetary competition and hence inter-agency conflict.

16. The **degree of uncertainty and/or overlap of agency mandates** may indicate higher likelihood of impasses and/or incomplete or distorted implementation, due to agency polarization and/or jurisdictional uncertainty.

17. The **degree of differences of interests of stakeholder groups served by different agencies** may indicate impasses and/or destructive conflict due to inter-group polarization; it may also indicate inter-agency conflict based on the need to serve different constituencies, which in turn may cause incomplete or distorted enactment of initiatives.

18. The **degree of social isolation of implementers (ethnic differences between administrators and local stakeholders; narrowness of contact with local stakeholders)** may indicate limited responsiveness to stakeholders' needs and wants, increasing the likelihood of distorted implementation, avoidable deprivations and destructive conflict.

19. The **low levels of bureaucratic salaries compared to benchmarks** may indicate restriction through partial incorporation, greater temptation

of bureaucratic corruption, increasing the likelihood of distorted or incomplete enactment, avoidable stakeholder deprivations, selfish violations of the agent's responsibility, and/or destructive conflict.

20. The **extent of prosecutions for bureaucratic corruption** may indicate the degree of such corruption (although it may also indicate ongoing and successful anticorruption initiatives, for political tactics against opponents); higher likelihood of selfishness and agents' neglect of responsibility to pursue farsighted objectives.

21. The **prevalence of weak punishments for shortsighted administrative decisions** may indicate weak monitoring and sanctions against selfish shortsighted decisions.

22. The **degree of overlap between political divisions and the targets of prosecution** may indicate the strength of the government leaders' motive to emasculate political opposition, and/or the likelihood of destructive conflict.

23. The **degree of inconsistency of invocation outcomes across similar contexts** may indicate invocation problems with the administrative and/or court systems.

24. The **degree of intractability of conflict over invocation outcomes** may indicate invocation problems with the administrative and/or court systems.

Indicators focusing on stakeholder or political groups:

1. The **degree of divergence of expectations among stakeholders** may indicate greater likelihood of impasses.

2. The **extent of discrepancies in analyses and projections available to stakeholders** may indicate high uncertainty, possibly increasing the likelihood of unwillingness to support or acquiesce to initiatives.

3. The **extent of conflict among group interests** may indicate higher divergence of stakeholders' perceived interests, higher likelihood of impasses, and/or destructive inter-group conflict.

4. The **extremeness of group demands** may indicate either polarization of perceived interests and/or general group relations or the negotiating strategy of taking extreme positions; all could lead to impasses.

5. The **extent of communications projecting fears of future initiatives due to passage of the current initiative** may indicate a greater likelihood of impasses.

6. The **sparseness of communication of stakeholder preferences** may indicate fear of triggering government retribution, and therefore lack of opportunity to avoid avoidable harm.

7. The **extent of stakeholder communications denouncing government favoritism toward other groups** may indicate inter-group polarization and a higher likelihood of destructive inter-group conflict.

8. The **difference in intensity of current rhetoric and past outcomes of negotiations** may indicate how far apart negotiators' actual positions are.

9. The **degree of differences in defining and using key symbols** may indicate the potential for disruptive policy disagreements.

10. The **degree to which policy issues are heavily emotional and symbolic to stakeholders** may indicate a higher likelihood of impasses and/or destructive inter-group conflict.

11. The **degree to which stakeholders denounce constitutive policymaing arrangements** may indicate greater likelihood of impasses and/or destructive conflict.

12. The **degree of disparaging communications about other groups** may indicate higher likelihood of ethnic or religious antagonism, destructive violence, and/or policy impasses.

13. The **degree of communications conveying polarized ideologies and critiques of other groups' positions** may indicate higher likelihood inter-group polarization, of destructive violence, and/or policy impasses.

14. The **degree of fear of future deprivations communicated by particular stakeholder groups** may indicate concern that current policy initiatives presage harsher initiatives.

15. The **shortness of stakeholders' planning horizons** may indicate their pure or strategic impatience, and/or their vulnerability.

16. The **degree of economic or political role overlap** may indicate severe economic or political competition, possibly increasing the likelihood of sufficient feelings of threat to provoke aggressive actions.

17. The **degree of close group proximity, for example, through recent migration,** may indicate cultural clashes and/or economic or political competition.

18. The extent of **communications that others are allied with the government** may indicate the belief that the government favors these other groups, increasing the likelihood of aggressive confrontations with other groups and the government.

19. The **degree of stakeholders' socioeconomic marginality** may indicate socioeconomic vulnerability that increases the likelihood of strategic impatience.

20. The **prevalence of communications calling for broad punishment of other groups** may indicate collective guilt attribution and the impulse to vicarious retribution.

21. The **degree of disparaging communications about other political parties or factions** may indicate partisan motives to disrupt initiatives.

22. The **extent of communications negatively over-simplifying out-group characteristics, including exploitative roles,** may indicate stereotyping and endorsement of collective culpability; hence increasing the likelihood of destructive inter-group conflict.

23. The **degree of discrepancies between government appraisals and other appraisals** may indicate partisan motivations to undermine the government's popularity through inappropriately negative appraisal, perhaps exacerbated by withholding appraisal information.

24. **Low levels of communication from stakeholders regarding initiatives,** possibly due to fears of government retaliation, may indicate inadequate intelligence resulting in poorly designed, hence higher risk, initiatives.

25. The **degree of provocateurs' mobilization success** may indicate a high risk of highly- resourced provocateurs to mobilize inter-group violence, violence against the government, and/or government action against the mobilized groups.

26. The **prevalence of demonstrations against government measures** may indicate stakeholder resistance, distrust, and/or assessment of deprivation.

Indicators focusing on relations between national and subnational governments:

1. The **degree of discrepancies between the goals of national policy-makers and the subnational decisions** may indicate conflicts of objectives among levels.

2. The **degree of overlap and/or inconsistencies of mandates of national and subnational governments** may indicate jurisdictional uncertainty due to decentralization.

3. The **degree of scarcity of information held by subnational government officials shared with national government** may indicate conflict between the governmental levels.

4. The **differences in political affiliations of top-level national and subnational officials** may indicate a potential for subnational resistance to national initiatives.

5. The **importance of the central government's motive to shed costs** may indicate a higher risk of ineffective decentralization.

6. The **degree of political and ideological differences between natural and subnational leaders** may indicate greater risk of conflict, ineffectiveness of decentralized government performance, and/or constitutive crisis.

The key term in each of the above entries is "may indicate" – emphasizing the fact that indicators of this sort point to possibilities, not certainties.

FINAL THOUGHTS

All of the considerations outlined in this book indicate that successful development policies, programs, and projects require not only carefully designed content, but also awareness of how the decision process works and what challenges it faces. Initiatives that look good on the desk of the planner are often derailed or distorted as they go through the steps from idea to reality. If they are aware of these challenges, development practitioners, whether in or out of government, whether domestic or foreign, can play crucial, constructive roles in shaping both policy initiatives and policy processes. The question is whether they can take full advantage of the tools available to avert pitfalls, to adopt optimal procedural tactics, or to press for improved policymaking institutions. Sensitivity to the challenges, and awareness of useful indicators, are not enough; knowing what questions to ask is not the same as being able to answer them. The indicators offered throughout the book, and summarized in this chapter, probably come close to being comprehensive in pointing to the questions that must be answered to diagnose risks and opportunities. Yet, some of the answers require considerable effort to understand the perspectives not only of policymakers at various levels, but of stakeholders as well. Some of the indicators (e.g., the extent of prosecutions for bureaucratic corruption) may have opposite implications (e.g., either rising corruption, or successful anticorruption initiatives through more intensive prosecutions). In short, the questions are designed to direct deeper examination, often with the help of informants who are closer to the context.

References

African Economic Outlook 2012. African Development Bank. www.african economicoutlook.org.

Agrawal, Arun, and Jesse Ribot. 2006. Recentralizing while decentralizing. In David Cameron, Gustav Ranis, and Annalisa Zinn, eds., *Globalization and Self-Determination: Is the Nation-State under Siege?* London: Routledge, pp. 301–332.

Ahsan, Muhammad. 2003. An analytical review of Pakistan's educational policies and plans. *Research Papers in Education* 18(3): 259–280.

Akhtari, Mitra, Diana Moreira, and Laura Trucco. 2015. *Political turnover, bureaucratic turnover, and the quality of public services.* Harvard University Working Paper. http://scholar.harvard.edu/files/makhtari/files/akh tari_moreira_trucco_dec_27.pdf

Al Ramiah, Ananthi, Miles Hewstone, and Katharina Schmid. 2011. Social identity and intergroup conflict. *Psychological Studies* 56(1): 44–52.

Alderman, Harold, and Ruslan Yemtsov. 2013. How can safety nets contribute to economic growth? *World Bank Economic Review* 28(1): 1–20.

Alston, Lee, Marcus André Melo, Bernardo Mueller, and Carlos Pereira. 2004. *Political Institutions, Policymaking Processes and Policy Outcomes in Brazil.* Washington, DC: Inter-American Development Bank.

Amon, Joseph, Richard Pearshouse, Jane Cohen, and Rebecca Schleifer. 2013. Compulsory drug detention centers in China, Cambodia, Vietnam, and Laos: Health and human rights abuses. *Health and Human Rights* 15(2): 124–37.

Andersson, Krister, Clark Gibson, and Fabrice Lehoucq. 2004. The politics of decentralized natural resource governance. *Political Science and Politics* 37 (3): 421–426.

Andrews, Matthew, and Anwar Shah. 2003. Citizen-centered governance: A new approach to public sector reform. In Anwar Shah, ed., *Bringing Civility in Governance* 3. Washington, DC: World Bank.

Angel, Shlomo. 2000. *Housing Policy Matters: A Global Analysis.* New York: Oxford University Press.

Anisimova, Alla, and Ol'ga Echevskaya. 2012. Sibirskaya identichnost' kak politicheskoye vyskazyvaniiye (Siberian identity as a political proclamation). *Pro et Contra* May–June: 66–75.

Anyaegbunam, Chike, Paolo Mefalopulos, and Titus Moetsabi. 2004. *Participatory Rural Communication Appraisal: Starting with the People: A Handbook*. Rome: United Nations Food and Agriculture Organization.

Araral, Eduardo. 2014. Policy and regulatory design for developing countries: a mechanism design and transaction cost approach. *Policy Sciences* 47(3): 289–303.

Aresti, Maria. 2016. *Oil and Gas Revenue Sharing in Bolivia*. New York: Natural Resource Governance Institute, May. www.resourcegovernance.org/analysis-tools/publications/revenue-sharing-case-study-oil-and-gas-revenue-sharing-bolivia

Ascher, William. 1999. *Why Governments Waste Natural Resources: Policy Failures in Developing Countries*. Baltimore: Johns Hopkins University Press.
    2009. *Bringing in the Future: Strategies for Farsightedness and Sustainability in Developing Countries*, Chicago: University of Chicago Press.

Ascher, William, and Natalia Mirovitskaya. 2015. *Development Strategies and Inter-Group Violence: Insights on Conflict-Sensitive Development*. New York: Palgrave Macmillan.

Auer, Peter, and Natalia Popova. 2003. *Labour market policy for restructuring in Turkey: The need for more active policies*. International Labour Office Employment Paper 51. Geneva: International Labour Office.

Augoustinos, Martha, and Iain Walker. 1998. The construction of stereotypes within social psychology from social cognition to ideology. *Theory & Psychology* 8(5): 629–652.

Bagaka, Obuya. 2008. Fiscal decentralization in Kenya: The constituency development fund and the growth of government. Proceedings of Twentieth Annual Conference of the Association for Budgeting and Financial Management, Chicago.

Bagde, Surendrakumar, Dennis Epple, and Lowell Taylor. 2016. Does affirmative action work? Caste, gender, college quality, and academic success in India. *American Economic Review* 106(6): 1495–1521.

Bardach, Eugene. 1981. Problems of problem definitions in policy analysis. In John Crecine, ed., *Research in Public Policy Analysis and Management*. Vol. 1. Greenwich, CT: JAI Press, pp. 161–171.

Bardhan, Pranab. 2002. Decentralization of governance and development. *Journal of Economic Perspectives* 16(4):185–205.

Barrientos, Armando. 2012. Social transfers and growth: What do we know? What do we need to find out? *World Development* 40(1): 11–20.
    2013. *Social Assistance in Developing Countries*. Cambridge: Cambridge University Press.

Basdeo, M. Vinesh, and Omphemetse S. Sibanda. 2013. The dilemma of unfunded mandates for local government in South Africa. In Conference Proceedings Published by the South African Association of Public Administration and Management (SAAPAM). Pretoria, South Africa: Tshwane University of Technology.

Batkin, Andy, Nick Chapman, Jurrien Toonen, Maheen Sultan, and Muriel Visser. 2006. *Evaluation of DFID Country Programmes: Country Study: Bangladesh 2000–2005*. London: United Kingdom Department of International Development, May.

Baud, Isa, Michaela Hordijk, Paul van Lindert, Gery Nijenhuis, and Guus van Westen. 2010. *Towards Improved Local Governance Through Strengthened Local Government: Evaluation of the LOGO South Programme 2007–2010*. The Hague: VNG-International.

Beh, LooSee. 2007. The politics of administrative reform: Malaysia and China in perspective. In Émile Kok-Kheng Yeoh and Evelyn Devadason, eds., *Emerging Trading Nation in an Integrating World: Global Impacts and Domestic Challenges of China's Economic Reform*. Kuala Lumpur: Institute of China Studies, University of Malaya, pp. 197–232.

Benmaamar, Mustapha. 2006. *Financing of road maintenance in Sub-Saharan Africa: Reforms and progress towards second generation road funds*. Sub-Saharan Africa Transport Policy Program. No. 6. RMF Series Discussion Paper. Washington, DC: World Bank.

Benton, Allyson. 2009. What makes strong federalism seem weak? Fiscal resources and presidential–provincial relations in Argentina. *Publius: The Journal of Federalism* 39(4): 651–676.

Bercovitch, Jacob, Victor Kremenyuk, and William Zartman, eds. 2008. *Sage Handbook of Conflict Resolution*. London: Sage.

Berger, Stefan, and Hugh Compston, eds. 2002. *Policy Concertation and Social Partnership in Western Europe*. New York: Berghan Books.

Bhadra, Gautam. 1988. *The mentality of subalternity: kantanama or rajdharma*. CSSSC Occasional Paper No. 104. Calcutta: Centre for Studies in Social Sciences.

Bharadwaj, Prashant, Leah Lakdawala, and Nicholas Li. 2013. *Perverse Consequences of Well Intentioned Regulation: Evidence from India's Child Labor Ban. No. w19602.* Cambridge, MA: National Bureau of Economic Research.

Biglaiser, Glen, and David Brown. 2005. The determinants of economic liberalization in Latin America. *Political Research Quarterly* 58(4): 671–680.

Bird, Richard, and Pierre-Pascal Gendron. 2006. *Is VAT the best way to impose a general consumption tax in developing countries?* Andrew Young School of Public Policy International Studies Program Working Paper 06–17. Atlanta: University of Georgia.

Bird, Richard, Jorge Martínez Vázquez, and Benno Torgler. 2008. Tax effort in developing countries and high income countries: The impact of corruption, voice and accountability. *Economic Analysis and Policy* 38(1): 55–71.

Blake, Charles. 1996. The politics of inflation-fighting in new democracies, *Studies in Comparative International Development* 31(2): 37–57.

Boonyarattanasoontorn, Jaturong. 2006. Do poverty alleviation policies contribute to the welfare of poor people in rural communities? A case study of six villages in chiang rai province. *Thammasat Review* 11(1): 87–114.

Borras, Saturnino, and Jennifer Franco. 2010. Contemporary discourses and contestations around pro-poor land policies and land governance. *Journal of Agrarian Change* 10(1): 1–32.

Boughton, James. 2003. *Who's in Charge? Ownership and Conditionality in IMF-Supported Programs*. Washington, DC: International Monetary Fund.

Bradley, John R., 2007. Iran's ethnic tinderbox. *The Washington Quarterly* 30(1): 181–190.

Brandon, Anthony. 2014. *Review of international protected area management effectiveness (PAME) experience*. Report for the Association for Water and Rural Development (AWARD) [USAID / RESILIM / AID-674-A-13–00008], October 21.

Bräutigam, Deborah. 2004. The people's budget? Politics, participation and pro-poor policy. *Development Policy Review* 22(6): 653–668.

Brewer, Garry D., and Ronald D. Brunner. 1975. *Political Development and Change: A Policy Approach*. Chicago: Free Press.

Brewer, Garry D., and Peter deLeon. 1983. *The Foundations of Policy Analysis*. Pacific Grove, CA: Brooks/Cole.

Brömmelhörster, Jörn, and Wolf-Christian Paes, eds. 2003. *The Military as an Economic Actor: Soldiers in Business*. London: Palgrave Macmillan.

Broussard, Nzinga. 2013. Ethiopia: Averting violence through its quest for growth. In William Ascher and Natalia Mirovitskaya, eds., *The Economic Roots of Conflict and Cooperation in Africa*. New York: Palgrave Macmillan, pp. 85–106.

Brouwer, Stijn. 2015. *Policy Entrepreneurs in Water Governance*. Basel: Springer International Publishing, 2015.

Brown, Graham, Frances Stewart, and Arnim Langer. 2007. *The implications of horizontal inequality for aid*. World Institute for Development Economics Research Paper. United Nations University,

Brunner, Ronald, and Amanda Lynch. 2010. *Adaptive Governance and Climate Change*. Boston, MA: American Meteorological Society.

Brunner, Ronald, Toddi Steelman, Lindy Coe-Juell, Christina Cromley, Christine Edwards, and Donna Tucker, eds. 2005. *Adaptive Governance: Integrating Science, Policy, and Decision Making*. New York: Columbia University Press.

Brussets Emily, Birthe Nautrup, Yulia Immajati, and Susanne B. Pedersen. 2004. Assistance to Internally Displaced Persons (IDPs) in Indonesia. Sida Evaluation 04/27. Department for Co-operation with Non-governmental Organisations and Humanitarian Assistance. www.oecd.org/dataoecd/29/23/35223588.pdf

Caiden, Naomi, and Aaron Wildavsky. 1980. *Planning and Budgeting in Poor Countries*. New Brunswick, NJ: Transaction Publishers.

Carvalho, Ernani, and Natalia Leitao de Melo. 2012. Brazilian public prosecution office and independence. Paper presented at the American Political Science Association, New Orleans.

Cernea, Michael. 2003. For a new economics of resettlement: A sociological critique of the compensation principle. *International Social Science Journal* 55(175): 37–45.

2007. Financing for development: Benefit-sharing mechanisms in population resettlement. *Economic and Political Weekly* 42(12): 1033–1046.

Céspedes, Luís, Eric Parrado, and Andrés Velasco. 2014. Fiscal rules and the management of natural resource revenues: The case of Chile. *Annual Reviews Resource Economics* 6(1): 105–132.

Chandavarkar, Rajnarayan. 2007. Customs of governance: Colonialism and democracy in twentieth century India. *Modern Asian Studies* 41(3): 441–470.

Chandoevit, Worawan. 2010. What Thais want from welfare state. *Thai-ASEAN News Network*. June 24. https://archive.li/Ao6xV.

Chanmorchan, Proudfong, Teppawan Pornwalai, Christina Popivanova, and Nard Huijbregts. 2015. *Thailand's Child Support Grant Programme*. Bangkok: UNICEF and the Thailand Development Research Institute.

Chauvel, Richard. 2011. Policy failure and political impasse: Papua and Jakarta a decade after the "Papuan Spring." In Peter King, Jim Elmslie, and Camellia Webb-Gannon, eds., *Comprehending West Papua*. Sydney: University of Sidney Centre for Peace and Conflict Studies, pp. 105–146.

Cheema, G. Shabbir, and A. Dennis Rondinelli, eds. 2007. *Decentralizing Governance: Emerging Concepts and Practices*. Washington, DC: Brookings Institution Press.

Cheikhrouhou, Hela, W. Britt Gwinner, John Pollner, Emanuel Salinas, Sophie Sirtaine, and Dimitri Vittas. 2007. *Structured Finance in Latin America*. Washington, DC: World Bank.

Chin, James. 2011. History and context of public administration in Malaysia. In Evan Berman, ed., *Public Administration in Southeast Asia: Thailand, Philippines, Malaysia, Hong Kong, and Macao*. Boca Raton, FL: CRC Press, pp. 141–154.

Chomba, Geoffrey, Green Mbozi, David Mundia, Mike Simpamba, Billy Mwiinga, Cynthia Donovan, and Stanely Mushingwani. 2002. Improving the transfer and use of agricultural market information in Zambia: A user needs assessment. Food Security Research Project Working Paper 6. www.aec.msu.edu/agecon/fs2/zambia/index.htm.

Clark, Susan G. 2011. *The Policy Process: A Practical Guide for Natural Resource Professionals*. New Haven, CT: Yale University Press.

Cohen, John. 1987. *Integrated Rural Development: The Ethiopian Experience and the Debate*. Uppsala: Scandinavian Institute of African Studies.

Commission for the Implementation of the Constitution (Kenya). 2011. *Second quarterly report on the implementation of the Constitution*. Nairobi: Commission for the Implementation of the Constitution.

Commission on Legal Empowerment of the Poor. 2008. *Making the Law Work for Everyone*. New York: UN Development Programme.

Contreras-Hermosilla, Arnoldo. 2003. Barriers to legality in the forest sectors of Honduras and Nicaragua. Consultancy report. www.talailegal-centroamerica.org. https://scholar.google.com/scholar?as_q=&as_epq=+Barriers+to+legality+in+the+forest+sectors+of+Honduras+and+Nicaragua+&as_oq=&as_eq=&as_occt=any&as_sauthors=&as_publication=&as_ylo=&as_yhi=&btnG=&hl=en&as_sdt=0%2C14.

Cordes, Till, Tidiane Kinda, Priscilla S. Muthoora, and Anke Weber. 2015. *Expenditure rules: Effective tools for sound fiscal policy?* IMF Working Paper No. 15–29. Washington, DC: International Monetary Fund.

Cornell, Agnes. 2014. Why bureaucratic stability matters for the implementation of democratic governance programs, *Governance* 27(2): 191–214.

Cordova, Efrén. 1987. Social concertation in Latin America. *Labour and Society* 12(3): 409–423.

Cororaton, Caesar, and Erwin Corong. 2009. *Philippine Agricultural and Food Policies: Implications for Poverty and Income Distribution.* Washington, DC: International Food Policy Institute.

Correa, Diego, and José Antonio Cheibub. 2015. The anti-incumbent effects of conditional cash transfer programs, *Latin American Politics & Society* 58(1): 49–71.

Dahana, Abdullah. 1997. Comments. In Leo Survadinata, ed. *Ethnic Chinese as Southeast Asians.* London: Palgrave Macmillan, pp. 66–72.

Darkoh, Michael, and Joseph Mbaiwa. 2002. Globalisation and the Livestock Industry in Botswana, *Singapore Journal of Tropical Geography* 23(2): 149–166.

Daseking, Christina, Atish Ghosh, Timothy Lane, and Alan Thomas. 2004. *Lessons from the Crisis in Argentina.* IMF Occasional Paper 236. Washington, DC: International Monetary Fund.

Davin, Thomas. 2016. Child support grant proves essential. *Bangkok Post* March 4. www.google.com/#q=%22Child+Support+Grant+Programme%22+thailand.

Davis, Lucas. 2014. The economic cost of global fuel subsidies. *American Economic Review, Papers and Proceedings* 104 (5): 581–585.

Dawis, Aimee. 2009. *The Chinese of Indonesia and Their Search for Identity.* Amherst, NY: Cambria Press.

De Brauw, Alan and John Hoddinott. 2011. Must conditional cash transfer programs be conditional to be effective? The impact of conditioning transfers on school enrollment in Mexico. *Journal of Development Economics* 96(2): 359–370.

De Janvry, Alain. 2010. Agriculture for development: New paradigm and options for success. *Agricultural Economics* 41(suppl 1): 17–36.

De Janvry, Alain, and Elisabeth Sadoulet. 2010. Agriculture for development in Africa: Business-as-usual or new departures? *Journal of African Economies* 19.suppl 2: ii7–ii39.

De Oliveira, Francisco, Eduardo Barreto, and Kaizô Beltrão. 2001. Brazil: The Brazilian social security system. *International Social Security Review* 54(1): 101–112.

DeBono, Kenneth. 1987. Investigating the social-adjustive and value-expressive functions of attitudes: Implications for persuasion processes. *Journal of Personality and Social Psychology* 52(2):279–287.

Del Granado, Francisco Javier Arze, David Coady, and Robert Gillingham. 2012. The unequal benefits of fuel subsidies: A review of evidence for developing countries. *World Development* 40 (11): 2234–2248.

Denson, Thomas F., Brian Lickel, Mathew Curtis, Douglas M. Stenstrom, and Daniel R. Ames. 2006. The roles of entitativity and essentiality in judgments of collective responsibility. *Group Processes & Intergroup Relations* 9(1): 43–61.

Dery, David. 2000. Agenda setting and problem identification. *Policy Studies* 21 (1): 37–47.

Development Partners Working Group on Decentralization and Local Governance. 2011. *Busan and Beyond: Localizing Paris Principles for More Effective Support to Decentralization and Local Governance Reforms.* Bonn:

DeLoG Secretariat, GIZ. www.delog.org/cms/upload/pdf/DeLoG_Busan_ and_beyond.pdf.

Dim, N. U., Okorocha, K A., and Okoduwa V. O. 2016. Project failure in the Nigerian construction industry: Cases of highway construction projects by the Nigerian Federal Ministry of Works. *Project Journal.* https://projectjournal.co .uk/2016/04/01/has-nigeria-become-the-worlds-junk-yard-of-abandoned-and-failed-mega-projects-worth-billions/.

Dixon, Annette. 2009. *Financial and Social Protection in Thailand. World Bank Workshop.* Washington, DC: World Bank. September 11. www.worldbank .or.th/WBSITE/EXTERNAL/COUNTRIES/EASTASIAPACIFICEXT/THAIL ANDEXTN/0,,contentMDK:22317568~menuPK:50003484~pagePK:2865 066~piPK:2865079~theSitePK:333296,00.html?cid=EXTEAPMonth1.

Domingo, Maria Oliva, and Danilo R. Reyes. Performance management reforms in the Philippines. In Evan Berman, ed., *Public Administration in Southeast Asia: Thailand, Philippines, Malaysia, Hong Kong, and Macao.* Boca Raton, FL: CRC Press, pp. 397–428.

Drazen, Allan. 2002. Conditionality and ownership in IMF lending: A political economy approach, *IMF Economic Review* 49(1): 36–67.

2008. Is there a different political economy for developing countries? Issues, perspectives, and methodology, *Journal of African Economies* 17(suppl 1): 18–71.

Dreher, Axel. 2006. IMF and economic growth: The effects of programs, loans, and compliance with conditionality. *World Development* 34(5): 769–788.

2009. IMF conditionality: theory and evidence. *Public Choice* 141(1–2): 233–267.

Dressel, Björn. 2010. Judicialization of politics or politicization of the judiciary? Considerations from recent events in Thailand. *The Pacific Review* 23(5): 671–691.

Dunning, David, Dale W. Griffin, James D. Milojkovic, and Lee Ross. 1990. The overconfidence effect in social prediction. *Journal of Personality and Social Psychology* 58(4): 568.

East African Magazine. 2006. Doubts over cassava project. September 11, 2006. www.nationmedia.com/eastafrican/current/Magazine/Magazine110920062 .htm.

Eaton, Kent. 2003. Can politicians control bureaucrats? Applying theories of political control to Argentina's democracy. *Latin American Politics and Society* 45(4): 33–62.

Eaton, Kent, Kai Kaiser, and Paul Smoke. 2011. *The Political Economy of Decentralization Reforms in Developing Countries: Implications for Aid Effectiveness.* Washington, DC: World Bank.

Ebel, Robert, and François Vaillancourt. 2001. Fiscal decentralization and financing urban governments: Framing the problem. In Mila Freire and Richard Stren, eds., *The Challenge of Urban Government Policies and Practices.* Washington, DC: World Bank, pp. 155–170.

Edwards, Kari, and Edward E. Smith. 1996. A disconfirmation bias in the evaluation of arguments. *Journal of Personality and Social Psychology* 71(1):5–24.

Eisenhardt, Kathleen. 1989. Agency theory: An assessment and review. *The Academy of Management Review* 14(1): 57–74.

Elizondo, Carlos. 2011. *Stuck in the Mud: The Politics of Constitutional Reform in the Oil Sector in Mexico*. Houston: James A. Baker III Institute for Public Policy.

Erikson, Robert S. 2007. Does public ignorance matter? *Critical Review* 19(1): 23–34.

Estache, Antonio, and Danny Leipziger. 2009. Fiscal policy, distribution, and the middle class, in Antonio Estache and Danny Leipziger, eds., *Stuck in the Middle: Is Fiscal Policy Failing the Middle Class?* Washington, DC: Brookings Institution Press.

ETH Zürich. 2016. *EPR Atlas: Kenya*. Zürich: ETH Zürich. https://growup.ethz .ch/atlas/Kenya.

European Commission. 2007. *Supporting decentralization and local governance in third world countries*. Reference document 2. Brussels: European Commission.

Ezrow, Natasha. 2011. *The Importance of Parties and Party System Institutionalization in New Democracies*. Essex, UK: University of Essex Institute for Democracy & Conflict Resolution Briefing Paper (IDCR-BP-06/11) file:///C:/ Users/wascher/AppData/Local/Temp/06_11.pdf.

Farole, Thomas. 2011. *Special Economic Zones in Africa: Comparing Performance and Learning from Global Experience*. Washington, DC: World Bank.

Fearnside, Philip. 2016. Environmental policy in Brazilian Amazonia: Lessons from recent history. *Novos Cadernos* 19(1): 27–46.

Festré, Agnès, and Pierre Garrouste. 2015. Theory and evidence in psychology and economics about motivation crowding out: A possible convergence?. *Journal of Economic Surveys* 29(2): 339–356.

Findley, Roger W. 1988. Pollution control in Brazil. *Ecology Law Quarterly* 15 (1): 1–68.

Fischer, Frank, and Gerald J. Miller, eds. 2006. *Handbook of Public Policy Analysis: Theory, Politics, and Methods*. Boca Raton, FL: CRC Press.

Fiszbein, Ariel, Norbert Schady, and Francisco HG Ferreira. 2009. *Conditional Cash Transfers: Reducing Present and Future Poverty*. Washington, DC: World Bank.

Flanigan, Shawn Teresa, and Cheryl O'brien. 2015. Service-seeking behavior, perceptions of armed actors, and preferences regarding governance: Evidence from the Palestinian Territories. *Studies in Conflict & Terrorism* 38(8): 622–651.

Flyvbjerg, Bent, Massimo Garbuio, and Dan Lovallo. 2009. Delusion and deception in large infrastructure projects: Two models for explaining and preventing executive disaster. *California Management Review* 51(2): 170–193.

Flyvbjerg, Bent, Mette Holm, and Søren Buhl. 2005. How (in)accurate are demand forecasts in public works projects?: The case of transportation. *Journal of the American Planning Association* 71 (2): 131–146.

Franceschet, Susan. 2010. Explaining domestic violence policy outcomes in Chile and Argentina. *Latin American Politics and Society* 52(3): 1–29.

Franceschet, Susan, and Jennifer Piscopo. 2013. Federalism, decentralization, and reproductive rights in Argentina and Chile. *Publius: The Journal of Federalism* 43(1): 129–150.

Frank, Jonah. 2010. *Towards a Fiscal Pact: The Political Economy of Decentralization in Bolivia*. Washington, DC: World Bank.

Frederick, Shane, George Loewenstein, and Ted O'Donoghue. 2002. Time discounting and time preference: A critical review. *Journal of Economic Literature* 40:351–401.

Frey, Dieter. 1986. Recent research on selective exposure to information. In Leonard Berkowitz, ed. *Advances in Experimental Social Psychology*, vol. 19. New York: Academic Press, pp. 41–80.

Friedrich, Carl J. 1941. *Constitutional Government and Democracy*. Boston: Little, Brown and Company.

Fyfe, Alec. 2007. *The Use of Contract Teachers in Developing Countries: Trends and Impact*. Geneva: International Labour Office.

Giacchino, Stephen. 2003. Bridging the politico-administrative divide. Doctor of Business Administration thesis, Cranfield University School of Management, March.

Gillis, Malcolm, ed. 1989. *Tax Reform in Developing Countries*. Durham, NC: Duke University Press.

Gimpelson, Vladimir, and Daniel Treisman. 2011. Misperceiving inequality. NBER Working Paper 21174. www.nber.org/papers/w21174.

González, Lucas. 2008. Political power, fiscal crises, and decentralization in Latin America: Federal countries in comparative perspective (and some contrasts with unitary cases). *Publius: The Journal of Federalism* 38(2): 211–247.

Goredema, Charles. 1997. The Attorney-General in Zimbabwe and South Africa: whose weapon-whose shield. *Stellenbosch Law Review* 8: 45–64.

Government of Ghana. 2015. Address challenges of GETFund and related matters affecting students – NUGS. www.ghana.gov.gh/index.php/media-center/news/2194-address-challenges-of-getfund-and-related-matters-affecting-students-nugs.

Grindle, Merilee, and John Thomas. 1991. *Public Choices and Policy Change: The Political Economy of Reform in Developing Countries*. Baltimore, MD: John Hopkins University Press.

Grosh, Margaret, Carlo Del Ninno, Emil Tesliuc, and Azedine Ouerghi. 2008. *For Protection and Promotion: The Design and Implementation of Effective Safety Nets*. Washington, DC: World Bank.

Gwartney, James, Joshua Hall, and Robert Lawson. 2014. *2014 Economic Freedom Dataset*. Vancouver: Fraser Institute. www.freetheworld.com/datasets_efw.html.

Gwynne, Robert, and Kay Cristobal. 2014. *Latin America Transformed: Globalization and Modernity*. New York: Routledge.

Hamdan, Kamal. 2005. *Micro and small enterprises in Lebanon*. Economic Research Forum. Research Report Series 417. Beirut: Economic Research Forum.

Hamman, John, George Loewenstein, and Roberto Weber. 2010. Self-interest through delegation: An additional rationale for the principal-agent relationship. *American Economic Review* 100(4): 1826–1846.

Hammergren, Linn. 2006. "Rebuilding nation building": Latin American experience with rule of law reforms and its applicability to nation building efforts. *Case Western Reserve Journal of International Law* 38: 63–93.

Hanstad, Tim, Robin Nielsen, Darryl Vhugen, and Tajamul Haque. 2009. Learning from old and new approaches to land reform in India, in Hans P. Binswanger-Mkhize, Camille Bourguignon, and Rogier van den Brink, eds., *Agricultural Land Redistribution: Toward Greater Consensus*. Washington, DC: World Bank, pp. 241–263.

Haokip, Thongkholal. 2014. Inter-ethnic relations in Meghalaya. *Asian Ethnicity* 15(3): 302–316.

Harstad, Bård. 2008. Do side payments help? Collective decisions and strategic delegation. *Journal of the European Economic Association* 6(2-3): 468–477.

Heffernan, Claire, and Federica Misturelli. 2000. *The Delivery of Veterinary Services to the Poor: Preliminary Findings from Kenya*. Report of the DFID Project 7359 London: Department for International Development.

Heider, Fritz. 1958. *The Psychology of Interpersonal Relations*. New York: Wiley.

Helmke, Gretchen, and Frances Rosenbluth. 2009. Regimes and the rule of law: Judicial independence in comparative perspective. *Annual Review of Political Science* 12 (2009): 345–366.

Henley, David. 2010. *Three principles of successful development strategy: outreach, urgency, expediency*. Paper delivered at the 3rd plenary Tracking Development Conference, Putrajaya, Malaysia, May. www.institutions-africa.org/trackingdevelopment_archived/resources/docs/Henley-three-principles.pdf.

Herbert, Ross. 2002. Implementing NEPAD: A Critical Assessment. *In African Report-Assessing the New Partnership*. Ottawa: North-South Institute, 93–134.

Herbst, Jeffrey. 2005. Mbeki's South Africa. *Foreign Affairs* 84(6):93–105.

Hirschman, Albert O. 1963. *Journeys toward Progress: Studies of Economic Policy-Making in Latin America*. New York: Twentieth Century Fund.

1975. Policymaking and policy analysis in Latin America A return journey, *Policy Sciences* 6: 385–402.

Hodler, Roland, and David Knight. 2011. Ethnic fractionalisation and aid effectiveness. *Journal of African Economies* 21(1): 65–93.

Holzner, Claudio. Clientelism and democracy in Mexico: The role of strong and weak networks. 2006. In Hank Johnston and Paul Almeida, eds, *Latin American Social Movements: Globalization, Democratization, and Transnational Networks*, Guilford, CT: Roman and Littlefield, pp. 77–94.

Howlett, Michael. 2011. *Designing Public Policies: Principles And Instruments*. New York: Routledge.

Hu, Shaohua. 2006. Revisiting Chinese Pacifism. *Asian Affairs: An American Review* 32(4): 256–278.

Huidrom, Raju, M. Ayhan Kose, and Franziska Ohnsorge. 2016. *Challenges of fiscal policy in emerging and developing economies*. Centre for Applied Macroeconomic Analysis Working Paper, Crawford School of Public Policy. Canberra: Australia National University.

ICRA Research Services. 2015. *Expenditure Priorities and Medium-Term Fiscal Roadmap of Central Government Expected to Be Clarified by 2015–16 Budget*. New Delhi: ICRA Research Services.

IEAG (Independent Expert Advisory Group on a Data Revolution for Sustainable Development). 2014. *A World That Counts: Mobilising the Data Revolution for Sustainable Development*. New York: United Nations, November.

Ifeka, Caroline. 2001. Playing civil society tunes: Corruption & misunderstanding Nigeria's "real" political institutions. *Review of African Political Economy* 89:461–465.

International Regional Information Network. 2011. Nyanza's forgotten IDPs. www.irinnews.org/report/91946/kenya-nyanzas-forgotten-idps.

Islam, Tazul. 2016. *Microcredit and Poverty Alleviation*. London: Routledge.

Ismahan, Mustafa, and F. Gulcin Ozkan. 2011. The political economy of public spending decisions and macroeconomic performance. *International Journal of Economic Perspectives* 5(2): 163–174.

Jaffrelot, Christophe. 2011. *Religion, Caste, and Politics in India*. London: C. Hurst & Company.

James, Deborah. 2000. "After years in the wilderness": The discourse of land claims in the New South Africa. *The Journal of Peasant Studies* 27(3): 142–161.

James, Laura. 2015. *Recent Developments in Egypt's Fuel Subsidy Reform Process*. Geneva: International Institute for Sustainable Development. http://search.iisd.org/gsi/sites/default/files/ffs_egypt_lessonslearned.pdf

Janis, Irving. 1972. *Victims of Groupthink: A Psychological Study of Foreign Policy Decisions and Fiascos*. Boston: Houghton Mifflin Company.

Jingyan, Yuan. 2013. The politics of public goods provision in rural China. PhD diss., National University of Singapore.

Jiri, Jonas. 2002. *Argentina: The Anatomy of a Crisis*. ZEI, Zentrum für Europäische Integrationsforschung. Bonn: Rheinische Friedrich-Wilhelms-Universität.

Johnson, Adrienne. 2014. *Green Governance or Green Grab? The Roundtable on Sustainable Palm Oil (RSPO) and Its Governing Processes in Ecuador*. LDPI Working Paper 54. Amsterdam: The Land Deal Politics Initiative.

Jones, Bryan D., Frank R. Baumgartner, and Jeffery C. Talbert. 1993.The destruction of issue monopolies in Congress. *American Political Science Review* 87 (3): 657–671.

Jones, Harry, Nicola Jones, and Louise Shaxson. 2012. *Knowledge, Policy and Power in International Development: A Practical Guide*. Bristol, UK: Policy Press.

Jones, Harry, Nicola Jones, Louise Shaxson, and David Walker. 2013. *Knowledge, Policy and Power in International Development: A Practical Framework for Improving Policy*. ODI background note. London: Overseas Development Institute.

Joshi, Anuradha. 1999. *Progressive bureaucracy: An oxymoron?: The case of joint forest management in India*. Rural Development Forestry Network Paper 24a. London: Overseas Development Institute.

Kabiri, Ngeta. 2007. Global environmental governance and community-based conservation in Kenya and Tanzania. PhD diss., University of North Carolina.

Kahan, Dan, Donald Braman, John Gastil, Paul Slovic, and C. K. Mertz. 2007. Culture and identity-protective cognition: Explaining the white-male effect in risk perception. *Journal of Empirical Legal Studies* 4(3): 465–505.

Kahan, Dan M., Hank Jenkins-Smith, and Donald Braman. 2011. Cultural cognition of scientific consensus. *Journal of Risk Research* 14(2): 147–174.

Kahneman, Daniel, and Shane Frederick. 2002. Representativeness revisited: Attribute substitution in intuitive judgment. In Thomas Gilovich, Dale Griffin, and Daniel Kahneman, eds., *Heuristic and Biases: The Psychology of Intuitive Judgment*. New York: Cambridge University Press, pp. 49–89.

Kalra, Aditya. 2014 India slashes health budget, already one of the world's lowest. Reuters December 23. http://in.reuters.com/article/india-health-budget-idINKBN0K1oYo20141223.

Kamungi, Prisca, Johnstone Oketch, and Chris Huggins. 2005. Land access and the return and resettlement of IDPs and refugees in Burundi. In Chris Huggins and Jenny Glover, eds. *From the Ground Up: Land Rights, Conflict and Peace in Sub-Saharan Africa*. Pretoria: African Centre for Technology Studies/Institute for Security Studies.

Kamugisha, Dennis. 2014. The liaison between central and local governments: Is it inclined in a symbiotic fashion to ease service delivery in Tanzania. *International Journal of Social Sciences and Entrepreneurship* 1(10): 274–291.

Kantai, Parselelo. 2003. A deal in the Mara. *Ecoforum* 26(1): 41–46.

Katz, Daniel. 1960. The functional approach to the study of attitudes. *Public opinion quarterly* 24(2):163–204.

Kaufman, Robert. 1972. *The Politics of Land Reform in Chile, 1950–1970*. Cambridge, MA; Harvard University Press.

Keene-Mugerwa, Lilian. 2011. Human rights of the working poor in Uganda's informal sector. In Dan Banik, ed., *The Legal Empowerment Agenda: Poverty, Labour and the Informal Economy in Africa*. Surrey, UK: Ashgate, pp. 159–176.

Kehl, Jenny R. 2012. Institutions to bridge troubled waters, In Michelle Williams, ed., *The Multicultural Dilemma: Migration, Ethnic Politics, and State Intermediation*. New York: Routledge, pp. 136–152.

Khotsing, Thannaphat. 2013. *The Community Title Deed Policy Implementation*. Bangkok: National Institute of Development Administration. http://libdcms .nida.ac.th/thesis6/2556/b183163.pdf.

Killian, Bernadeta. 2008. The state and identity politics in Zanzibar: Challenges to democratic consolidation in Tanzania. *African Identities* 6(2): 99–125.

Kinsey, Bill, and Hans Binswanger. 1993. *Characteristics and Performance of Settlement Programs: A Review*. Washington, DC: World Bank.

King, Elisabeth. 2013. *From Classrooms to Conflict in Rwanda*. New York: Cambridge University Press.

Kivumbi, George, and Francis Kintu. 2002. Exemptions and waivers from cost sharing: Ineffective safety nets in decentralized districts in Uganda. *Health Policy and Planning* 1 7(suppl 1): 64–71.

Knight, Mark. 2004. Guns, camps and cash: Disarmament, demobilization and reinsertion of former combatants in transitions from war to peace. *Journal of Peace Research* 41(4): 499–516.

Knott, Jack, and Gary Miller. 2006. Social welfare, corruption and credibility: Public management's role in economic development. *Public Management Review* 8(2): 227–252.

Kombe, Wilbard J., and Volker Kreibich. 2012. Bringing the state back into urban growth regulation – The Tanzanian experience1. *Trialog* 80: 13–17.

Kothari, Ashish, and Neema Pathak. 2009. *Conservation and Rights in India: Are We Moving Towards any Kind of Harmony?* Pune/Delhi: Kalpavriksh – Environmental Action Group, May. http://kalpavriksh.org/images/LawsNPolicies/conservationnrights%20in%20india_paper%20for%20rrg.pdf.

Krasner, Stephen D. 2010. The durability of organized hypocrisy. In Hent Kalmo and Quentin Skinner, eds., *Sovereignty in Fragments: The Past, Present and Future of a Contested Concept.* Cambridge: Cambridge University Press, pp. 96–113.

Kus, Basak. 2014. The informal road to markets: neoliberal reforms, private entrepreneurship and the informal economy in Turkey. *International Journal of Social Economics* 41(4): 278–293.

Lai, Cynthia, Delia Catacutan, and Agustin Mercado Jr. 2016. *Decentralizing Natural Resource Management: Emerging Lessons from ICRAF Collaboration in Southeast Asia.* Manila: International Centre for Research in Agroforestry.

Larrousse, Delphine, Bhavna Mathur, and Aleen Saunders. 2006.*Using the Facilities Accessibility of Pay and Use toilets in Madanpur Khadar Resettlement Colony of Delhi* New Delhi: Council for Social Development.

Lasswell, Harold D. 1932. The triple-appeal principle: A contribution of psychoanalysis to political and social science. *American Journal of Sociology* 37: 523–538.

  1963. The decision process: Seven categories of functional analysis, reprinted in Nelson Polsby, Robert Dentler, and Paul Smith, eds., *Politics and Social Life.* Boston: Houghton Mifflin, pp. 93–105.

  1971. *A Pre-view of Policy Sciences.* New York: Elsevier.

Lasswell, Harold D., and Abraham Kaplan. 1950. *Power and Society.* New Haven: Yale University Press.

Lasswell, Harold D., and Myres McDougal. 1992. *Jurisprudence for a Free Society.* Dordrecht: Kluwer, and New Haven, CT: New Haven Press.

Lavers, Tom. 2013. The Political Economy of Social Policy and Agrarian Transformation in Ethiopia. PhD diss., Bath University.

Leaf, Michael. 2002. A tale of two villages: Globalization and peri-urban change in China and Vietnam. *Cities* 19(1): 23–31.

Leibold, Annalisa. 2011. Aligning incentives for development: The World Bank and the Chad-Cameroon Oil Pipeline. *Yale Journal of International Law* 36 (1): 167–205.

Lickel, Brian, Norman Miller, Douglas M. Stenstrom, Thomas F. Denson, and Toni Schmader. 2006.Vicarious retribution: The role of collective blame in intergroup aggression., *Personality and Social Psychology Review* 10(4): 372–390.

Linz, Juan. 1990. The perils of presidentialism, *Journal of Democracy* 1(1): 51–69.

Litvack, Jennie, Junaid Ahmad, and Richard Bird. 1998. *Rethinking Decentralization in Developing Countries*. Washington, DC: World Bank.

Litvack, Jennie, and Jessica Seddon, eds. 2002. *Decentralization Briefing Notes*. Washington, DC: World Bank.

Lo, Carlos Wing-Hung, Gerald E. Fryxell, and Wilson Wai-Ho Wong 2006. Effective regulations with little effect? The antecedents of the perceptions of environmental officials on enforcement effectiveness in China, *Environmental Management* 38(3): 388–410.

Loevinsohn, Michael. 2013. *Natural Experiments: An Under-Appreciated Evaluation Resource?* Centre for Development Impact Practice Paper Number 2, March. Brighton: Institute of Development Studies.

Loewenstein, George F., and Dražen Prelec. 1993 Preferences for sequences of outcomes, *Psychological Review* 100(1): 91–108.

Loveman, Brian. 1976. *The Struggle for the Sountryside: Politics and Rural Labor in Chile, 1919–1973*. Bloomington: University of Indiana Press.

Lund, Michael. 2009. Conflict prevention: Theory in pursuit of policy and practice. In Jacob Bercovitch, Victor Kremenyuk, and William Zartman, eds., *Sage Handbook of Conflict Resolution*. London: Sage.

Macdonald, Laura. 1997. *Supporting civil society: The Political Role of Non-Governmental Organizations in Central America*. Basingstoke: Macmillan.

2016. Globalizing civil society: Interpreting international NGOs in Central America. In Timothy Shaw and Larry Swatuk, eds., *The South at the End of the Twentieth Century: Rethinking the Political Economy of Foreign Policy in Africa, Asia, the Caribbean and Latin America*. Bastingstoke, Hamstead: Macmillan, pp. 210–225.

Maddock, Rodney, Elkin Castaño, and Frank Vella. 1992. Estimating electricity demand: The cost of linearising the budget constraint. *Review of Economics and Statistics* 74(2): 350–354.

Madrid, Raúl. 2003. Labouring against neoliberalism: Unions and patterns of reform in Latin America. *Journal of Latin American Studies* 35(1): 53–88.

Mahala, Peter. 2013. Unions: Healthy Competition? *Farmers Weekly*. Pinegowrie, South Africa. http://farmersweekly.co.za/article.aspx?id=40684&h=Unions:-healthy-competition.

Mahannop, Narong. 2004. The development of forest plantations in Thailand, in Thomas Enters and Patrick B. Durst, eds., *What Does It Take? The Role of Incentives in Forest Plantation Development in Asia and the Pacific.* . Bangkok: UN Food and Agriculture Organization, pp. 211–236.

Makinde, Taiwo. 2005. Problems of policy implementation in developing nations: The Nigerian experience, *Journal of Social Sciences* 11(1): 63–69.

Malle, Bertram. 1999. How people explain behavior: A new theoretical framework. *Personality and Social Psychology Review* 3(1): 23–48.

Martínez Valle, Adolfo. 2016. The Mexican experience in monitoring and evaluation of public policies addressing social determinants of health. *Journal of Global Health Action* 9(1):1-5.

Mashaw, Jerry. 1989. The economics of politics and the understanding of public law. *Chicago-Kent Law Review* 65: 123–160.

Massie, Roy. 2008. Responding to the health needs of the internally displaced persons: An analysis of the Indonesian health system. PhD diss., Queen Margaret University.

Matli, Moeketsi. 2005. *The Social Impacts of a large Development Project: The Lesotho Highlands Water Project.* Bloemfontein, South Africa: University of the Free State Faculty of Natural and Agricultural Sciences.

McGibbon, Rodd. 2004. *Secessionist challenges in Aceh and Papua: Is special autonomy the solution?* Policy Studies 10. Washington, DC: East-West Center.

McLean, Joanne and Steffen Straede. 2003. Conservation, relocation and the paradigms of park and people management: A case study of Padampur villages and the Royal Chitwan National Park, Nepal. *Society and Natural Resources* 16(6): 509–526.

McNeil, Mary. 1972. Lateritic soils in distinct tropical environments: Southern Sudan and Brazil, in M. Taghi Farvar and John P. Milton, eds., *The Careless Technology: Ecology and International Development*, New York: Doubleday, pp. 591–608.

Michels, Robert. 1915/1949. *Political Parties: A Sociological Study of the Oligarchical Tendencies of Modern Democracy*, trans. Eden Paul and Cedar Paul. Glencoe: The Free Press.

Mills, Anne, Mariam Ally, Jane Goudge, John Gyapong, and Gemini Mtei. 2012. Progress towards universal coverage: The health systems of Ghana, South Africa and Tanzania. *Health policy and planning* 27, suppl 1: i4-i12.

Mishan, Edward J. 1984/2013. *Introduction to Political Economy.* London: Routledge.

Mogues, Tewodaj. 2013. *Political Economy Determinants of Public Investment Decision-making in Agriculture: Lessons from and for Africa.* Washington, DC: International Food Policy Research Institute.

Mokone, Mokote. 2010. *The World Bank, NEPAD and Africa's development.* Johannesburg: University of the Witwatersrand. http://146.141.12.21/bit stream/handle/10539/9823/MA%20Research%20Report%20Mokete% 20Mokone.pdf?sequence=3http://citeseerx.ist.psu.edu/viewdoc/download? doi=10.1.1.352.7633&rep=rep1&type=pdf.

Molina-Millan, Teresa, Tania Barham, Karen Macours, John A. Maluccio, and Marco Stampini. 2016. *Long-Term Impacts of Conditional Cash Transfers in Latin America: Review of the Evidence.* Washington, DC: Inter-American Development Bank.

Molle, François, and Chu Thai Hoanh. 2009. *Implementing Integrated River Basin Management: Lessons from the Red River Basin, Vietnam.* Colombo, Sri Lanka: International Water Management Institute.

Montgomery, John D., Harold D. Lasswell, and Joel S. Migdal, eds. 1979. *Patterns of policy: Comparative and Longitudinal Studies of Population Events.* New Brunswick, NJ: Transaction Publishers.

Mosley, Paul, Farhad Noorbakhsh, and Alberto Paloni. 2003. *Compliance with World Bank conditionality: Implications for the selectivity approach to policy-based lending and the design of conditionality.* Nottingham: University of

Nottingham Centre for Research in Economic Development and International Trade. Research Paper. March 20.

Mousseau, Demet. 2006. Democracy, human rights and market development in Turkey: Are they related? *Government and Opposition* 41(2): 298–326.

Muhumuza, William. 2008. Pitfalls of decentralization reforms in transitional societies: The case of Uganda, *Africa Development* 33(4):59–81.

Muñoz-Piña, Carlos, Alain De Janvry, and Elisabeth Sadoulet. 2003. Recrafting rights over common property resources in Mexico. *Economic Development and Cultural Change* 52(1): 129–158.

Muntemba, Shimwaayi, and Alexander Amuah. 2000. *Building Networks of Service-Providing Institutions Sourcebook*. Washington, DC: World Bank.

Muscat, Robert. 2002. *Investing in Peace: How Development Aid Can Prevent or Promote Conflict*. Armonk, NY: ME Sharpe.

Nacif, Benito. 2006a. *The Fall of the Dominant Presidency: Lawmaking under Divided Government in Mexico*. México City: Centro Investigación y Docencia Económicas.

2006b. *¿Qué hay de malo con la parálisis? Democracia y gobierno dividido en México*. México City: Centro Investigación y Docencia Económicas.

Nagan, Winston. 1990. South Africa in transition: Human rights, ethnicity and law in the 1990s. *Villanova Law Review* 35: 1139–1173.

Naidoo, Vinothan, and Annelie Maré. 2015. Implementing the National Development Plan? Lessons from co-ordinating grand economic policies in South Africa. *Politikon* 42 (3): 407–427.

Nakamura, Robert. 1987. The textbook policy process and implementation research. *Policy Studies Review* 7(1): 142–154.

Nakayama, Mikiyasu and Furuyashiki, Kumi. 2009. Renting submerged land for sustainable livelihood rehabilitation of resettled families: Cases of Jintsugawa Dams in Japan. *International Journal of Water Resources Development* 25(3): 431–439.

Nandi, Anulekha. *Women in Iran*. 2015. Saratoga Springs, NY: Saratoga Foundation for Women WorldWide.

Nankani, Gobind. 2004. *NEPAD: Multistakeholder Dialogue, Johannesburg*. Washington, D.C.: World Bank.

Naughton-Treves, Lisa, Nora Alvarez-Berríos, Katrina Brandon, Aaron Bruner, Margaret Buck Holland, Carlos Ponce, Malki Saenz, Luís Suarez, and Adrian Treves. 2006. Expanding protected areas and incorporating human resource use: A study of 15 forest parks in Ecuador and Peru, *Sustainability: Science, Practice, & Policy* 2(2): 32–44.

Neira, Eduardo, Hernán Verscheure, and Carmen Revenga. 2002. *Chile's Frontier Forests: Conserving a Global Treasure*. Washington, DC: Global Forest Watch, World Resources Institute.

Nellis, John. 2012. *The international experience with privatization: Its rapid rise, partial fall and uncertain future*. Calgary: University of Calgary School of Public Policy, Research Paper No. 12–3.

Nickerson, Raymond S., 1998. Confirmation bias: A ubiquitous phenomenon in many guises. *Review of General Psychology* 2(2): 175.

Norden, Deborah L. 2012. Sowing conflict in Venezuela: Political violence and economic policy. In William Ascher and Natalia Mirovitskaya, eds., *Economic Development Strategies and the Evolution of Violence in Latin America*. New York: Palgrave Macmillan, pp. 153–180.

Nordstrum, Lee E. 2015. *Effective Teaching and Education Policy in Sub-Saharan Africa: A Conceptual Study of Effective Teaching and Review of Educational Policies in 11 Sub-Saharan African Countries*. RTI International, Technical report no. 19, August.

Obeed Al-Azawi, Ali A., and Frank Ward. 2017. Groundwater use and policy options for sustainable management in Southern Iraq. *International Journal of Water Resources Development* 33(4): 628–648.

Obi, Cyril. 2007. *Oil and Development in Africa: Some Lessons from the Oil Factor in Nigeria for the Sudan*. Copenhagen: Danish Institute for International Studies.

Ocampo, Geneviva. 2009. *Paraguay: Development of an anti-crisis plan*. Social Watch 133. www.socialwatch.org/sites/default/files/paraguay2009_eng.pdf.

Odularu, Gbadebo. O. 2009. Export diversification as a promotion strategy for intra-ECOWAS trade expansion. *African Journal of Business Management* 3 (2): 32–38.

Oduro, Razak. 2015. Beyond poverty reduction: Conditional cash transfers and citizenship in Ghana. *International Journal of Social Welfare* 24(1): 27–36.

O'Gara, Chloe, Lisa Long, and Emily Vargas-Barón. 2008. Policy options for early childhood development. In William Cummings and James Williams, eds., *Policy-Making for Education Reform in Developing Countries: Policy Options and Strategies*, vol. 2. Lanham, MD: Rowman & Littlefield, pp. 27–64.

Okafor, Emeka Emmanuel, and Yusuf Abdulazeez. 2007. Gender-sensitive projects for sustainable development in Nigeria: A critical assessment. *Journal of Social Sciences* 15(3): 235–248.

Organisation for Economic Development and Co-operation. 2016. *Development Co-Operation Report 2016: The Sustainable Development Goals as Business Opportunities*. Paris: OECD Publications.

Orphanides, Athanasios, and John Williams. 2007. Robust monetary policy with imperfect knowledge. *Journal of Monetary Economics* 54(5): 1406–1435.

Ortiz, Isabel. 2007. *Social policy*. UN Department of Economic and Social Affairs Policy Notes.

Ortmann, Gerald. 2005. Promoting the competitiveness of South African agriculture in a dynamic economic and political environment. *Agrekon* 44(3): 286–320.

O'Shannassy, Michael. 2011. Malaysia in 2010. *Asian Survey* 51(1): 173–185.

Pacheco, Regina Silvia. 2013. Arm's length bodies in Brazil: Contradictions and challenges. *Public Organization Review* 13(2): 131–141.

Padmanabhan, Vijay. 2002. Democracy's baby blocks: South Africa's electoral commissions. *New York University Law Review* 77: 1157–1194.

Pagés, Carmen, Gaëlle Pierre, and Stefano Scarpetta. 2009. *Job Creation in Latin America and the Caribbean: Recent Trends and Policy Challenges*. Washington, DC: World Bank and Palgrave Macmillan.

Panday, Devendra Raj. 1989. Administrative development in a semi-dependency: The experience of Nepal, *Public Administration and Development* 9(3): 315–329.

Pannarunothai, Supasit, Patmasiriwat, Direk, and Srithamarongsawat, Samrit. 2004. Universal health coverage in Thailand: Ideas for reform and policy struggling. *Health Policy* 68 [Nonthaburi].

Park, Donghyun, Sang-Hyop Lee, and Minsoo Lee, eds. 2015. *Inequality, Inclusive Growth, and Fiscal Policy in Asia*. Abington, UK: Asian Development Bank and Routledge.

Petchmark, Panthip, Somsook Boonyabancha, and Mitsuhiko Hosaka. 2011. Social security through community welfare funds in Thailand. In James Midgley and Mitsuhiko Hosaka, editors, *Grassroots Social Security in Asia: Mutual Aid, Microinsurance and Social Welfare*, New York: Routledge, pp. 95–109.

Pierce-Colfer, Carol J., Heru Komarudin Komarudin, Laura German, Simon Nyangas, Yulia Siagian, and Joseph Tanui. 2007. *Participatory forest management, equity and local governance – Keynote address*. Addis Ababa: International Conference on Participatory Forest Management (PFM), Biodiversity and Livelihoods in Africa: pp. 116–128.

Pieterse, Edgar, and Mirjam Van Donk. 2002. Incomplete ruptures: The political economy of realising socio-economic rights in South Africa. *Law, Democracy & Development* 6(2): 193–229.

Poteete, Amy R. 2002. Who seeks participation and why? The adoption of participatory policy-making techniques in Botswana and Uganda. https://ostromworkshop.indiana.edu/papers/poteete_120202.pdf.

Prado, Fernando Almeida, Simone Athayde, Joann Mossa, Stephanie Bohlman, Flavia Leite, and Anthony Oliver-Smith. 2016. How much is enough? An integrated examination of energy security, economic growth and climate change related to hydropower expansion in Brazil. *Renewable and Sustainable Energy Reviews* 53: 1132–1136.

Priest, Julia. 2014. Participatory Rural Appraisal: Lessons for Countries in the North. www.researchgate.net/publication/242446398_Participatory_Rural_Appraisal_Lessons_for_Countries_in_the_North.

Prilles, Wilfredo. 2005. Kaantabay Sa Kauswagan: Empowering the urban poor in Naga City, Philippines. *Open House International* 30(4): 56.

Pritchett, Lant, Michael Woolcock, and Matt Andrews. 2010. *Capability traps? The mechanisms of persistent implementation failure*. Washington, DC: Center for Global Development Working Paper No. 234.

Psacharopoulos, George. 1989. Why educational reforms fail: A comparative analysis, *International Review of Education* 35(2): 179–195.

Raczynski, Dagmar, and Gonzalo Muñoz-Stuardo. 2007. Chilean educational reform: The intricate balance between a macro and micro policy. In William Pink and George Noblit, *International Handbook of Urban Education*. Dordrecht: Springer Netherlands, pp. 641–663.

Reeder, Glenn, John Pryor, Michael Wohl, and Michael Griswell. 2005. On attributing negative motives to others who disagree with our opinions. *Personality and Social Psychology Bulletin* 31(11): 1498–1510.

Regalia, Ferdinando, and Marcos Robles. 2005. *Social Assistance, Poverty and Equity in the Dominican Republic*. Washington, DC: Inter-American Development Bank.

Rennkamp, Britta. 2012. *Sustainable development planning in South Africa: A case of over-strategizing?* Berlin Conference, Berlin. www.diss.fu-berlin.de/docs/servlets/MCRFileNodeServlet/FUDOCS_derivate_000000002429/Rennkamp-Sustainable_development_planning_in_South_Africa-389.pdf.

Republic of Chile. 1980. Constitution of the Republic of Chile, Official Version. http://confinder.richmond.edu/admin/docs/Chile.pdf.

Rich, Bruce. 2013. *Foreclosing the Future: The World Bank and the Politics of Environmental Destruction*. Washington, DC: Island Press/Center for Resource Economics.

Richter, Iris. 2016. *Experiences from the Implementation of Social Land Concessions in Cambodia*. Bonn: Deutsche Gesellschaft für Internationale Zusammenarbeit, January. www.giz.de/de/downloads/giz2016-en-lessons-learned.pdf.

Riggs, Fred. 1964. *Administration in Developing Countries: The Theory of Prismatic Society*. Boston: Houghton-Mifflin.

Robbins, Paul. 2000. The rotten institution: Corruption in natural resource management. *Political Geography* 19: 423–443.

Roberts, John. 2003. Managing public expenditure for development results and poverty reduction. Overseas Development Institute Paper 203. London: Overseas Development Institute.

Rodden, Jonathan. 2002. The dilemma of fiscal federalism: Grants and fiscal performance around the world, *American Journal of Political Science* 46(3): 670–687.

Rodríguez, Francisco. 2006. The anarchy of numbers: Understanding the evidence on Venezuelan economic growth. *Canadian Journal of Development Studies/Revue canadienne d'études du développement* 27(4): 503–529.

Rodrik, Dani. 2008. *Normalizing Industrial Policy*. Washington, DC: World Bank, 2008.

Rondinelli, Dennis. 1981. Government decentralization in comparative perspective: Theory and practice in developing countries. *International review of administrative sciences* 47(2): 133–145.

2006. Government decentralization and economic development: The evolution of concepts and practices. *Research in Public Policy Analysis and Management* 15: 433–445.

Root, Hilton, Harry Jones, and Leni Wild. 2015. *Managing Complexity and Uncertainty in Development Policy and Practice*. London: Overseas Development Institute.

Rosado Marzán, César. 2009. Of labor inspectors and judges: Chilean labor law enforcement after Pinochet (and what the United States can do to help). *St. Louis University Journal of Law* 54: 497–523.

Ross, Michael. 2013. *The oil Curse: How Petroleum Wealth Shapes the Development of Nations*. Princeton, NJ: Princeton University Press.

Sabatier, Paul. 1988. An advocacy coalition framework of policy change and the role of policy-oriented learning therein, *Policy Sciences* 21(2): 129–168.

1999. The need for better theories. In Paul Sabatier, ed., *Theories of the Policy Process*. Boulder CO: Westview Press, pp. 1–17.

Sah, Baua Lal. 2013. *Implementation Status of Female and Disadvantaged Group Education Scholarship Program*. Bakhundol, Lalitpur, Nepal: Social Inclusion Research Fund, May.

Sahani, Nihi Sharma. 2015. Forest guard shortage makes it hard to check poaching, *Hindustan Times*, Dehradun, August 12.

Samuels, David, and Scott Mainwaring. 2004. Strong federalism, constraints on the central government, and economic reform in Brazil. In Edward Gibson, ed., *Federalism and Democracy in Latin America*. Baltimore: Johns Hopkins University Press, pp. 85–130.

Sarr, Babacar. 2015. Assessing public sector performance in developing countries: four essays on public financial management and public service delivery. PhD diss., Université d'Auvergne-Clermont-Ferrand I.

Schelling, Thomas C. 1980. *The Strategy of Conflict*. Cambridge, MA: Harvard University Press.

Schon, Donald. 1979. Generative Metaphor: A Perspective on Problem-Solving in Social Policy. In Andrew Ortony, ed., *Metaphors and Thought*. Cambridge: Cambridge University Press, pp. 254–283.

Scialabba, Nadia, and Douglas Williamson. 2004. *The Scope of Organic Agriculture, Sustainable Forest Management and Ecoforestry in Protected Area Management*. Rome: UN Food and Agriculture Organization.

Selway, Joel. 2011. Electoral reform and public policy outcomes in Thailand: The politics of the 30-baht health scheme. *World Politics* 63(1): 165–202.

Shaw, Kurt. 2004. *Legitimacy in Colombian shantytowns. Essay prepared for the International Seminar on Urban Conflict and Possibilities for Transformation*, Medellin, Colombia, September 5–7. Shine A Light. http://shinealight.org/legitimacy.pdf.

Shirley, Mary M., and Lixin Colin Xu. 1998. Information, incentives, and commitment: An empirical analysis of contracts between government and state enterprises. *Journal of Law, Economics, & Organization* 14(2): 358–378.

Silva, Eduardo. 1996. Democracy, market economics, and environmental policy in Chile, *Journal of Interamerican Studies and World Affairs* 38(4): 1–33.

Simmons, Carolyn, Barbara Bickart, and John Lynch. 1993. Capturing and Creating Public Opinion in Survey Research. *Journal of Consumer Research* 20(2): 316–329.

Sinha, Priyanka. 2014. The disinvestment policy in India – Through a prism of politics, *Journal of Institute of Public Enterprise* 37(1/2): 6–6.

Soetarto, Endriatmo, MT Felix Sitorus, and Yusup Napiri. 2001. *Decentralisation of Administration, Policy Making and Forest Management in Ketapang District, West Kalimantan*. Bogor, Indonesia: CIFOR.

South African National Planning Commission. 2012. *National Development Plan 2030*. Johannesburg: The Presidency of the Republic of South Africa.

Starr, Pamela K. 2014. Mexico's problematic reforms, *Current History* 113(760): 51.

Stewart, Frances. 2005. Horizontal inequalities: a neglected dimension of development. In World Institute for Development Economics Research, *Wider*

Perspectives on Global Development. London: Palgrave Macmillan, pp. 101–135.

Subbarao, Kalinidh, and Kaushik Rudra. 1996. *Protecting the Disadvantaged in a High Growth Economy: Safety nets in Thailand*. Washington, DC: World Bank.

Sugiri, Agung. 2009. Financing slum upgrading in Indonesia: Can sustainability reinvestment help? In Happy Santosa, Sri Yuwanti, and Erika Yuni Astuti, eds., *Informal Settlements and Affordable Housing IV*. Madrid: 3rd International Meeting of the International Council for Research and Innovation in Building and Construction.

Suhardiman, Diana, Mark Giordano, Edwin Rap, and Kai Wegerich. 2014. Bureaucratic reform in irrigation: A review of four case studies. *Water Alternatives* 7(3): 444–463.

Swanson, Darren, Stephan Barg, Stephen Tyler, Henry Venema, Sanjay Tomar, Suruchi Bhadwal, Sreeja Nair, Dimple Roy, and John Drexhage. 2010. Seven tools for creating adaptive policies. *Technological Forecasting and Social Change* 77(6): 924–939.

Taber, Charles, and Milton Lodge. 2006. Motivated skepticism in the evaluation of political beliefs. *American Journal of Political Science* 50(3): 755–769.

Tabbush, Constanza. 2010. Latin American women's protection after adjustment: A feminist critique of conditional cash transfers in Chile and Argentina. *Oxford Development Studies* 38(4): 437–459.

Taber, Charles S., and Milton Lodge. Motivated skepticism in the evaluation of political beliefs. *American Journal of Political Science* 50(3): 755–769.

Tadem, Teresa. 2009. Localizing and globalizing advocacies and alternatives: A comparative analysis of five global civil society movements. In Teresa Tadem, ed., *Localizing and Transnationalizing Contentious Politics: Global Civil Society Movements*. Lanham, MD: Lexington Books, pp. 219–258.

Tajfel, Henri, and John C. Turner. 1979. An integrative theory of intergroup conflict. In William Austin and Stephen Worchel, eds. *The Social Psychology of Intergroup Relations*. Monterey, CA: Brooks/Cole, pp. 33–47.

Tantivess, Sripen, and Gill Walt. 2008. The role of state and non-state actors in the policy process: The contribution of policy networks to the scale-up of antiretroviral therapy in Thailand. *Health Policy and Planning* 23(5): 328–338.

Tanwir, Maryam, and Azam Chaudhry. 2015. The performance evaluation system in Pakistan's civil service. *Africa's Public Service Delivery and Performance Review* 3(2): 81–103.

Tate-Campbell, Ruth. 2010. HIV and AIDS education for displaced burmese in thailand: Politics, policy and practice. *Journal of Education for International Development* 4(3). www.equip123.net/JEID/articles/4_3/Tate_Campbell.pdf.

Tobias, Jutta, and Karol Boudreaux. 2011. Entrepreneurship and conflict reduction in the post-genocide Rwandan coffee industry. *Journal of Small Business & Entrepreneurship* 24 (2): 217–242.

Tommasi, Mariano. 2011. Latin America: How state capacity determines policy success. *Governance* 24(2): 199–203.

Tsebelis, George. 2002. *Veto Players: How Political Institutions Work*. Princeton, NJ: Princeton University Press.

Turner, Mark, and David Hulme. 1997. *Governance, Administration, and Development: Making the State Work.* Sterling, VA: Kumarian Press.

Tyler, Geoff, Peter Hazell, Andrew Dorward, Jonathan Kydd, and Mike Stockbridge. 2008. *Experiences with Commercial Agriculture: Background Paper for the Competitive Commercial Agriculture in Sub-Saharan Africa (CCAA) Study.* Washington, DC: World Bank and UN Food and Agriculture Organization.

Ugwuanyi, Bartholomew, and Emma E. O. Chukwuemeka. 2013. The obstacles to effective policy implementation by the public bureaucracy in developing nations: The case of Nigeria. *Singaporean Journal of Business Economics and Management Studies* 1(8): 34–43.

UN Conference on Trade and Development. 2007. *Economic development in Africa: Reclaiming policy space: Domestic resource mobilization and developmental states, overview by the UNCTAD Secretariat.* Geneva, July.

UNESCO 2011. *Financing education in Sub-Saharan Africa: Meeting the Challenges of Expansion, Equity, and Quality.* Montreal: UNESCO Institute for Statistics.

UNICEF 2013. *Child Support Grant in Thailand: Frequently Asked Questions.* New York: UNICEF.

Utting, Peter. 2006. *Reclaiming Development Agendas: Knowledge, Power, and International Policy Making.* Basingstoke, UK: Palgrave.

Van Ginkel, Maarten, Jeff Sayer, Fergus Sinclair, Aden Aw-Hassan, Deborah Bossio, Peter Craufurd, Mohammed El Mourid, Nasri Haddad, David Hoisington, Nancy Johnson, Carlos León Velarde, Víctor Mares, Andrew Mude, Ali Nefzaoui, Andrew Noble, K. P. C. Rao, Rachid Serraj, Shirley Tarawali, Raymond Vodouhe, and Rodomiro Ortiz. 2013. An integrated agro-ecosystem and livelihood systems approach for the poor and vulnerable in dry areas. *Food Security* 5(6): 751–767.

Varshney, Ashutosh. 2003. *Ethnic Conflict and Civic Life: Hindus and Muslims in India.* 2nd edn. New Haven, CT: Yale University Press.

Vian, Taryn, Derick W. Brinkerhoff, Frank G. Feeley, Matthieu Salomon, and Nguyen Thi Kieu Vien. 2012. Confronting corruption in the health sector in Vietnam: Patterns and prospects. *Public Administration and Development* 32 (1): 49–63.

Whaites, Alan, Eduardo Gonzalez, Sara Fyson, and Graham Teskey. 2015. *A Governance Practitioner's Notebook: Alternative Ideas and Approaches.* Paris: OECD.

Wang, Juan. 2007.The politics of poverty mis-targeting in China. *Journal of Chinese Political Science* 12(3): 219–236.

Weingast, Barry, Kenneth Shepsle, and Christopher Johnsen. 1988. The political economy of benefits and costs: A neoclassical approach to distributive politics, *Journal of Political Economy* 89: 642–664.

Weyland, Kurt. 1996. *Democracy Without Equity: Failures of Reform in Brazil.* Pittsburgh, PA: University of Pittsburgh Press.

Wildavsky, Aaron 1964. *Politics of the Budgetary Process.* Boston, MA: Little-Brown.

1997. *The New Politics of the Budgetary Process.* Boston, MA: Addison Wesley Publishing Company.

Winichakul, Thongchai. 2008. Toppling democracy. *Journal of Contemporary Asia* 38(1): 11–37.

Wolf, Jr., Charles, Xiao Wang, and Eric Warner. 2013. *China's Foreign Aid and Government-Sponsored Investment Activities: Scale, Content, Destinations, and Implication.* Santa Monica, CA: RAND Corporation.

Wood, Graeme. 2006. Iran: A Minority Report. *Atlantic Monthly* 298(5) (December): 46–47.

World Bank. 2009. *Implementation completion and results report (IBRD-73370 IBRD-74330) on loans in the amounts of US$86.4 million and US$104.8 million of additional financing to the Republic of Colombia for a social safety net project.* Washington, DC: World Bank.

2015. *World Development Report 2015.* Washington, DC: World Bank.

World Bank and Inter-American Development Bank 2005. *Infrastructure in Latin America: Recent Developments and Key Challenges.* World Bank, Washington D.C.

World Bank Group Independent Evaluation Group. 2009. *The World Bank Group Program of Support for the Chad-Cameroon Petroleum Development and Pipeline Construction.* Report No.: 50315. Washington, DC: World Bank. http://siteresources.worldbank.org/INTOED/Resources/ChadCamReport.pdf.

2012. Independent Evaluation Group Implementation Completion and Results Report Review, Tunisia Employment Development Policy Loan 2010–2011. Washington DC: World Bank. http://lnweb90.worldbank.org/oed/oeddoclib .nsf/DocUNIDViewForJavaSearch/8525682E00686037852579D400653102? OpenDocument.

2015. *The State of Social Safety Nets 2015.* Washington, DC: World Bank.

World Values Survey. 2016. World Values Survey Wave 6: 2010–2014 Online Data Analysis. www.worldvaluessurvey.org/WVSOnline.jsp.

World Wildlife Fund. 2004. *Are Protected Areas Working? An Analysis of Forest Protected Areas.* Gland, Switzerland: World Wildlife Fund, June.

Zekri, Slim, and Ariel Dinar. 2003. Welfare consequences of water supply alternatives in rural Tunisia. *Agricultural Economics* 28(1): 1–12.

Zeng, Douglas Zhihua. 2015. *Global experiences with special economic zones: Focus on China and Africa.* World Bank Policy Research Working Paper 7240. Washington, DC: World Bank.

Index